# UNDERSTANDING MARKETS AND STRATEGY

*To Paula, Hannah and Oliver*

MALCOLM MORLEY

# UNDERSTANDING MARKETS AND STRATEGY

## How to exploit markets for sustainable business growth

KoganPage

First published in Great Britain and the United States in 2014 by Kogan Page Limited



2nd Floor, 45 Gee Street
London EC1V 3RS
United Kingdom
www.koganpage.com

1518 Walnut Street, Suite 1100
Philadelphia PA 19102
USA

4737/23 Ansari Road
Daryaganj
New Delhi 110002
India



ISBN 978 0 7494 7152 1
E-ISBN 978 0 7494 7153 8

**British Library Cataloguing-in-Publication Data**

A CIP record for this book is available from the British Library.

**Library of Congress Cataloging-in-Publication Data**

CIP data is available.

Library of Congress Control Number: 2014015339.

Typeset by Amnet
Printed and bound in India by Replika Press Pvt Ltd

# CONTENTS

# ACKNOWLEDGEMENTS

I owe a debt of thanks to all who have taught me. I have been on a journey of discovery which has exposed me to seminal works by Peter Drucker on management, Michael Porter on competitive strategy, Henry Mintzberg on strategy processes, Malcolm McDonald on marketing, Gerry Johnson, Kevan Scholes and Cliff Bowman on strategic management, Gary Hamel and CK Prahalad on strategic competencies, Peter Senge on learning organizations, J Barney, R Rumelt and B Wernerfelt on the resource-based view of strategy, Abraham Maslow's hierarchy of needs and many others. I'd like to acknowledge the work of all of these great researchers and authors in this ever-evolving field of study.

Like all academic study, however, theory needs to be brought to life by inspirational tutors and the opportunity to apply it in practice. I have been fortunate to have had the opportunity to gain experience of putting theory into practice to enable me to continuously develop and contextualize it. Hopefully readers will be able to see how this process has worked in the pages of this book and be able to use and make the models, tools and techniques their own.

I'd like to particularly acknowledge those chief executives and senior managers from so many diverse companies with whom I've worked over many years. I'd like to thank them for sharing their problems with me and their willingness to be both challenged and to challenge their organizations. Understanding markets and strategy needs to continuously evolve. So too does the need to ensure that leaders and managers and their organizations do not get constrained in their thinking and action by taken-for-granted assumptions and the "comfort" of success.

Economies and markets throughout the world are at different stages of recovery and will continue to change. There is a huge need to ensure that all those within companies understand markets and strategy. Hopefully this book will help with this challenge.

I am grateful to the team at Kogan Page for their support throughout the process of publication.

*Malcolm Morley*
*m.morley@ucs.ac.uk*

# Introduction

Many books have been written about marketing but few on how to understand markets and how to develop competitive and corporate strategies for them. Marketing is too frequently approached as a separate issue rather than as part of the strategic competitive approach of companies. This has meant that many companies have started on a marketing journey without understanding the terrain over which they must travel. This has been illustrated many times over by the generic approaches to marketing that are seen in so many companies. An approach that often costs a lot but delivers little. A poor return on investment that baffles and disappoints those signing off the expenditure.

One of the lessons I have learned in working with a wide range of companies is that too often there's a fundamental misunderstanding of markets and how to understand them. I have also learned that managers have an impatience to jump straight to action rather than seek to understand the context for that action. There is almost a macho imperative to be seen to be doing something even if it isn't quite understood why it should be done.

Whilst time is money and competition sometimes requires an immediate response to the action of others, it's a senior manager's thirst for action – even if it is action that has not been thought through – that is too frequently seen to impel choice. Action needs to be a product of – and consistent with – a market-focused competitive strategy based upon a competitive and corporate analysis and evaluation. Inconsistent, ad hoc reactive action confuses the market and those within the organization charged with delivering success. *Understanding Markets and Strategy* provides the tools and techniques to ensure that decisions are taken within a credible market-focused strategy.

I've seen many grandiose marketing strategies that have been developed without really understanding what creates and makes a market work and the key strategic issues affecting both the market and the ability of the companies to compete. These marketing strategies are typified by an internal and seller focus to competition ('our products are better than theirs') and on a narrow band of product features and price.

In these circumstances underperformance against unrealistic sales targets regrettably becomes the norm – not a good place to be, as these organizations lag behind the market and do not have a role in influencing it. Even where companies have technically brilliant products, if they do not put them in the context of the market they will not sell. Understanding markets (and not just marketing) is vital to competitive success, as is being able to recognize what the company must do corporately to develop its ability to compete in markets. The company's products and services must be put into the context of the market rather than the company seeking to put the market into the context of the company and its products and services.

This book is very straightforward in its objective. It seeks to provide practical help for senior managers (and those aspiring to become senior managers) to enable them to understand markets and to develop strategies to enable their companies to compete to win; to really enable markets to be understood so that marketing strategies and plans can be developed in context, and investment in products, services and marketing can be pursued with real prospects for success in practice. It is based on my experience of what managers need to make a difference to the success of companies. The practical tools, techniques and knowledge within this book can be used internationally.

Over many years as a book reviewer for the Chartered Management Institute in the UK and variously as an international management consultant, board director and academic I've read many management books. As a student I read voraciously on strategy but was often left wondering how theory was applied in practice. *Understanding Markets and Strategy* is written for practitioners and students who want to avoid marketing spin and to have practical tools and techniques to help them to understand markets and strategy. It is written particularly to help managers to help their companies to compete to win. It is not a marketing strategy book.

The contents are structured in a way that builds understanding but also allows the reader to dip in and out of the text to get to grips with different aspects of markets and strategy. Each chapter will challenge and stimulate the reader's thinking but also help with that thinking to enable them to apply what is written to their company.

The reader will look at markets in a new way and be able to put their company and their ambitions into the market context. At the end of each chapter there is a series of practitioner's tips to help the reader apply what they have learnt in their own organization. There are also practitioner's questions to help the reader start the conversations required within their company to address the fundamental issues that are often ignored in the dash for action. These questions will help the reader to create an agenda for change and to achieve a shared understanding of key issues within their company. As we all know, journeys of discovery need to be shared if a common understanding and shared commitment to competitive strategy are to be achieved within companies and they are to lead to effective action.

The book takes the reader through the context and attractiveness of markets, how to analyse them, how to evaluate key strategic issues relevant to them, how to develop scenarios for them, how to develop strategies for them, how to understand the competitive dynamic and how to compete to win. It also explores corporate strategies to support the competitive strategy and how to manage strategic change.

The knowledge, tools and techniques in *Understanding Markets and Strategy* will challenge and change how managers think and act. It will form an important part of the development that all managers need to support them in achieving their potential and to achieve what they and their companies want to achieve. As with all books, however, the realization of that potential is in the hands of the reader, who must convert knowledge and intent into effective action.

# So, what is a market?

01

## Introduction

No book about understanding markets and the strategies for them can really start before defining what a market is and what needs to be in place before it can operate. This chapter defines a market and provides an understanding of when one exists and when one doesn't.

It is important to understand both, as it is clear that confusion about this leads to investment in sales and marketing that is wasted. It is also the case that until a market is understood, developing strategies for it can only be generic. Generic strategies are like firing a gun and hoping to hit something as someone else at some time has hit something. Companies that are successful in markets not only fire but take aim at a defined target knowing that they are within range and have both the right gun and the right ammunition with which to hit the target.

The chapter also deals with the unrealized and realized value of markets, the types of buyers and sellers in markets, market processes for sales and the role of knowledge in markets. At the end of the chapter, readers should be able to look at their own companies and ask searching questions to ensure that they and others within the company understand the nature of the market that they are seeking to compete within.

## Defining a market

As a boy in the school holidays I was often found on a Monday in a small town called Bakewell, in the heart of the glorious Derbyshire countryside. Apart from the world-renowned Bakewell tart, the reason that I was there was for the market.

In my mind at that point in time the market consisted of two parts. The first was a livestock market where farmers were selling cows, sheep, pigs, etc and the second was a general non-livestock market selling everything from food to textiles. Little did I know that even at that tender age I was, if only in a rudimentary way, segmenting markets!

In outline, the people at the market on a Monday were:

- Tourists who wanted to see and to experience the market. They generally looked at what the non-livestock market had to offer and only had a limited interest in the livestock market.
- Local people who lived in the town and who used the market to provide an alternative to the permanent shops.
- Farmers who were there to sell their livestock and to socialize.
- Farmers' wives and their families who were there to shop both in the non-livestock market and in the permanent shops and who were interested in a whole range of non-livestock goods and services.
- Buyers in the livestock market who were of three types principally:
  - butchers buying in small volumes for their businesses;
  - meat wholesalers buying in larger volumes for their businesses;
  - farmers buying animals to rear, eg calves to fatten for future sale.
- The auctioneers who provided the facilities and means for the sale of livestock to take place.
- Hauliers who provided transport for the livestock to and from the market.
- Market stallholders who were there to sell their non-livestock goods and services.
- Permanent shop, pub and restaurant proprietors, etc who were there to sell their non-livestock goods and services.
- Veterinarian and environmental health professionals who were there to regulate animal welfare and hygiene.
- The police who were there to ensure that public order was kept.
- Other public service providers, such as refuse collectors or street cleaners, who were there to maintain the public realm.

The stalls were only set up on a Monday and were dismantled the same day, leaving the permanent shops to trade for the rest of the week. The market stall traders moved on to a different location every day. The livestock market took place only on Mondays.

On Mondays the population of the town more than doubled and went from being a small rural idyll in the middle of glorious countryside to being a bustling, busy centre of commerce. But were all of the people above part of the market? Unless a market is capable of being clearly defined, it is not possible to analyse and evaluate it, never mind exploit it. All of the people who attended the Bakewell 'market' had a diverse range of needs and expectations. Those wishing to meet and influence those needs – and to convince buyers to buy from them – need to be able to define and understand what a market is and how their offer relates to it.

I have read many definitions of a market. Some of these definitions are more like a complex linguistic tour of the management lexicon rather than a guide for managers and students to understand markets. Any definition needs to be capable not only of being understood but of being used in practice. This chapter seeks to provide a readily understandable and useful definition. As the narrative unfolds the reader will be able to use the definition to provide a strategic context for companies and thus develop competitive and corporate strategies that will enable them to exploit the markets that they compete in.

## Market definition

> *A market is the interface of a buyer (or buyers) with the willingness and ability to buy and a seller (or sellers) with the willingness and ability to sell products and services.*

Without the willingness *and* ability to buy and the willingness *and* ability to sell there is no market.

Let's stay with the Bakewell Monday market as an example. Those who visited Bakewell for the 'buzz' of the livestock market might have had the ability to buy (they could afford to buy) but they did not have the willingness to buy. They were merely *Market Tourists* and were not part of the market. They did not have the willingness *and* ability to buy.

The wholesalers who bought and sold livestock in large quantities setting the benchmark prices on the day of the market were part of the market as they had both the willingness and ability to buy. Indeed they may be categorized as the *Market Buyer Principals*.

Market Buyer Principals are those who create market price and non-price benchmarks. They can either increase unit prices through their volume buying where the supply is restricted, reduce the unit price through their bulk buying where the supply is plentiful or reduce unit price by not buying, to leave an oversupply in the market. They might stipulate that they will only buy if certain conditions are met, eg sheep are sold in lots of 20 and that there are a minimum of number of animals available to buy, to make it worth them going to the market. Market Buyer Principals have power in the market over the suppliers to the market and over the non-market principal buyers.

Those buyers who play by the Market Buyer Principals' benchmarks and who aren't able to change them or who wait until the Market Buyer Principals have got what they want or until they have decided not to buy are the *Market Buyer Followers*. These Market Buyer Followers often choose not to, or cannot, compete with the Market Buyer Principals. They often watch the Market Buying Principals very closely and try to get the benefits of the benchmarks they create. Market Buyer Followers, however, are still an important part of the market as they have both the willingness and ability to buy.

There are also *Market Buyer Independents*. These are buyers who act independently for themselves, focusing solely on their individual needs. They determine at the point of purchase what they are willing and able to spend to buy what is on offer. They might choose to take on a Market Buyer Principal; to pay a premium price or forgo something that they want. They cannot create a benchmark for a market, nor do they follow others. They make up their own minds and decide what, when and where to buy (or not) at the interface with the sellers, in competition with other buyers.

The same relates to sellers within the market. There are *Market Seller Principals* who have sufficient volume in the market to be able to set benchmark prices for sales and *Market Seller Followers* whose pricing follows the prices set by the Market Seller Principals. To a lesser extent there are *Market Seller Independents* who take a more ad hoc approach to their sales. The roles and power of buyers and sellers and their effect on the market dynamic are covered in detail in Chapter 09.

Those who visit markets but who don't have the willingness and/or ability to buy or to sell are *Market Tourists*. They often create confusion and noise and may contribute to the environment of the market but not economically to it.

> *Cumulatively, Market Buyer and Seller Principals, Market Buyer and Seller Followers and Market Buyer and Seller Independents are known as the* Market Participants.

*If you are not a Market Participant then you are only an observer of the market.* Note in the definition the reference to buyers and sellers. A bilateral relationship between a buyer and a seller is a negotiation. Negotiation is one of the fives types of buy or sell processes in a market.

The five types of buy or sell processes in a market are:

1. a bilateral negotiation between a buyer and a seller;
2. competition between sellers for a buyer's decision to buy;
3. competition between buyers for a seller's products and services;
4. no negotiation and acceptance of the terms of the seller by the buyers;
5. no negotiation and acceptance of the terms of the buyer by the seller.

A market requires either more than one willing and able buyer with at least one willing and able seller or at least one willing and able buyer with more than one willing and able seller. In both cases the market only exists where there is a potential buy or sell interface between the buyers and the sellers. Just having a willingness and ability to buy or to sell does not create a market. There has to be an interface between buyers and sellers where there is a potential for the willingness and ability to buy or to sell to lead to a sale.

In the case of the Bakewell livestock market there were a small number of Market Buyer Principals, a larger number of Market Buyer Followers and a very small number of Market Buyer Independents. Livestock is not normally something bought in a commercial auction without prior intent and constraints regarding price. There were also a large number of Market Follower Sellers. No seller had a sufficient proportion of the available livestock to be a Market Seller Principal, such that if they withdrew their stock it would affect the dynamic of the market and drive prices up. There were a small number of Market Tourists who were interested in seeing what was going on and to see the animals but they did not form part of the market, only part of the environment surrounding the market.

In terms of the Bakewell non-livestock market, whilst there was an interface between willing and able buyers and willing and able sellers the buying and selling relationship was bilateral, which meant at best that it was a negotiation. The shop owners and stall operators (the sellers) offered goods and services for a set price. Buyers individually either offered that price or sought to negotiate a better deal. The buyers had the willingness and ability to buy and the sellers had the willingness and ability to sell but they were engaged in a bilateral negotiation and not a competitive bidding process as with the livestock market. Such negotiations, except in monopoly situations, are informed by the potential for competition.

In the non-livestock market it was the availability of alternative suppliers of the goods and services required by the buyers, the buyers' knowledge about those alternative suppliers and the willingness and ability of the buyers to access the alternative suppliers that determined where the power lay in the bilateral negotiation. Where the buyer had the knowledge, willingness and ability to access alternative suppliers of goods and services, a competition was created for the supply of those goods and services with the buyer having power to negotiate. Where, however, the buyer did not have knowledge of alternative suppliers or the willingness and ability to access them, the seller then had power to negotiate (or not).

In markets information is of vital importance as it determines where power lies between buyers and sellers, between buyers and between sellers. Knowledge of – and access to – alternative buyers for sellers and alternative sellers for buyers creates competition. This competition is a vital component of markets that managers need to understand if they are to exploit them. Competition as part of the market dynamic is explored in greater depth in Chapters 10 and 15.

*Total realized market value is the value of sales derived from the interface of buyers and sellers. The power of buyers and sellers in markets reflects their knowledge of alternative sellers and buyers, their willingness and ability to access them and their willingness and ability to use that knowledge in the buying or sales process.*

## Knowledge in markets

The issue of knowledge and the power it conveys in markets can be illustrated by reference to stock markets. Trading in stocks and shares is regarded by some as gambling. People buy stocks and shares based upon their knowledge and their hopes and beliefs about the future performance of the stocks and shares. Insider trading where an individual gets access to confidential information and acts upon it for gain is outlawed as it puts those with that knowledge at an unfair advantage in the market and can distort the market, leading to those without that knowledge suffering loss or indeed the demise of a company.

Some individuals and companies invest heavily in developing expertise to analyse company accounts and in developing an expert understanding of markets and the companies competing within them. This then gives them a higher level of knowledge than those who do not have access to such expertise.

Knowledge in the market is imperfectly distributed. This skewed distribution provides asymmetric competitive advantage and power in the market. Professional investors have significantly more knowledge of markets and the companies competing within them than general investors. Even the professionals, however, do not always get it right as their evaluation of the enhanced information that they have available to them is sometimes wrong or unexpected events have an unexpected impact. This is why even professional investors sometimes decide to be Market Buyer and Seller Followers rather than Market Buyer and Seller Principals. This is also why some funds and investors merely track the market. The returns may be lower but so too are the risks.

The benchmarks for the market for particular stocks and shares are created by those buying and selling large volumes of stocks and shares, the Market Buyer and Seller Principals. Some Market Buyer and Seller Principals take on 'icon status' and their actions are tracked closely by Market Buyer and Seller Followers. Warren Buffett is a Market Buyer and Seller Principal who has become known as the Sage of Omaha due to his ability to make great returns from the buying and selling of stocks and shares. When Warren Buffett buys or sells a particular stock and share he does so in large quantities and the Market Followers take note and often seek to emulate him. A successful and long track record generates confidence that he will get it right more often than he gets it wrong. Some Market Buyer and Seller Principals can increase or reduce the price of stocks and shares through what and when they choose to buy and to sell.

In this increasingly technology-reliant world where fractions of a second can make or lose money, Market Buyer and Seller Principals are being represented by computer programs that react to trigger levels for their decision-making. Huge volumes of stocks and shares can be traded, affecting a market based upon a mathematical trigger rather than on human judgement. This has led to some spectacular failings putting at risk companies and markets.

## What markets look like

The definition of a market can be represented diagrammatically as follows:

**FIGURE 1.1** The illustration of market definition

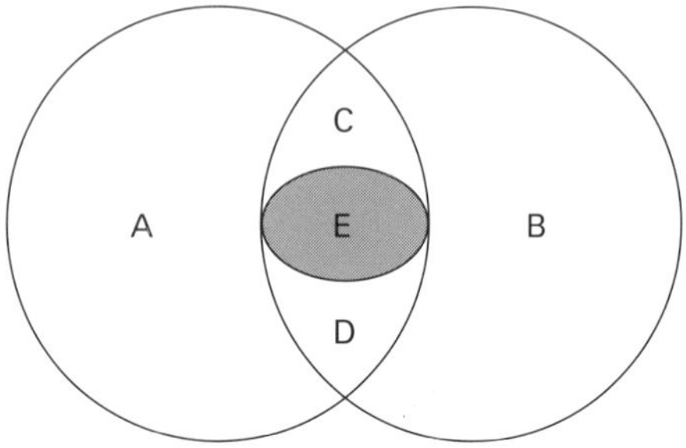


A represents the buyers with the ability to buy but not the willingness to buy. They've got the money but not the willingness to buy. Some of these will be Market Tourists whilst others will be inhibited by the price, the product and service benefit mix or the branding, etc. It is important that the barriers to buying are understood as a basis for developing options to overcome them.

B represents the sellers with the ability to sell but not the willingness to sell. They've got the products and services but not the willingness to sell. Some of these sellers will be Market Tourists whilst others will be inhibited by the competitive dynamic in the market, the volumes available, the margin available, etc.

C and D represent the buyers with the willingness and ability to buy and the sellers with the willingness and ability to sell but where sales have not been completed. This *unrealized value of the market* is represented by the purchasing power of the buyers in C and D. This is one of the two places (the other being E, below) where the five types of buy or sell market processes take place. It is where the Market Buyer and Seller Principals, Market Buyer and Seller Followers and Market Independents interact unsuccessfully to buy and sell.

E represents the sales completed and therefore the *realized value of the market* from the five buy or sell market processes. Sales illustrate the realized value of markets. The profile of the sales in terms of volume, prices, product and service benefit packages and timing illustrates what is happening and who is making it happen. Sales data provide valuable information about buyers, sellers, the economy, market trends, the impact of regulation, power in the market, market direction, channels to market and how the market is segmenting. Knowing who is buying and selling what, when and how enables the impact and intent of Market Buyer and Seller Principals and Market Buyer and Seller Followers to be identified and the market dynamic to be understood more fully.

The purchasing power of buyers in C + D + E represents the total value of the market. The total value of the market is determined by the cumulative value of the purchasing power of the buyers with the willingness and ability to buy. Marketing seeks to support the move of more of C and D into E.

Another way of looking at markets is to think of them in terms of mixing two chemicals, X and Y. Chemical X (a powder) represents willing and able buyers and chemical Y (a solution) represents willing and able sellers. Pour chemical X into a beaker containing chemical Y. Some of chemical X will react with some of chemical Y to create a new compound, Z, which floats in the unreacted remaining solution of chemical Y whilst an amount of chemical X just goes straight to the bottom of the beaker and remains unreacted. Chemical Z represents the realized value of the market. The potential unrealized value of the market is represented by the chemical X (the powder) that is at the bottom of the beaker.

Heating and/or stirring the remaining unreacted mixture of chemical X and chemical Y in the beaker creates more interactions between the chemicals and more reactions take place to produce more chemical Z. The more reactions there are, the more the realized value of the market increases. Similarly, if you add a catalyst to the mixture this promotes more reactions and speeds up the reaction process. The realized value of the market increases. An important role of marketing is to provide the heating or stirring and catalysts to the buyer/seller interface to create more sales.

The key for companies competing in markets is to find ways to increase the conversion rate of the chemicals for their products and services. Heating and/or stirring the mixture and/or adding a catalyst will be dealt with in Chapters 4 and 5.

> *Marketing should be seen as a catalyst to increase the willingness and ability of buyers to buy and the willingness and ability of sellers to sell to increase the sales completed.*

Competition in markets between buyers or between sellers is the norm and in the busy, noisy markets that companies operate within it is vital that they don't get distracted by those who have neither the willingness nor the ability to buy or to sell – the Market Tourists. A clear sign of companies being distracted by such 'noise' is the lack of focus in their marketing to support products and services and the confusion that it causes in buyers with the willingness and ability to buy.

Being able to define a market is important because it is the basis on which markets are segmented, sales are targeted and competitor-positioning strategies for products and services are developed. If your company cannot define the market, can it identify the products and services against which it is competing? Can it evaluate the size of demand and market shares within it? Can it understand the current and evolving needs of the buyers? Can it evaluate whether or not it can serve the market and chosen segments profitably? Can it determine what its competitive strategy should be?

The definition of the market and understanding the segments within it are vital for the company, both now and for the future. Understanding and being able to define the market are fundamental issues that companies need to address. Being able to define what a market is, however, is just the start. This definition needs to be used to create a meaningful context for the company and its products and services. It also needs to be able to be used to identify and evaluate the competitors, put their products and services in context and to inform the development of strategic options for competitive success.

As the future unfolds, so too the definition of the market needs to evolve. Competitive and corporate strategies need to be formulated looking forwards and not backwards. Unless managers can define and develop their understanding of markets there is a very real risk of their companies not fulfilling their potential and thus being adversely affected by competition.

Managers need to define markets not just in terms of products and services but in terms of the buyers' requirements in the market. They need to be able to identify and understand the impact and relationships between Market Buyer and Seller Principals, Market Buyer and Seller Followers, Market Buyer and Seller Independents and Market Tourists.

Managers must always remember that the past is only a guide to the future. Without being able to define and to understand the market now there is little chance of being able to make credible assumptions about the future development of the market.

> *Ask not what is affecting your company, ask rather what is affecting the buyers in the market, how the realized value of markets is achieved and how the unrealized potential of the market could be converted into the realized value of the market.*

If companies are to really exploit markets and to be successful they first have to be able to define the market and to understand the dynamic within it. They need to decide if they are to be a Market Buyer or Seller Principal, a Market Buyer or Seller Follower and whether they are interested in Market Buyer and Seller Independents. Most importantly they need to have a shared understanding within the company of the definition of a market and then bring that definition to life.

## Practitioner's tips

1. Make sure that throughout your company there is a clear understanding of when a market is created – at the interface of willing and able buyers and willing and able sellers.
2. Focus on what constitutes the willingness and ability to buy.
3. Focus on the characteristics of those with the willingness and ability to buy.
4. Recognize the difference between the unrealized value of the market and the realized value of the market.
5. Be realistic in evaluating the size of the market, the likelihood of converting potential but unrealized value into realized value and what might act as a catalyst to improve this process.
6. Recognize that if your company gets the definition of the market wrong it will not be able to compete successfully.
7. Recognize that any definition of the market has to be from the buyer's perspective and not from the seller's.
8. Recognize that if the company doesn't have an effective interface with buyers with the willingness and ability to buy, it cannot compete in the market.
9. Be clear about what your company requires if it is to be a willing and able seller.

10 Always remember that sellers who fail to deliver their promises affect the buyer's perception about the company's willingness and ability to sell and consequently their ability to be part of the market.

## Practitioner's questions

1. Do you know who the buyers with the willingness and ability to buy are in the market?
2. Can your company focus on those with the willingness and ability to buy?
3. Does your company know why buyers have the willingness and ability to buy?
4. Does your company know why buyers with the willingness and ability to buy don't buy from some or any of the competitors in the market?
5. Where is your company and where are its competitors in the realized market?
6. How strong are your company's products and services in converting those in the unrealized market to being in the realized market?
7. How strong are your company's competitors' products and services in converting those in the unrealized market to being in the realized market?
8. Does your company know how the potential value of the market can be increased?
9. Does your company have an effective interface with the willing and able buyers who buy and those that don't buy from your company?
10. Does your company know what catalysts work to improve the conversion rate from the unrealized value of the market into the realized value of the market for competitors?

# What makes markets attractive?

02

## Introduction

Attractiveness is in the eye of the beholder but whose eye is it? Attractiveness in terms of markets is often viewed very subjectively. Objective data are subjectively evaluated against criteria that are sometimes hard to understand and often more to do with the history of companies rather than the future of them.

Whether to stay in markets or to exit them can be very sensitive decisions. Decisions to stay in markets rather than manage exits from them can sometimes hinge on their evaluation as being attractive. This chapter looks at the unrealized and realized value of markets and criteria to be used when evaluating the attractiveness of markets.

## Attractive versus attraction

Horses can be led to water but they can't always be made to drink. The interaction of willing and able buyers and willing and able sellers may or may not result in sales. It is important to understand what the barriers are to preventing buyers buying and whether this is symptomatic of all buyers in the market or just of the buyer's perception of the seller. If it is symptomatic of the buyers in the market, it will affect the evaluation of the market as attractive for all sellers. If it is symptomatic of the buyer's evaluation of the seller's products and services, it will affect the evaluation of the attractiveness of the market for that seller.

In the latter case where the seller believes it is able to do something about its offer in the market to enable it to compete more successfully, the market could still be attractive to it. In the former case the market might not be attractive, as the seller might feel unable (or indeed be unable to invest sufficiently) to change buyer behaviour.

The unrealized value of the market consists of the purchasing power of those willing and able buyers that explore and consider buying through their interaction with willing and able sellers. The realized market value consists of the value of the sales that result from this interaction.

It is often stated that the value of markets – whatever the currency – is billions. There is an attraction to big numbers because surely the company can get a slice of those numbers. Managers see opportunity in big numbers. Some also have an attraction to new markets as this moves them from the problems and challenges of existing markets. Attraction relates to the power to attract, ie to appeal to the senses, to generate interest or to excite. Big numbers generate interest and excite.

*Attractive* relates to an evaluation of the properties that cause an attraction. *Attraction* creates interest, and an evaluation of what is of interest against criteria (hopefully more than just the senses) determines whether or not it is attractive. This applies to markets. Managers have an attraction to certain markets but they need to be clear about the criteria that they use to determine whether in fact they are attractive.

Having a large unrealized market value number creates attraction, eg the Indian and Chinese markets with their huge populations and developing economies. Evaluation of the attraction of the market and what it takes to compete successfully within it, however, may result in it not being attractive for a company. It might not wish to operate as part of a joint venture with a local company or have to agree to technology transfer or be willing to invest in those markets, putting at risk its current market performance.

Whilst many markets may cause attraction, not all of them are attractive. Unrealized market value figures need to be carefully interrogated to ensure that they are based upon credible data. A market's value should be based upon the realized value of sales over time. Where these data do not exist, or cannot be accessed, a market's value based upon potential sales is speculative at best and should be treated with caution.

Potential sales data are often based upon assumptions – assumptions about the economy; changes in legislation; the desirability of certain products and services; the relative strengths of competing products and services; changes in social patterns; the adoption of technological advances; etc. All may cause attraction but are they attractive? How do you judge?

Market research has become widely adopted to try to get a more scientific approach to these variables. Again, whilst market research is helpful it often comes with many caveats attached. It is important to recognize that market research is a support for judgement and risk-taking and not a replacement for them.

Sales data are a key competitive resource and are closely guarded unless there are reasons to disclose them, eg to give confidence to the stock market. Why would you normally let your competitors know how your sales are going? Whilst you may want to create an image of market domination or progress you need sales data to inform your decision-making and not that of your competitors!

> *There can be a big difference between the realized value of a market and the total value of a market. Be clear about the credibility of the data upon which the unrealized and realized market values are based and the assumptions made in formulating those values.*

Few markets are homogeneous and are often segmented in terms of the products and services required by buyers and by their geographical coverage. The value of the potential and realized markets for 'X' in Mexico might be very different to the total and realized value of the markets for 'X' in England. Where markets exist is dealt with in Chapter 3. It is important to be clear about the limits that are being applied to the definition of the market. The definition needs to be real rather than theoretical.

Converting a market's total value into realized value has many barriers. Believing that you have a good understanding of the total value of markets is only part of the equation. You need to understand the barriers to converting unrealized value into realized value and how you can overcome those barriers. You also need to decide whether the market is sufficiently attractive for you to invest and take the risks necessary to overcome them.

The value of a market in terms of sales is different from the attractiveness and profitability of markets for sellers. Some markets operate on very low margins that require very large volumes of sales to make the desired quantum of profit, eg supermarkets. Other markets exist on low volume, high margins, eg haute couture. The market dynamic can have a significant impact on profitability and its attractiveness. Whilst the total value of markets might be significant and attractive, the ability to realize acceptable levels of profit from it might be very different.

Managers sometimes see attraction in turnover and market share. It is surely profitability, however, that is attractive. Whilst having a bigger market share than a competitor might be seen as attractive, it is sometimes better to have a lower market share and greater profitability. A 5 per cent net profit on a market share equivalent of £1 billion is better than having a 2 per cent net profit on a market share equivalent of £2 billion.

Turnover sometimes comes to be regarded as a proxy for attractiveness. Let's look at an example.

## CASE STUDY

### Attractive through profit, not just turnover

In the years after the Velvet Revolution in the Czech Republic I did some consultancy with a number of companies that were taking advantage of their new commercial freedoms. One particular company I helped was considering withdrawing from one of its important markets where it had traditionally been successful. Before it withdrew from the market I was asked to identify why, despite the market being regarded as attractive and generating a high turnover for the company, it had got into difficulties and whether it could take action that would enable it to stay in the market and benefit from its attractiveness.

Context is all. In the past under the communist regime the prevailing culture was supply-side led. The company, prior to its transfer to the commercial sector, had a production target and it was judged in terms of meeting its production target. I found, however, that whilst the company's managers had been freed from the previous constraints and were free to pursue a commercial approach to the business, the company's culture was still dominated by a supply-side and production culture. Talking to the managers of the company I found that they all focused on turnover. Production equated to turnover, which equated to attractiveness. The turnover had become a proxy for the attractiveness of the market.

Digging deeper into the company and the assumptions and beliefs of the mangers that guided their decision-making, I found that there was a lack of understanding of the terms 'fixed costs', 'variable costs' and 'profit margin'. Perhaps as a legacy from the past, the managers believed that the vast majority of their costs were fixed rather than variable.

The company's products and services were competitively priced and had been generating a high turnover. An analysis of the company's cost base revealed that its cost of production and overheads were very high. To maintain sales volume and turnover, prices had been reduced with the result that the profit margin on sales that was previously small had all but gone. Insufficient profit on sales was being generated to provide the money necessary for investment in the development of the product and service portfolio, in marketing and in providing a return for the shareholders.

The buyers' perceptions of the products and services they wanted were changing. The company's competitors had adjusted their cost bases in the light of the competition and were able to sustain lower prices whilst also having money to develop their products and services. This led to buyers' perceptions of the company's products and services changing. The company's previous good value proposition was being seen increasingly as neither good nor of value.

The company did not have the money available to develop its products and services to match the changing buyer requirements. It saw its previous price advantage eroded and its high cost base meant that it could not respond to price competition without losing money. The company's turnover was consequently suffering and its high cost base was not capable of being sustained. Increasingly it was not able to compete in the market profitably. As turnover went down the cash flow and working capital became more difficult and the company's view of the attractiveness of the market reduced.

The total and realized value of the market had not changed significantly but the ability of the company to compete successfully within the market had changed. Changing the company's definition of the attractiveness of the market and getting it to focus on the profitability of turnover, rather than just turnover, required organizational, cultural as well as strategic change.

To managers many things provide an attraction but we have to be able to determine what is really attractive. It is stated that attractiveness is in the eye of the beholder. Sometimes it is necessary to change how the eye of the beholder looks at the world to really understand the difference between attraction and attractiveness!

# Clarifying what constitutes attractiveness

A number of different criteria can be used to define market attractiveness. Companies have to decide whether the total market value and the realized market value provide them with the opportunity to achieve a profitable return whether as an existing competitor in the market or as a new entrant to the market.

## *Responding to customers*

It is also the case that it is sometimes important or necessary for companies to be in markets because their major buyers in the market want them to be there, eg international companies often want to deal with international service providers to ensure consistency and to simplify relationships. If you aren't present in the markets that the buyer is in then you can't compete for that buyer's business. Similarly, significant buyers might only want to deal with sellers who provide a multifaceted 'solutions' package of products and services. If they don't provide a coordinated comprehensive 'solution' in those markets then they can't compete for that buyer's business. In these cases the definition and evaluation of attractiveness for sellers are *supra-market* and focused on the profitability of meeting the seller's requirements in aggregate across markets and across market segments.

## *Understanding total and realized market value versus price*

The definition of market attractiveness needs to be actively understood and acted upon within the company to avoid different parts of the company approaching the market in different ways. One of the ways of developing this shared understanding is the development and use of the total and realized market value versus price graph. An example is provided in Figure 2.1.

Developing this graph enables perceptions about the potential and realized values of the market to be tested at different price levels within the team. Whilst accepting that price is only one determinant of demand it is a useful tool to use in surfacing different perceptions in teams about market attractiveness.

*There is a difference between the total value of a market and the realized value of a market at different price points. The attractiveness of markets will be affected by whether the company can profitably get the value of sales required at the price points at which it can compete to provide an acceptable level of return on investment.*

Too often teams focus internally (both in terms of the company and their roles within it) rather than externally on the market. Discussing perceptions about the elasticity of buyer demand with price in a market is a good starting point for developing an external focus. This external focus can then be used to put the company's products and services in context and to discuss what the company would need to do to compete profitably at different price points and market values.

The graph in Figure 2.1 starts at the minimum price for the product and service in the market. There is often an assumption that demand will continue to increase as the price reduces. Whilst buyers want to get a good deal it is often the case that if products and services are perceived as too cheap it undermines confidence in those products and services. Buyer perception of value can act as a self-regulator of buyer price sensitivity.

**FIGURE 2.1** The total and realized market value versus price graph

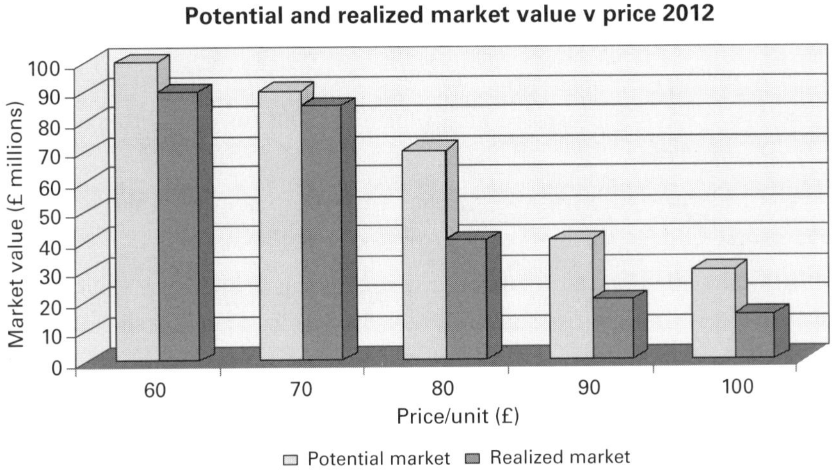

Price is also tempered by the concentration of the buyers (a small number of high-volume buyers can drive prices down) and the concentration of the sellers (a small number of sellers can drive prices up). The minimum price in the market is determined by the willingness and ability of buyers to buy at a price, the willingness and ability of sellers to sell at that price and who has the power in the market.

In the illustration above the minimum price is £60 per unit. No seller at that time was willing and able to sell below that price. This could change over time, however, as a seller is able to reduce costs or adopts a loss leader market penetration strategy or a buyer exercises its power over the sellers, eg supermarkets exercising their power over suppliers.

The graph illustrated shows a significant drop in both the total and realized value of the market above £70 with further significant drops above £80. This demonstrates that seeking to achieve premium prices may not be attractive, as the size and value of the total and realized markets at these prices may not be sufficient to enable them to be exploited profitably. The graph indicates that the market may only be attractive if the company believes that it can gain sufficient market share profitably at £60–£70 per unit to generate the returns on investment it requires.

The key to the above is not the production of a definitive graph but its use to surface and address different perceptions about the market and the company's approach to it. I have found that this approach can uncover very real differences in the views of managers about the attractiveness of markets including:

- There is an emotional attachment rather than economic approach to the market (this market was how the company started and is the heart of the company).
- There are differing levels of optimism about the company's ability to compete.
- Speculative assumptions about the intentions of competitors are being made.
- Unshared optimistic assumptions are being made about the future total value in the market or growth rate of the market.
- Unshared optimistic assumptions are being made about the ability of the company to convert unrealized value into realized value in the market.
- There are differing views on the nature and potential impact of the barriers to exit and whether or not they can and should be addressed.
- There are differing views on the nature and impact of barriers to entry for new competitors.

- There are differing views on buyer loyalty and buyers' willingness and ability to switch to other sellers.
- A lack of a shared understanding of the developing needs of the buyers in the market.
- Previously unstated views that the market isn't attractive and that the company should withdraw.

Companies must have a shared understanding of the attractiveness of markets and this understanding must effectively guide their actions. Developing a *total and realized market value versus price* graph and answering the questions below facilitates a realistic dialogue about markets, their attractiveness and the ability of companies to make a profit within them.

## Practitioner's tips

1. Be clear about the definition of the market and that the differences between attraction and attractiveness are understood.
2. Get each team member to record their assumptions about the minimum price and total and realized value of the market before the team gets together to discuss them.
3. Discuss as a team the assumptions underlying each individual's differing assessment of the difference between the total market value and the realized market value at different price points.
4. Identify whether there are other major variables that are likely to affect the differences between the total and realized market values. If there are then use them as part of the discussion.
5. Identify what makes the market attractive, not just for your company but for all competitors.
6. Don't put your company's products and services into the discussion until you've done the above.
7. Remember that your company's products and services don't operate in isolation; you must consider the products and services of others.
8. Make sure that you know not just the current unit cost and margin of your company's products and services but the ability of your company to change them if necessary.
9. Remember that this isn't a science and that you are making assumptions.

10 Make sure that at the end of the discussion there's a shared understanding of the market; how attractiveness is defined; whether or not the market is attractive to the company; whether anything needs to change to make it attractive; the questions that still need to be addressed; and ensure that there is a shared commitment to answer these questions.

## Practitioner's questions

1. Is there a shared understanding of the company's definition of the market and the criteria for market attractiveness?
2. As price rises how do the total and realized market values rise or fall?
3. As the relationship between total and realized market value changes how does this impact on your company's profitability?
4. Where is your company relative to its competitors in terms of price and profitability?
5. Is the market stable or changing? If it's changing how is it changing?
6. What does your company need to do to be able to compete?
7. Is the value of the market attractive to your company at the price point at which it can compete?
8. What are the trends in the market in terms of price, total value, realized value, competitor market shares and the nature of competition?
9. What are the key variables that affect price, total market value and realized market value?
10. Can your company change the competitive dynamic and the relationship between total market value and realized market value?

# Where do markets exist?

03

## Introduction

The world has changed as a result of the huge advances in communications technology and the accessibility of the functionality that technology provides to people. Lifestyles have changed as a result of technological change and confidence has grown in the security of internet-based transactions.

These changes have been reflected in where markets exist, with significant implications for traditional marketplaces and the physical infrastructure and investment made to support them. This chapter explores these changes and what companies need to address to ensure that they do not get left behind and miss opportunities to compete.

## Markets and places

Many definitions of a market refer to the place where sellers and buyers of products and services come together to transact business, eg Bakewell market. The reference to 'a place' reflects the historical setting for markets being places where sellers and buyers congregated to barter and agree prices for the exchange of goods and services. Places where markets took place were referred to as market towns.

Whether it is rural Europe, the United States, Africa, Australia, Asia or India, market days remain a part of the social as well as economic fabric of the local society. Physical markets still attract people but the nature of markets has been extended far from the physical places where traditionally they have been located.

As has been seen from the definition of a market in Chapter 1, the mere physical or virtual presence of a company in a marketplace does not mean that the company is in a market. A market requires an interface between willing and able buyers with willing and able sellers.

Some companies confuse presence in a physical or virtual marketplace with being in a market. They are only in a market if they are part of the interaction between willing and able buyers with willing and able sellers, irrespective of where they are located. In the past the willingness and ability of the buyer to go beyond the high street were very limited. Today they are increasingly unlimited.

> *Physical and geographical boundaries increasingly do not define a marketplace. Marketplaces are increasingly defined by the willingness and ability of buyers to interact with willing and able sellers virtually rather than being defined by where they are physically located, as was traditionally the case.*

Today physical marketplaces only constrain the operation of a market where the willing and able buyers have a time-sensitive need for a product and service or do not have the inclination to 'shop around' for the best deal for them. This is why 'convenience' stores are able to charge a premium for products and why petrol stations in locations where there isn't an alternative supply for miles around are able to charge higher prices for the commodity of petrol.

As we know, where a market consists of a single seller – so-called 'monopolistic markets' – it leads to a distortion between the power of buyers and sellers. The seller is all-powerful for those products that the buyer needs or wants to buy. The marketplace in these situations is determined by the seller.

## Virtual marketplaces

The internet has transformed the buyer's willingness and ability to interact with sellers wherever they are located, as well as the boundaries of markets and the definition of marketplaces. This is evidenced increasingly by 'virtual marketplaces' where buyers in one country have their sale completed in another country's tax jurisdiction. Controversy is building over companies like Google and Amazon that generate huge sales from one country's buyers but pay little tax to that country's government whilst still operating within the law.

The development of virtual marketplaces has highlighted the difference between and separation of marketplace and market. Huge businesses have been created on the basis and convenience of providing virtual marketplaces for buying products and services. Amazon, eBay and the websites of traditional 'bricks-and-mortar' companies are transforming the look and use of high streets, as it is no longer an absolute requirement for retailers to have a physical presence in towns and cities for the operation of a market for their products and services.

Retailers have sought to adapt to this by providing a company-dedicated transactional website with collection from their high-street physical shops or through specialist logistic firms. The term 'transactional' is important because as with marketplaces of the past, markets for some goods and services and for some buyers require a social element to them.

Internet-based marketplaces have sought to address this need for a social element to purchasing by providing masses of information. Not all buyers, however, want to trawl through all of this information and prefer to talk directly to someone. Internet marketplaces have also sought to use the experience of those who have bought using the marketplace to reassure potential buyers of the quality and reliability of the product and service offer and its fulfilment. This is why websites such as Amazon include reader reviews of books and reviews of the seller's performance. Businesses have been created out of providing reviews of buyers' experiences, such as www.tripadvisor.co.uk.

One of the most sophisticated markets represented by the Stock Exchange in the UK has long migrated to being virtual. No longer do stockbrokers and traders know each other and negotiate with each other in person on the basis of 'my word is my bond'. They now rely upon virtual trades and computer-generated programs that do many thousands of trades in a fraction of a second when trigger points are reached.

In this case the place where the market is found has become an increasingly virtual platform for trading. This perhaps explains some of the difficulties experienced when computer programs have caused turmoil in the market – market-significant actions in seconds driven by programmed processes without judgement!

It is also the case that time has become a critical issue in some markets. The term 'time is of the essence' relates to days in some markets whereas in financial markets and trading situations it could relate to fractions of a second. It is important to understand the time context for different marketplaces and markets.

This time criticality has driven the automation of transaction processes. The nature and volume of the outputs from these transactional processes can have a significant impact on the viability and reputation of markets and upon the buyers and sellers within them. The transactional process software programs in these situations become a proxy for buyers and sellers testing their willingness and ability to trade. This is a long way from the traditional concept of a market and its reliance upon people and places.

> *The 'places' where markets exist have increasingly become virtual. Place relates to where and how the interface between willing and able buyers and willing and able sellers is facilitated. Different markets have different levels of time-critical dynamics; different levels of reliance upon technology; different levels of social interaction requirements and different levels and types of transactional functionality requirements.*

Despite all of the above, whilst the processes within a market may be increasingly transactional and automated, a market isn't an inanimate entity. A market consists of a living and dynamic collection of people as buyers or sellers – a dynamism affected by a number of economic and social variables that will be explored later.

The more automated the processes within a marketplace without oversight and judgement, the greater the risks for organizations. Automated processes need to be constantly reviewed and adjusted to reflect the changing market conditions and the risk profile of the organization.

> *Whilst inanimate transactional processes support markets they need to be managed to keep in touch with the market as it develops and to ensure that risk is managed. If the dynamism in markets is created by inanimate transactional processes organizational risk can rise.*

It is important to highlight at this point that the rise of comparison websites with sales functionality now means that different marketplaces are being created. Companies may now need to be in different virtual marketplaces to ensure that they can compete for business. Buyers want the opportunity to directly compare the offers of different sellers.

It is also important to highlight that companies that develop their brands and invest huge amounts of money in them do not want to be in some marketplaces. This is because they believe that the brand association with the marketplace can have a negative impact on their brand.

## CASE STUDY

### Burberry

Burberry is an aspirational branded clothing company experiencing tremendous success. In November 2013 the company announced that half-year sales were more than £1 billion for the first time.

The Burberry check is synonymous with the brand and instantly recognizable, conveying brand values consistent with its target higher socio-economic buyers. Burberry check is a design of distinction.

These brand values were undermined in the past by the adoption of the Burberry check by football hooligans and lower socio-economic groups known colloquially as 'chavs'. This created a major problem for Burberry, as counterfeit producers and copycats created a supply of low-cost, low-quality products using the iconic pattern. The once-exclusive Burberry brand was undermined as its trademark check was seen in the mass market, undermining its desirability amongst affluent buyers.

Burberry had also sought to grow using a licensing model. Twenty-three licensees around the world were each doing something different ranging from kilts to dog leads. It appeared that there was something for everyone but little of it was consistent with exclusiveness. This licensing had allowed the product range to proliferate and Burberry had lost control over its most important asset: its brand.

In 2006, new Chief Executive Angela Ahrendts countered this undermining of the brand by taking back control of it. The company spent millions buying back licences and it launched trademark infringement lawsuits against retailers stocking copycat designs. She recognized that ubiquity kills a brand based upon exclusivity and was determined to both control market access to the product and to ensure that wherever buyers came into contact with Burberry products they got a consistent, high-quality Burberry service.

➔

Burberry used endorsements from 'A-list' celebrities like Kate Moss to reposition the brand. It advertised heavily in magazines such as *GQ*, *Vogue* and *Harper's Bazaar* and adopted a viral, internet-based marketing approach. It was present at fashion weeks around the world and held exclusive events. Crucially, it controlled where its products could be purchased.

The availability of products in the 'grey' market that subsequently find a channel to marketplaces inconsistent with the brand's values is a constant challenge for companies seeking to protect their brands. Seeing a high-end fragrance in a discount store does not protect and support the brand values of the product. Control of channels to markets for sellers is of crucial importance to maintain brand integrity. Marketplaces need to be consistent with the objectives of sellers for their products and services.

## Managing multiple marketplaces

Companies need to be aware of the proliferation of marketplaces and, wherever possible, make positive choices about whether or not they compete within them. Increasingly, companies need to have marketing plans that embrace different types of marketplace. Different marketplaces have different competitive 'rules of the game' and different buyer expectations. Companies need to understand these 'rules of the game' and different buyer expectations and have the systems in place to ensure that they don't seek to apply old marketplace processes and responses to new marketplaces.

The physical proximity of marketplaces once implicit in the definition of a marketplace has long gone and it is only companies that are able to recognize and respond to the requirements of the new marketplaces that will survive and prosper. The marketplace is increasingly not just here but everywhere.

Presence in different marketplaces has to be driven by where the buyers want to be and where and how they make their 'buy' decisions. It is no accident, for example, that the value of space for advertising on websites is directly related to the nature and volume of traffic generated by those websites. Companies, in deciding where to advertise, have to be clear about where the buyers they wish to attract congregate and how the presence of the company's products and services on those websites, etc will be viewed by buyers.

It is no longer adequate to have one approach to the marketplace and to marketing. Different marketplaces require different approaches and managers need to make choices about how they can support the buyer's perception of the brand and accessibility to it. Can the company afford not to have multiple marketplace plans and strategies?

As important as being clear about the strategy for multiple marketplaces is the need to ensure that expectations generated in them are delivered in practice. An internet-based marketplace will soon be undermined if physical order fulfilment is unreliable, as will bricks-and-mortar marketplaces if the shelves remain empty.

In developing different strategies for different marketplaces the challenges for organizational culture, resources and linkages between company activities need to be understood. A buyer wishing to proceed to buy a product using an internet-based marketplace will want to be able to transact the purchase seamlessly, in a timely way and with absolute confidence in the security of the transaction. They also do not want to make a selection only to find a click-through which states: 'Sorry, currently not in stock'. Companies need to be clear about the buyer's criteria for each marketplace, how they meet those criteria and how they compare with other companies competing within that marketplace.

## Practitioner's tips

1. The 'place' in marketplace reflects the requirements of buyers. Merely being in a marketplace does not mean that your company is in a market.
2. Companies need to have a strategy to influence and plan for changes in where the 'place' in marketplace is likely to be in the future.
3. Don't be constrained by past investment when investing in the marketplace for the future.
4. Remember that all fixed costs are variable in the long term. Nothing is set in stone and everything can be changed, including where your company has its marketplace and how it uses the marketplaces of others.
5. Technology makes everything possible at a price and with a risk. Be clear about what your company needs to do to meet the requirements of buyers, what it's prepared to spend in getting it and the risks of both investing and not investing.

6 Put the efficiency and economy of transactional technology-based processes in the context of the needs of buyers.
7 Don't forget that buyers often want more than just access to the purchase of a product and service and that the marketplace needs to be able to provide it.
8 Don't just abandon physical infrastructure; think about how it can be used in a new marketplace context.
9 Be clear about which marketplaces you need to be in and those that you don't want to be in.
10 Make sure that you know how and under what conditions your products and services are being offered, to ensure that the marketplace is not undermining your brand and objectives.

## Practitioner's questions

1 Where are the marketplaces that your company needs to be in now?
2 What are your company's objectives for the marketplaces in (1) above and are they being met?
3 Is your company clear about the marketplaces that it does not want to be in and taking steps to ensure that it is not in those marketplaces?
4 Where will be the marketplaces that buyers will use in the future be?
5 Do you have a plan for developing a presence in these marketplaces of the future to at least match the pace of buyer migration to them?
6 If your company has created its own virtual marketplace, are you clear what functionality and support buyers want from the operation of the marketplace and how your company compares with those requirements and the offer of other marketplaces?
7 If a marketplace has international reach, are the company's products and services offered in a way consistent with different international marketplace requirements?
8 Is your company able physically to service marketplaces with international reach to the level required by buyers and provided by other sellers?

9 Are your company's presence and investment in marketplaces being driven by technology or using technology to support the achievement of corporate objectives?

10 What is the risk profile of the company arising out of its presence in different marketplaces both individually and cumulatively?

# Have to buy or discretionary buy?

04

## Introduction

Buyers buy for different reasons. Some buy because they have to buy and others buy because they would like to buy; they are in a discretionary buy situation. Some are compelled by need and some by desire. It is important that companies understand the motivations of buyers to buy so that they can decide how they might market their products and services in a more focused and effective way and improve their competitive offer relative to others.

This chapter looks at the human dynamics of *have to buy* and *discretionary buy*. Particular reference is made to Maslow's hierarchy of needs and the challenges for managers in taking an external buyer perspective of products and services that are identified.

## Understanding have to buy and discretionary buy

Buying can be divided into *have to buy* and *discretionary buy*. *Have to buy* constrains the markets that the buyers can be active within. *Discretionary buy* provides buyers with flexibility and choice in relation to the markets that they can be active within. An objective of marketing is to convince those with a willingness and ability to buy that what the company offers is a *have to buy* rather than a *discretionary buy*. Examples might include: 'I have to buy a mobile phone because it's a necessity of life.' The mobile phone has moved from being a *discretionary buy* for most people to being a *have to buy* item. An iPhone is a discretionary buy as there are lots of cheaper phones with less functionality or the same functionality. The marketing and branding associated with Apple products, however, seek to convince those who have a willingness and ability to make a discretionary buy of a mobile phone to buy the Apple iPhone. The marketing is aimed at not only encouraging buyers to make a discretionary buy but to convince them that the Apple iPhone is a *have to buy* bundle of product and services.

If I *have to buy* an Apple iPhone I will only be active in markets selling Apple iPhones and those marketplaces selling them. Competition for my willingness and ability to buy will be focused around *where* I have to buy and not *what* I have to buy. In the example above, the competition is not between Apple iPhones and other phones but between marketplaces selling Apple iPhones.

Where those in a *have to buy* situation are not constrained by only having to buy an Apple iPhone then the market (and thus the competition) is between a much wider range of phones and not just in marketplaces selling Apple iPhones. The less specific the buyer's requirements, the more diverse the products and services competing for the willingness and ability of buyers to spend on buying a phone.

## Motivation to buy

In understanding what to buy the motivation of buyers needs to be understood. A useful tool in gaining this understanding is Maslow's hierarchy of needs. Maslow (1954) identified that people have a hierarchy of needs that affects their motivation. These levels start with physiological needs and develop through safety, 'belongingness', esteem, through to self-actualization. The theory expounds that individuals seek to fulfil their needs in the lower sections of the hierarchy before considering the higher sections of the hierarchy.

It has been found, however, that individuals can in fact seek to fulfil higher sections of the hierarchy before all of their needs in the lower sections of the hierarchy are fulfilled. In part, marketing, access to credit and societal changes have been responsible for this development. It has also been found that the focus of individuals varies with context, eg at times of war (Tang and West 2002), and that it varies across age groups (Goebel and Brown 1981).

Buyers increasingly want products and services now rather than waiting until they have saved up enough money to buy them. Access to credit meant that they were able to buy products and services now, and marketing encouraged a 'me too' buyer demand. Whilst this led to economic growth, it did so on the back of unsustainable levels of personal debt. It was this debt, encouraged and supported by financial institutions, that subsequently proved toxic for those institutions and for the buyers incurring the debt as economies around the world went into recession.

Whilst the resulting economic recession severely affected demand in the market it is interesting to note that as the economies around the world are at various stages of recovery so too is the level of debt funding it. It seems that the underlying societal changes of the 'me too' and 'now' culture have not gone away but were merely put into abeyance until confidence started to grow and access to credit became easier.

Understanding the psychology of the motivation of buyer behaviour is important. Understanding how these motivations change over time and in different contexts is also important. Different buyers in different market segments can have different motivations that affect their buying behaviour.

Continuing the example of the mobile phone, it can be seen that some people who might be considered to have not satisfied the lower sections of the Maslow hierarchy believe that an iPhone is a *have to buy*. Indeed such is their willingness to secure the *have to buy* phone that they acquire the ability to do so through borrowing money. Companies seeking to increase sales seek to provide willing buyers with the ability to buy through the credit terms that they offer.

A way to illustrate this is provided by a three-step process:

Step 1 involves defining the target buyers and then identifying whether the products and services are *have to buy* or *discretionary buy*.

Step 2 then takes the competing products and services (this can be done for products and services that are *have to buy* or *discretionary buy)* and puts them in the context of Maslow's hierarchy of needs. This provides a context for the 'buy' decisions being sought and the approach needed to marketing.

Step 3 seeks to identify how the competing brands for the competing products and services are perceived by the buyers. This again helps to hone the marketing mix, the understanding of market segmentation and what the company may need to focus upon in terms of product and service development.

Undertaking this process enables the company to address the following questions:

1. Can marketing help to convince willing and able buyers that the company's products and services are *have to buy* rather than *discretionary buy*?
2. Can marketing convince willing and able buyers that the company's products and services meet their Maslow hierarchy requirements?

3 Can marketing convince willing and able buyers that the company's brand has a competitive edge over its rivals?

This process and these questions enable an externally focused dialogue to be initiated within the company that provides a context for evaluating the objectives of and the balance in the marketing mix for the company's products and services.

Step 1: Identifying whether the products and services are *have to buy* or *discretionary buy*.

**FIGURE 4.1** Categorizing products and services for have to buy or discretionary buy

| Competing products and services ↓ | Have to buy | Discretionary buy |
|---|---|---|
| A | | |
| B | | |
| C | | |
| D | | |

Step 2: Identifying how the competing products and services relate to Maslow's hierarchy.

**FIGURE 4.2** Competing products and services and Maslow's hierarchy

| | | Competing products and services |
|---|---|---|
| Maslow's hierarchy | Self-actualization | |
| | Esteem | |
| | Belongingness | |
| | Safety | |
| | Physiological | |

Step 3: Placing the competing brands in Maslow's hierarchy.

**FIGURE 4.3** Brands and Maslow's hierarchy

| | | Brands of competing products and services |
|---|---|---|
| Maslow's hierarchy | Self-actualization | |
| | Esteem | |
| | Belongingness | |
| | Safety | |
| | Physiological | |

It is vital in undertaking the three steps above that the company's focus is external and as objective as possible. Only in this way will useful information be collected that will enable the marketing and product and service development strategies to evolve successfully. Knowing your own company's products and services is essential. Knowing them in the context of willing and able buyers in the market is vital. This is an ongoing process.

> *Knowing whether your company's products and services are* **have to buy** *or* **discretionary buy** *is an important first step in understanding willing and able buyers. This needs to be built upon by then seeking to understand the motivation of willing and able buyers to enable the company's product and service development and marketing to be focused.*

A phone's base functionality was verbal communication. Increasingly, verbal communication has become merely part of the functionality of the mobile communications, information gateway and entertainment device called a phone. The size of the market for the standalone traditional base functionality for phones (only being able to speak to someone) has shrunk in many parts of the world to zero. I might *have to buy* a phone but today I want it as part of a mobile portfolio of functionality.

The phone market has been redefined by these changes with a level of non-verbal communications functionality becoming a norm. It could be argued that there isn't a phone market any more but a mobile communications market segmented by functionality. The past *discretionary buy* functionality segments in the market and the dynamism of the competition within and between these market segments has been redefined and continues to evolve with the product development outputs of sellers and their ability to convince willing and able buyers of the ability that these advances have to meet their Maslow hierarchy of needs.

The more the functionality and the benefits of products and services evolve, the more segmented the market becomes and the more the boundaries between *have to buy* and *discretionary buy* change. Companies need to understand the impact of these changes on the motivations or Maslow hierarchy of needs of willing and able buyers. They also need to be able to develop their marketing and product and service offer on an ongoing basis in this context. Those with the greatest understanding and the ability to respond to the evolving needs of buyers get the best results.

## Competition not substitutes

In *discretionary buy* contexts, particularly willing and able buyers can be active in several markets. I might consider buying a computer or I might consider buying a television. If I have the willingness and ability to buy either or both and start actively exploring both, I am part of both markets. Whether or not I choose to buy either or both or neither is another issue, as is the choice of market and the marketplace in which I buy.

If I am in a *discretionary buy* situation and I buy a computer but not a television, have I bought a substitute product for a television? The answer is no. I have decided to buy in one market and not another. There may be a whole range of reasons for deciding to buy a computer and not a television. Other people might make a different decision or buy kitchen equipment rather than a computer or something else. The key is to understand which products and services are likely to be competing for the money the buyer has a willingness and ability to spend. It is about competition for willingness and ability to spend and not whether or not one product is a substitute for another.

Sellers need to understand whether or not their products and services are *have to buy* or *discretionary buy* to understand what their products and services are competing against. Only then can they start to address the competition and marketplaces. They also need to understand how they might develop their products and services to enable them to compete in *discretionary buy* markets. This is particularly important if the historical 'core' *have to buy* market is shrinking and/or becoming increasingly competitive.

> *There is no such thing as substitute products and services, only competing products and services. Sellers need to identify whether they are in a* **have to buy** *or a* **discretionary buy** *situation to enable them to understand the products and services that are competing against each other.*

Sometimes generic terms are used to describe markets, eg 'the consumer products market'. Whilst this might be a convenient nomenclature there is a danger that the extensive variety of buyers, products and services in such a market definition diminishes both its credibility and its practical use. Such a broadly defined market definition will contain a large number of segments with often very different competitive dynamism and a widely differing range of buyer willingness and ability to buy. It is like saying that I know the market is segmented like the colours of a rainbow but I'm going to only focus on what the characteristics are in the red section of the rainbow.

Some market segments will be dominated by *have to buy* buyers whereas others will be dominated by *discretionary buy* buyers. The key is to know how to define the market in a way that facilitates useful analysis and evaluation that can guide the development of effective marketing and competitive strategies.

It is hard to compete successfully if the company does not have a clear understanding of what its products and services are competing against. Competing in market segments dominated by *have to buy* buyers can be very different from competing in market segments dominated by *discretionary buy* buyers.

> *The company should seek to define markets in ways that reflect competing products and services and not just by using generic terms representing aggregated products and services.*

Life is full of choices. The choices that buyers make in a *have to buy* context can be different from those that they make in a *discretionary buy* context. Through understanding the motivation of buyers, a buyer's perception of a product and service can be changed from looking at it as a *discretionary buy* to looking at it as a *have to buy*. This can change the dynamic of competition. Apple products have continuously evolved in recent years and have been regarded as *have to buy* rather than *discretionary buy* for significant numbers of willing and able buyers. This has made it extremely difficult for other companies to compete. This to a lesser extent is the power of brands – I'm a Mercedes man and will only buy Mercedes cars. I only wear Paul Smith clothes or buy Apple computers.

## Practitioner's tips

1. If you sell in a *have to buy* context what your company's products and services are competing against should be clear. If you sell in a *have to buy* context you may still have to compete in many marketplaces.
2. If you sell in a *discretionary buy* context you are likely to be competing in several markets. If you sell in a *discretionary buy* context you are also likely to have to compete in many marketplaces.
3. Understanding whether you're in a *have to buy* or a *discretionary buy* context should have an impact on how the company addresses its approach to the market(s) and marketplaces.
4. Products and services need to be put into the context of the motivations and needs of willing and able buyers (eg using Maslow's hierarchy of needs) to enable the company to understand the *have to buy* and *discretionary buy* context.
5. In a *have to buy* context there cannot be a substitute product and service for what has to be bought, only competing products and services.
6. In a *discretionary buy* context there isn't a substitute product and service, only competing products and services for the money that the buyers are willing and able to spend.
7. Understand that one of the roles of marketing is to convince willing and able buyers that they are in a *have to buy* context rather than a *discretionary buy* context.

8. Understand which aspects of the product and service offer are more susceptible to being perceived as *have to buy* rather than *discretionary buy*.
9. Generic market descriptions are not helpful and companies need to be clear about which products and services are competing against each other.
10. Companies need to understand in the context of *have to buy* and *discretionary buy* how their products and services need to be developed and marketed to change the perceptions and motivations of willing and able buyers in respect of their products and services.

## Practitioner's questions

1. Are your company's products and services viewed by buyers as a *have to buy* or a *discretionary buy*?
2. If your company's products and services are a *discretionary buy*, against what are they competing?
3. Can your company convince willing and able buyers that its products and services are in a *have to buy* rather than a *discretionary buy* situation with reference to Maslow's hierarchy of needs?
4. Can your company develop its products and services to include sufficient functionality/features/benefits to extend the markets in which they can compete?
5. Is your company clear about which markets its products and services are competing in and the marketplaces in which it needs to be present to compete?
6. Are your company's products and services evolving at least as fast as the buyer's definition of the norm for the functionality/features/benefits of the products and services they want?
7. How is your company engaging with and tracking the changing buyer requirements and perceptions of buyers in the market?
8. How is your company engaging with and tracking the changing use of marketplaces by buyers?
9. Is your company viewed as a leader or a follower in the market?
10. Can and should your company's products and services create a compelling buyer benchmark for the *have to buy* and *discretionary buy* buyers?

# Products and services

05

## Introduction

This chapter explores how products are as inseparable from services as services relate to products. It recognizes that the organizational paradigm and strategy in some companies become too dominated by products or services and that this consequently leads to an inadequacy in portfolio development and approach to meeting the needs of buyers. Competitive advantage lies in providing solutions to the needs of buyers and recognizing that these solutions are a combination of products supported by services or services that support products.

In the case of services supporting products it may be the case that the product is not provided by the company providing the service, eg the service is maintaining a printing press for a buyer where the product is the production of packages for a wide variety of foodstuff containers. Service providers need to understand how the services they provide contribute to the product to which the service is provided.

This chapter explains how too narrow a focus on either products or services is a missed opportunity to improve competitiveness and to capture and retain buyers.

## The nature of products and services

Managers often talk in terms of their companies selling products. This is inaccurate and leads to missed opportunities and underperformance in sales. Companies sell products and services. Products and services can't be separated. Every product has some form of service attached to it even in self-service situations.

When we buy petrol we serve ourselves and may even pay for the fuel at the pump but we expect to be able to pay with confidence that our details will be kept secure and that the transaction will be accurate. We expect to be able to get the volume of fuel we want, for the pump to be clean, to have paper towels and gloves available if we need them and for everything to work properly and safely. We expect to have access to someone to put things right if they don't work properly.

When we buy something over the internet, we expect to be able to pay for it in a secure environment, to be able to get the information we want about it, for it to be available and for it to be delivered in the timescale in which it has been promised. All products are supported by services. Products and services are inextricably linked.

Companies that focus only on products and insufficiently on the services to support them often lose out in competitive situations. Take, for example, the difference between websites selling the same product. One is easy to use, provides lots of information in a user-friendly way and has a high customer satisfaction rating. Another website selling the same product has a much lower customer satisfaction rating and provides the minimum information. If the prices of the products are similar which website is likely to see more buyers?

Price difference is often marginal. I will often, however, not buy from the cheapest seller but from the one with the best customer rating. The sellers are being differentiated on the basis of previous buyers' perceptions of customer service. Differentiation and competitive advantage are being created not by the product but by the services supporting and linked to the product.

## CASE STUDY

### Disney

Disney is an international brand with a portfolio of products and services that transcends generations and has converted what could be defined by many as a *discretionary buy* into a *have to buy*. As every parent of young children knows when there's a new Disney film, whether with existing characters or with new characters, seeing the film and buying the products associated with it become a must: a *have to buy* for many parents.

Disney has become incredibly skilled at supporting its products with services. This is no more evident than at its theme parks where its characters are brought to life and supported by the Disney service experience whether through hotels, food outlets, merchandise stores, the interaction with the Disney characters or the amusement rides.

Disney promotes its theme parks as 'The Happiest Place on Earth'. The product and service offer creates an emotional reaction seeking to convert a *discretionary buy* into a *have to buy.* This conversion, however, would not be possible just through the product alone. It has to be a combination of product and service. Far fewer people would be converted from *discretionary buy* to *have to buy* if the excellent services supporting the theme park were not in place. If characters such as Mickey Mouse were not welcoming to children and their parents in the theme parks and did not 'live' their roles, Disney parks would soon have underperformed as a *have to buy.*

The Disney services support and bring to life the Disney products. When Disney creates a new character or develops a new product it concentrates on the total product and service portfolio and how it can provide a compelling combination of products and services that converts a *discretionary buy* into a *have to buy.*

Your company can have the most technologically advanced product in the world but without the services necessary to support it the product will not fulfil its commercial potential. The conversion of a *discretionary buy* into a *have to buy* can also be undermined by the services attached to a product. Buyers are often retained in an increasingly converging product specification world by the differentiation created by the services that support them.

> *Products and services exist together. Services support products. You need to understand both and how value is created by both for the buyers and the recipients of them. Commodity products will only compete on price unless the services supporting them enable them to become differentiated.*

In a service context value is created at the interface of the service provider and service recipient whereas this is not necessarily the case with how products create value.

The relationship between front and back offices similarly illustrates this point. No front office can survive without a back office and vice versa. It may be that different elements of the front and back offices exist in different organizations but they are inextricably linked. The reputation and effectiveness of companies rest just as much on services as they do on products. The hotel may have the best facilities in the world but if the customer service is poor its reputation is soon undermined. Never think of just product or service; always think of both.

A market operates on the basis of the provision of both products and services. There are no markets just for products. The emphasis and importance of the products and services might vary but they will both need to be addressed.

Where your company's products are being sold by others, eg by an agent or through retailers, the reputation of your company will rest not only on the functionality, design, quality and reliability of the product being sold but on the services provided by the company selling your company's product.

## CASE STUDY

### Penetrating a new market segment

A major manufacturer of large trucks wanted to improve its sales performance and decided to review and improve its marketing strategy and to identify how it could penetrate a new market segment. In short the company wanted more of its trucks on the road.

The company faced the market through franchisees. The product was first class technically with its engine producing the best-in-class fuel economy. Its brand was well regarded by buyers in the market and it was competitive financially. The success of the franchises, however, varied significantly. This degree of difference could not be shown to be merely because of differences in the geographical territories covered.

The largest demand for the trucks was in the 'haul-away' market segment. This involved waste or construction spoil being transported from wherever it was created or stored to where it was to be disposed of or used. The trucks had a reputation for being reliable and robust workhorses. The company had failed, however, to successfully penetrate the container haulage market segment.

The container haulage market segment required trucks to haul containers to and from ports and to make deliveries throughout Europe. Whilst fuel economy and reliability were key requirements of this market segment and the trucks were leaders in these functionalities they were not successfully penetrating this market segment. Analysis found that buyers bought trucks (the product) not only for their technical functionality but for the confidence that they could have in the franchisee's 'in franchise territory' service but also for the service coverage provided through the manufacturer for 'out of franchise' and European use of the truck.

The availability of the truck to carry loads, often loads with a 'time is of the essence' nature, eg foodstuffs, was crucial. This meant that the buyers were looking for flexible and quick turnaround times for vehicle servicing, preferably overnight, and fast and reliable breakdown services throughout both the UK and the rest of Europe.

The service support for the product and the perceptions of those providing those services were absolutely crucial to the buy decision in the container haulage market segment. Whilst the product was technically leading and had an edge in the very important fuel economy performance, this was not capable of being fully exploited because of the perceptions about the supporting services.

The franchisees were independent businesses. The truck franchise was often only one of the businesses owned by the franchisees. This meant that the sale of the trucks and the services to support them competed for investment against the other businesses owned by the franchisees. The truck manufacturer had to convince and incentivize the franchisees to invest in the services to support the sale of the trucks. It had to get them to a position of shared understanding of the market and the aspirations of the truck manufacturer for it. It also had to ensure that there was a seamless and trouble-free access to services in the rest of Europe.

The franchisees needed to develop a shared understanding of the market, its segmentation and how the truck manufacturer saw its future competitive positioning within it. They then needed to develop the product and service portfolio to enable them to exploit the market opportunities more effectively.

➔

The truck manufacturer was reliant upon the franchisees' commitment to the product and their willingness and ability to invest in the behaviours and services to support it. It had to be a symbiotic relationship based upon mutual understanding and intent to invest to drive the product and service portfolio forwards to change perceptions about the brand and to provide solutions to the buyers in different market segments.

It was not only the potential buyers in the container haulage market segment that had to be convinced but also the franchisees. Products and services will not be sold successfully if those selling them do not have confidence in them and do not see them as providing a profitable return on their investment. The franchisees needed to have confidence that if they sold into the container haulage market segment the services in the rest of the country and abroad would not let their buyers down. In the haul-away market segment the trucks travelled largely within the franchisees' territory and problems could be put right by them. The container haulage market segment did not provide that comfort and control.

Lessons learned:

1. In a B2B (business-to-business) market situation, business one supplying business two needs to understand the market from business two's perspective.
2. In a franchise situation there needs to be a shared understanding of the market and market segments and of how the products and services are perceived in them from the market's perspective.
3. There has to be a shared understanding of the franchisor's and franchisee's objectives for, and approach to, the market and the market segments within it.
4. There has to be a shared commitment and intent to invest in both products and services to meet the buyer's needs and the tangible delivery of that commitment through both investment and behaviours.
5. Different market segments require different product and service benefits and the perceptions of the brand as having strengths in one market segment may be seen as a weakness in others.
6. Irrespective of how good the product is, if the buyer's buy decision is heavily weighted on the services to support it then the product will

not be successful and able to compete with those products that may not have the technical superiority but which have (or are perceived as having) superior services to support them.

Managers need to fully understand that a product's competitiveness and success can be significantly affected by the services supporting it.

## Premium pricing

If premium prices are to be achieved there has to be a discernible difference in both the product and the services supporting them. Just having a differentiated product is not enough. One well-known brand that acknowledges this is Aston Martin:

The Aston Martin website states:

> With nearly a century of history, Aston Martin has developed into an automotive icon, a marque synonymous with luxury, heritage and authentic craftsmanship. Alongside these core values comes passion, passion about the cars we produce and a passion shared by our enthusiastic owners. All of our models are, and will continue to be hand-built and bespoke, using high technology processes within a very modern environment.
>
> Remaining at the forefront of contemporary manufacturing, every car produced embodies design and engineering excellence. Renowned around the world, we enter the next decade with the promise of radical innovation and change, without losing the core qualities that make our strong, independent British brand so widely revered.
>
> 'An Aston Martin combines three important elements: power, beauty, soul. Aston Martins are truly special – they always have been and always will be.' (Dr Ulrich Bez – CEO)

It is clear from the above and from the products themselves that the intent is clear. Aston Martin cars are beautiful premium products that ooze quality, design, engineering excellence, craftsmanship and luxury. The company seeks to make a connection not just with the product but with the emotions of the buyers. To generate a brand loyalty based upon being associated with something special. Something that is set apart not just by technical excellence but by design and style. It seeks to generate the feeling that those who drive an Aston Martin are special.

To reinforce and give credibility to this brand promotion requires services to match the product and the hyperbole. The cars are sold from well-appointed premises that are consistent with the brand values of the product. Price is not the deciding factor in the buyer's decision to buy. Indeed as a premium-priced product in demand there is often very little negotiation flexibility for the buyer in the price. The salespeople are selected for their confidence and ability to convey the brand image to those with the means to pay the premium prices of the product. After-sales services have to be first class.

To support product excellence and achieve premium pricing require a level of service that has to be unparalleled. Failure to deliver on the service will undermine the brand and make potential buyers less likely to be willing to pay the premium pricing.

There is no better illustration than when a brand becomes part of the lexicon. An example is Rolls-Royce and the saying: 'You get a Rolls-Royce service.' It's not just about the product but about the service to support the product. Premium pricing relates to both the product and the service.

Products, particularly premium-price products, are competitively susceptible to the services that are provided as part of the product and service portfolio offered to buyers. The most technically advanced and differentiated products can be totally undermined by the services that accompany them before a sale is completed, during the sales process and post sale. If the perception of buyers is that the service they receive does not match the brand values of the product or that the service promise made will not be delivered post sale the ability of the product to compete successfully and to achieve premium prices will be undermined.

*Premium-priced differentiated products need the support of differentiated services.*

## Products and services cocktail

For even the most basic of products buyers buy a cocktail of products and services. Whilst sometimes this is done subconsciously on a taken-for-granted basis buyers soon recognize where and when these taken-for-granted requirements are not met. The more sophisticated the product and the newer the product, the more important is the buyer's confidence in the services provided to support that product.

Take, for example, a hotel chain that wants to buy one thousand televisions. Not only does the buyer want televisions that meet a technical specification but the buyer wants to buy them:

1. when they want them;
2. with a choice of brands;
3. with other electrical products that they might want;
4. with a range of functionality to choose from to meet their needs, ranging from generic television channels to smart technology for different hotel room offers;
5. with access to advice should they want it;
6. with guaranteed problem-resolution times to ensure that the end user is not inconvenienced or given a negative perception about the hotel;
7. with choice as to the way that they pay for them;
8. with the ability to return them without hassle if they aren't the right televisions;
9. with the abilty to get reimbursement if required;
10. with the right to complain and get a satisfactory resolution to their complaint if necessary;
11. with the expectation of being treated courteously, with respect and as if their custom was valued.

Similarly, if buyers shop on the internet they want all of the above plus confidence of delivery in terms of what they have ordered, the state in which it is delivered, the timeliness of delivery, the security of payment, the security of data and the ability to return products that are not required. They are not just buying televisions but televisions supported by a range of services.

## CASE STUDY

### Marks & Spencer plc

Marks & Spencer in the UK gained competitive advantage in the past through not only having a range of products that were attractive to buyers but through its shopping experience. This shopping experience included a novel (at the time), hassle-free, return-or-exchange-of-products service. Customers

← returning products were not treated with suspicion as if they were at fault but instead were valued and treated with respect, not only when they bought products but also when they returned them.

Marks & Spencer was able to achieve premium prices based not only on the design and quality of its products but also on its services. Its brand became known for quality and service and it was consequently able to leverage the brand to diversify into other product and service areas. Such was its dominant success that it became known as a bellwether for the UK economy.

A significant factor in the rivals of Marks & Spencer being able to close the competitive gap with it was when they recognized, and invested in, the services that supported the products that they sold. Today buyers expect great products and great customer service as a taken-for-granted norm. If sellers want to gain and retain their customers they must recognize and act upon this buyer requirement.

Today Marks & Spencer is struggling to attain its former competitive advantage as it cannot differentiate on the basis of its services. It is also the case that its competitors have not only improved their service support for their products but that Marks & Spencer's products (particularly non-food) are not as compelling for buyers as in the past. Many of Marks & Spencer's branded products were regarded by many buyers as a *have to buy* but today are increasingly seen as a *discretionary buy.* Buyers can get comparable products and services from more competitors than ever before. The ability of Marks & Spencer to achieve premium pricing has been eroded.

Companies that struggle to compete on either product or service will lose their competitive advantage. Those that struggle to compete on both product and service put themselves at risk of failure. Buyer retention requires products and services that convert *discretionary buy* into *have to buy.* Marks & Spencer is no longer in this position.

Get the services supporting products wrong and it undermines the intrinsic value of the product offer. Getting the customer interfacing services right requires non-customer-facing services to be in place. The televisions described above need to be designed, manufactured, quality-tested, packaged, stored, transported and put into the right channels for the market. Having no product in the channel is a cardinal sin in selling as is non-delivery or untimely delivery of a product ordered via the internet.

In the past, a perennial problem reported by Bloomberg for Walmart, a major US retailer was stockouts: products not being available on the shelves. This meant that expensive shelf space responsible for generating sales and profit became a cost and not an income generator. Stockouts undermine customer confidence and loyalty and the brand is eroded. Walmart has now invested heavily to address this issue as it was a significant contributor to the loss of its competitive position and affected its profitability.

As Dudley (2013) reported:

> Once a paragon of logistics, the world's largest retailer has been trying to improve its restocking efforts since at least 2011, hiring consultants to walk the aisles and track whether hundreds of items are available. It even reassigned store greeters to replenish merchandise.
>
> Wal-Mart's inability to keep its shelves stocked coincides with slowing sales growth.

A key indicator of a company's health and managerial effectiveness in the retail market in particular is stockouts. Stockouts are self-inflicted wounds that create a risk for the company. If a company can't keep its shelves (physically and virtually) full of product, never mind sell the right product, there's a major problem. It is important to recognize the non-customer-facing services as part of the seller's offer in the market and as part of its definition of the business that it's in.

Sellers need to have processes and activities linked together to enable them to meet the requirements of buyers. Those sellers that don't recognize this and who have fragmented such processes and activities are at higher risk of failure and of losing out to competitors. Rather than having a buyer-focused value creation system, such companies merely remain a series of internal seller-focused activities. The value creation system is more likely to be transactionally based with external relationships for the provision of services at a higher risk of process failure than more coherently and effectively linked buyer-focused competitors.

## Value creation

Products have an intrinsic value creation role – they must 'do what it says on the tin' – but require extrinsic value creation services linked to them to ensure that value is created for buyers. Buyers initially focus on the intrinsic value of the product but then quickly focus on the extrinsic value creation of the services supporting them. Successful sellers recognize this and define value and the business that they're in from the buyer's perspective.

> *Value creation for buyers relates to both the product's intrinsic functionality/features/properties and to the extrinsic services supporting those products. Companies need to understand (and be able to deliver) both the intrinsic and extrinsic components of value creation from the buyer's perspective.*

Without the extrinsic value-creating services the product's intrinsic value will not be accessible to buyers nor realized by them. At its simplest indicative level the buyers will be unaware of them (marketing); unable to get access to them (logistics); unable to buy them (financial processes) or be advised about how they meet their needs (technology and human resources).

As much care, attention and investment is required for extrinsic value creation services as for intrinsic value creation product functionality/features/properties. This care must include how these services link together not only with the product but with each other. The competitive proposition of the company and its products can be totally undermined before the interface with the buyer occurs through a failure in the extrinsic value-creating services, eg stockouts.

> *The more fragmented the services supporting the product are, the more important it is to ensure that the linkages between them work effectively to ensure that the buyer's perception of the seller's offer is not undermined and competitive advantage is lost in the market.*

Electronic point-of-sale (EPOS) technology where data from the point of sale are collated and fed directly to the non-buyer service interface seeks to create the process links necessary to avoid stockouts and to provide market intelligence about what is selling and what isn't.

In businesses where the shelf life of products is limited, eg fashion products, it is vital that the products that are selling are available and those that are not are either incentivized or removed from sale. Even where buffer stocks are held, and particularly where the product has to be manufactured, this market intelligence has to be supported by effective extrinsic non-buyer interface services to ensure that the flexibility of supply matches the demand in the market. The more fragmented the extrinsic non-buyer interface services, the higher the risk of stockouts and missing opportunities to achieve sales.

In recognizing that products and services are inextricably linked it becomes clear that markets are created by willing and able buyers and sellers of products *and* services. These product and service combinations provide the buyer with value-creating *benefits*. Whilst the products and services can be regarded as inputs for buyers it is the outputs and outcomes that buyers are really interested in. These benefits are dealt with in Chapter 6.

As a consultant I was often struck by the product focus within organizations. This focus was frequently based upon the perception of the value and worth of the products (often the services supporting them were not considered of real relevance). I was often told that the company's product was technically superior to the competition; it was just a better product.

As an exercise to surface this issue I got groups of people from different functions within the same company together and got them individually to produce lists of how to define 'value' in terms of the company's product and services. I then got them to weight the list of 'value' components individually in terms of importance using the template below:

**FIGURE 5.1** Defining and weighting the components of value template

| Individual internally defined components of value | Individual weightings of importance |
| --- | --- |
| A | |
| B | |
| C | |
| D | |

When I then got them to share and compare their definitions and weightings with each other it soon became clear that the definition of value was almost always from an internal perspective. The definition also varied depending upon the function of the individual producing it and there was often a significant variation in the weightings applied to reflect the function. Different parts of the same company thought very differently about the value and importance of the same product and service components of the offer the company was making to buyers and the market.

It was clear that people thinking differently in the same company about the same things had great difficulty pulling together as a team. Having got to this point I then asked the question: Whose value is it anyway?

After discussion – sometimes lengthy discussion – it was agreed that value is defined by the buyer or customer. Grudgingly in some cases, it was accepted that an intrinsic attribute of a product only creates or adds value if a buyer or customer believes that it does. Having made this progress the exercise was then repeated from an external buyer perspective. Upon repeating the exercise a change in the definition of value, the components of it and the weightings applied to them often resulted. This provided a new context in which value was defined and products and services were evaluated. This resulted in agreed components of value being agreed from the buyer's perspective.

The next stage in this process was to get the delegates to provide their evaluation of competing products and services (including their own), highlighting any areas that the company needed to address if it were to improve the buyer's perception of value of its products and services and to increase its sales. The template below was used for this:

**FIGURE 5.2** Competitors and components of value template

| Weighted components of value | Competitor A | Competitor B | Competitor C | Competitor D | Competitor E |
|---|---|---|---|---|---|
| 1 | | | | | |
| 2 | | | | | |
| 3 | | | | | |
| 4 | | | | | |
| 5 | | | | | |

The above led to some sensitive but important differences in assumptions and issues being raised – it is often difficult to overtly recognize 'sacred cows' and to challenge them! Doing this, however, did lead to the identification of the key issues that the company needed to address if it was to improve its relative competitive position in the market from the buyer's perspective.

It enabled progress to be made in developing the product and service portfolio and in achieving a shared understanding of value within the company. The company's products were put into a different competitive context focused on the needs of the market (rather than internally) and led to changes in the way the company looked at the market, how it looked at competitors and how it learned corporately. It also led to improved team-working.

If the company as a team isn't clear about how value is created internally then how can it deliver value for buyers or even convince them to give the company a chance to do so?

> *Value is defined by willing and able buyers. It is against this buyer definition that different competing products and services in the market should be evaluated. Companies using internally focused definitions increase the risk of becoming out of touch with the market and not being able to convince buyers to even try their offer, never mind to buy it.*

Markets are created at the interface of willing and able buyers and sellers. Success in the market requires sellers to have a shared understanding within their companies of how the combination of the intrinsic value of products and the extrinsic value of services creates value for buyers.

## Practitioner's tips

1. Make sure that your company understands what the linkages are between the perception of the product's intrinsic value and the extrinsic services value required to support the product, and how they need to be present and work from the buyer's perspective.
2. Look at the company's offer to buyers from the buyer's perspective as a combination of intrinsic product and extrinsic services value creation.
3. Think about and develop, from a buyer's perspective, what the combination of products and services needs to be to enable the company to compete successfully in the market.
4. Remember that services create value at the interface of the service provider and the service recipient.

5. The intrinsic value of products is often not realized by the buyer until after purchase and perceptions of them can be affected significantly by the extrinsic service value created prior to the use of the product.
6. If your company's products are sold through an intermediary, make sure that your company has clear service standards for service provision in place and behaviours that support its product values.
7. If extrinsic services are key to the competitiveness and attractiveness of your company's products in the market, make sure that your company tests and invests in those services to ensure that they add to the buyer's perception of value rather than run the risk of them detracting from it.
8. Commodities with the same intrinsic product value compete only on price unless the extrinsic services supporting them can be differentiated and perceived as of greater value compared to competitors to buyers.
9. Remember that premium prices require not only premium products but also premium services.
10. How the intrinsic product value and extrinsic service value together create buyer value has to be understood throughout the company and create a shared framework for decision-making and behaviour.

## Practitioner's questions

1. What are the views within the company of the key intrinsic product value and extrinsic service value components of the company's offer to the market?
2. How are the different components in (1) above weighted within the company?
3. What are the causes and impacts of the differences arising out of (1) and (2) above?
4. Can the company develop an agreed list of weighted key intrinsic product value and extrinsic service value components of the company's sales offer?
5. How does the list in (4) above compare with the buyer's list?
6. What are the reasons for the differences between (5) and (4) above?
7. What can the company do to either change the buyer's perceptions or the company's offer or change the offer to the buyer relative to its competitors?

8 Are there clear understanding and commitment throughout the company to the buyers being the definers of value?

9 Does the company understand the practical implications of changing its thinking about the need to manage and develop the intrinsic value of its products and the extrinsic value of the services to support them?

10 Does the company have the willingness and ability to change what it does?

# Product and service benefits and price

06

## Introduction

This chapter explores the relationships between product and service benefits and the price that buyers are prepared to pay for them. It also explores movements in these relationships and what companies need to do to achieve these movements for their benefit.

## Ranking your products and services

Buyers buy product and service combinations. The potential buyer identifies and crystallizes the benefits they require and/or desire and then assigns a ranking of importance to the benefits required. I state 'identifies and crystallizes the benefits they require and/or desire', as some buyers are persuaded of what the benefits are that they need or want by finding out more about a product and service through their research, through the sales process or through marketing. Buyers can and do change their minds about what they need or want and a key part of salesmanship and the development of marketing plans is to get the buyers to crystallize their requirements in favour of the product and service being sold or marketed.

A buyer considering the purchase of a car for their family use, for example, might identify the following benefits and rank them for importance (10 being the highest score for ranking importance) in a benefit ranking table as per Figure 6.1:

**FIGURE 6.1** Benefit ranking table

| Benefit | Importance |
|---|---|
| Safety | 10 |
| Size | 9 |
| Reliability | 8 |
| Economy | 7 |
| Cost of repairs | 6 |
| Brand | 5 |
| Up to three years old | 4 |

This profile is then used, often subconsciously, as a template (known as the 'Buyer Benefit Template') against which to evaluate different cars within the maximum price the buyer is willing and able to spend on acquiring a car. Unless there is a standout benefit requirement that is a dealbreaker, buyers assess the overall package of benefits that different products and services offer. Marketing and the sales process can change the ranking of the different benefits required by the buyer. A skilled salesperson is able to influence and then crystallize the ranking of the benefit requirements of buyers in favour of the product and service offer they are selling.

*A Buyer Benefit Template provides a subjective (and often subconscious) template for buyers to assess competing products and services against. Sellers need to understand this template from a buyer's perspective.*

Understanding this buyer process is very important because it underlines the fact that products and services and indeed companies only have strengths if buyers believe that they are strengths. Too often sellers assess strengths and weaknesses from an internal rather than an external perspective. In the example above, only cars that match the buyer profile of benefits and importance will be regarded as having strengths for the buyer.

Every manager who has been on a management course will have come across a SWOT analysis, which is a tool to enable organizational Strengths, Weaknesses, Opportunities and Threats to be identified as a basis for developing organizational strategy and plans. The 'opportunities' and 'threats' part of this analytical tool will be dealt with in Chapter 8 on analysing and understanding markets.

Strengths and weaknesses can only be determined from an external perspective. You might think that your company and its products and services have a strength but if buyers don't, they will not buy. As value is defined by buyers so too are strengths and weaknesses.

*Strengths and weaknesses are defined externally by buyers and not internally by companies.*

Internal perceptions of strengths and weaknesses can be difficult to change.

## CASE STUDY

### Fast food

A fast food company believed that it provided world-class customer service that, combined with its products, provided an unbeatable product and service-versus-price offer. The company had been very successful in the United States and Western Europe and started to expand into Eastern Europe. Its traditional strengths were not delivering the success that it believed that they should. Indeed, Eastern Europe was providing a challenge to its perceptions of its strengths and weaknesses.

The performance statistics illustrated that the quality of the product was the same as everywhere else and that buyers did not have any concerns about it. The format of the restaurants was exactly the same as everywhere else. Apart from the language and the prices the buyer could be almost anywhere in the world. Indeed, many of the buyers were tourists from America and Western Europe who instantly recognized the brand.

The staff had been trained the same as everywhere else in the world. The locations of the restaurants were great. Everything seemed to be the same. The problem was that whilst the tourists wanted the reassurance of the familiarity of the offer that they could get anywhere in the world, there was no adaptation to the local context. It was the same as everywhere.

The company's perception of its product and service strength had stopped it seeing that its formula required an understanding that sameness – irrespective of context – can be both a strength but also a weakness. It believed that because of its success elsewhere it would be successful in the new context of Eastern Europe.

Local entrepreneurs had learned from their Western competitors quickly and offered a combination of high levels of customer service along with food with a local feel. The food was recognizable but more interesting.

Irrespective of what the Western company believed, the buyers' view prevailed and they didn't buy in the volumes desired from it to provide the returns that the company desired. The company had failed to understand that *strengths are defined by buyers* and their evaluations of competing products and services may differ in different segments of the same market and in different market contexts.

A company's strength in one market may need to be adapted to recognize the different buyer weighting of benefits for another market. Those companies that do not adapt their strengths, or are not capable of recognizing differences in buyer benefit requirements and weightings, will struggle to compete in different market contexts.

Buyers evaluate the strengths of competing benefits and of competing products and services. This means that strengths are relative to the buyer's subjective evaluation in their contexts. One company's products and services may be regarded as being a strength but not as big a strength as a competitor's products and services. As competitors change their product and service offer, buyer perceptions of strengths and weaknesses can change.

Understanding markets and developing strategies for them must lead to an evolution of the product and service benefit cocktail of the company. The company must ensure that its marketing plan convinces potential buyers that its products and services have changed to meet the buyer's evaluation of the relative strengths and weaknesses of competing products and services. Marketing is about changing buyer perceptions in favour of the product and service portfolio of benefits being marketed. Marketing, however, needs to be grounded in the buyer's reality in the market, within the context of the company's competitive strategy and reflect the company's ability to deliver the tangible outcomes promised by the marketing.

> *A buyer's perception of strengths and weaknesses of product and service offers from the same company may vary between different segments of the same market. Strengths and weaknesses are relative terms – relative to competing products and services. A buyer's perceptions can change over time and in response to marketing.*

## Market research

Market research is a useful tool to find out what potential and existing buyers think are the relative strengths and weaknesses of competing products and services. Getting an independent external organization to do this provides the best route to getting a true view of relative strengths and weaknesses.

I have found that it is very useful to do the strengths and weaknesses exercise internally first and then to compare the results with the external findings. The differences between internal and external perceptions have sometimes been quite marked.

Being able to accept the external perceptions and the differences with the internal perceptions of strengths and weaknesses is an important strength by itself. Too many managers find it too hard to accept the external findings of market research. There are a number of reasons for this, including:

- The belief that external perceptions undermine their personal reputation.
- They question past and current investment in the products and services.
- The insistence that the results are due to a timing issue as the market isn't quite ready for what's being offered.

- The belief that the market doesn't understand what's being offered and that the market is just wrong!

A way to surface the differences within the organization is to do a strengths and weaknesses exercise. This involves getting a group of managers to first of all identify and rank their perceptions of the buyer's benefit requirements. The managers then score their company's products and services against those buyer benefits and discuss any differences until an agreement is achieved. With the agreed scores for their company on one side the managers then need to score their competitors' products and services. This often causes the managers to reassess the scores for their company's products and services and to re-evaluate relative strengths and weaknesses.

The above, if handled correctly, can be a challenging but rewarding process that reveals differences in perceptions within the company and that enables the managers as a whole to move forward. Comparing the results from the above with the results from independent external market research can be similarly challenging but rewarding. I have found that successful companies are self-aware and get the ranking of buyer benefits right and are pretty accurate in assessing the strengths and weaknesses of their and competing products and services. Less successful companies are often those that are less self-aware and where there are significant differences in the internal understanding of buyer benefit rankings of the strengths and weaknesses of their and competing products and services.

*Successful managers and companies are self-aware in identifying buyer benefit requirements and how their and competitor products and services relate to them as strengths and weaknesses. They also have the ability to learn from the market and to adapt and change their product and service offer.*

Successful managers and companies have the ability to learn from the market and to adapt and change their product and service offer. Where there is a disconnect between the market's perceptions and internal perceptions, the company has to have the ability to make a significant investment (and has to have the time to invest) in changing market perceptions and/or adapt the products and services and invest in communicating how the product and service offer has changed to meet the market's needs.

## CASE STUDY

### Škoda

One company that has learned from market perceptions about its products and services, invested in product development and been given the time to change perceptions in the market is Škoda.

When Volkswagen bought Škoda, the Škoda brand was synonymous with poor quality and design. It had become the subject of unflattering jokes and buyers perceived it as having many weaknesses and few strengths. The dealerships selling Škoda were then few and mostly standalone so as not to confuse potential buyers about the other brands being sold by association.

Volkswagen understood the market and the competitive dynamic within it and developed a clear competitive strategy for it. It recognized that it had an opportunity to use the advantages of its core competencies and financial strength to deliver a different competitive product and service offer to the market.

Volkswagen understood that a value proposition had to be about more than price and that the benefits offered had to provide the profile of benefits required by the buyers to at least the range and quality of its competitors. It also recognized that the buyer's perception of weaknesses had to be changed, not only by the physical reality of vehicles not breaking down but through tangible evidence.

Volkswagen not only improved the design and physical reliability of the cars, but it also changed the portfolio of benefits offered to buyers relative to competing products and services and changed perceptions about the brand through successfully competing in rallies. Škoda has now become the most successful brand in the history of the International Rally Challenge, winning its third consecutive titles in both the drivers' and manufacturers' categories in 2012.

Škoda in the UK has won awards in various categories and its sales figures continue to grow. It has changed perceptions about its strengths and weaknesses relative to its competitors.

## Products, services and price

In making the buy decision, buyers don't just evaluate the relative strengths and weaknesses of different products and services, they also trade those relative strengths and weaknesses off against price. Buyers have an elasticity of price limits within their ability to pay, which is based upon their evaluation of the value that competing products and services create for them. This evaluation affects their willingness to pay.

Buyers have a *normal* and an *absolute* upper limit for what they are willing to pay for products and services whether they are in a *have to buy* or a *discretionary buy* situation. Both are within their ability to pay.

> *Buyers have a normal and an absolute upper limit to what they are willing to pay for products and services. The difference between the two is often determined by whether they are in a* have to buy *or a* discretionary buy *situation.*

The *normal* upper limit of price is what they would normally determine as the maximum that they would be willing to pay for the product and service offer. Whilst buyers have the willingness to pay a price at this maximum they often seek to negotiate with the seller to ensure that the price that they pay is below it. It is the buyer's normal evaluation of the price for the value that they will derive from the product and service offer. The lower the price at which they buy the product and service offer, the greater the value they determine they have achieved. Above this *normal* upper price limit, the willingness to buy normally ends unless the buyer is in a *have to buy* situation and still has the ability to pay more than the *normal* upper limit of price.

If the buyers are in a *have to buy* situation then their *normal* upper limit of what they are willing to spend will be revised upwards to the *absolute* upper limit of what they are both willing and able to pay. This extension of the price limit from the *normal* to the *absolute* upper limit of price is achieved often at the expense of reducing the spending on other products and services or through increasing the buyer's debt and hence ability to pay.

The operation of the elasticity of the buyer's spending limit between the *normal* and the *absolute* price limits is a product of the buyer's need to buy and the power of sellers within the market to maintain their prices. If the buyer is not able to buy the product and service benefits required within the *normal* price limit that they have set (or been set) they will either trade off some of their benefit requirements to achieve the price up to the *normal* price limit or trade-off paying more up to the *absolute* price limit for what they need to buy against buying another product and service. The latter reduces the amount available to be spent on other competing products and services.

A buyer might like to buy a smart TV (a *discretionary buy*) and a food processor (a *have to buy*) but can only afford a set amount of money. They *have to buy* a food processor with a certain degree of functionality, which is above their *normal* price limit. They buy the food processor and an ordinary television. They trade off the *discretionary buy* television functionality to enable them to buy the food processor above the *normal* price limit.

Buyers in a *discretionary buy* situation can sometimes go above their *normal* price limit to a higher *absolute* price limit by revising their price ceiling upwards when they convince themselves (or are convinced through salesmanship and marketing) that the *discretionary buy* has become a *have to buy* or that the value offered by the product and services is higher than the buyer originally believed (eg the salesperson convinces the buyer that there are additional benefits to the product and service offer for the price that the buyer had not identified). Again the buyers are generally only able to increase their price limit from the *normal* to the *absolute* price limit through reducing spending on buying another product and service or through increasing debt.

The buyer's process for evaluating product and service value and price is illustrated by the *Buyer Perceived Product and Service Benefit versus Price Matrix*. An example of this for an individual buyer is illustrated below for the *normal* price maximum. See also Bowman and Faulkner (1997).

**FIGURE 6.2** Buyer perceived product and service benefit versus price matrix

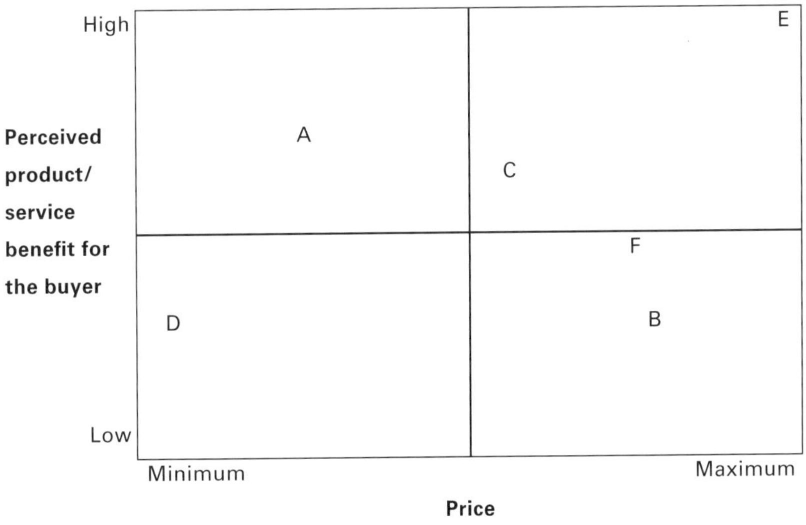

Product and service offers for products A to F are illustrated in the matrix. An individual buyer doing this evaluation will determine the trade-off that they are prepared to make, within their ability to pay, to gain the product and service benefit from the products and services for the price that has to be paid to acquire those benefits.

All six product and service offers are within the maximum *normal* price the buyer is prepared to pay. It might be expected that the buyer would seek to negotiate for buying product and service offer E as this provides a high degree of benefit value whilst being within the *normal* price maximum. If the product and service is a *have to buy* this could well be the case. If, however, product and service E is a *discretionary buy* the buyer might decide to negotiate for product and service A or C as both provide a reasonable degree of benefit fit at a lower cost. If this was acceptable this might mean that the buyer had more money to buy other *have to buy* products and services or other *discretionary buy* products and services. Individuals make individual choices based upon their individual contexts.

Sellers need, however, to be able to understand whether the individual buyer assessment above is illustrative of the likely requirements and behaviour of buyers in the market. These requirements and behaviours are identified through market research. Sampling the population of potential buyers with the willingness and ability to buy enables a profile of benefits to be created, price sensitivity to be identified and the positions of different product and service offers to be determined.

Plotting the different product and service offers on the *Market Perceived Product and Service Benefit versus Price Matrix* illustrates relative positions. The clustering of buyers for the market can be a guide to price elasticity. (See Figure 6.3.)

Some market researchers seek to make the results of their research more 'scientific' by applying numeric weightings and formulae to the buyer benefits identified. The reality is that buyer views are subjectively based. Giving these views a more 'scientific' numeric formula-based status is likely to increase complexity and provide a degree of certainty that doesn't exist in practice.

The Market Perceived Product and Service Benefit versus Price Matrix in Figure 6.3 illustrates relative positions of product and services A to F.

The distribution in the matrix indicates that there is varying elasticity in the price that buyers are willing to pay. D is seen generally as low price and providing low buyer value benefits. E is seen generally as high price and

**FIGURE 6.3** Market perceived product and service benefit versus price matrix

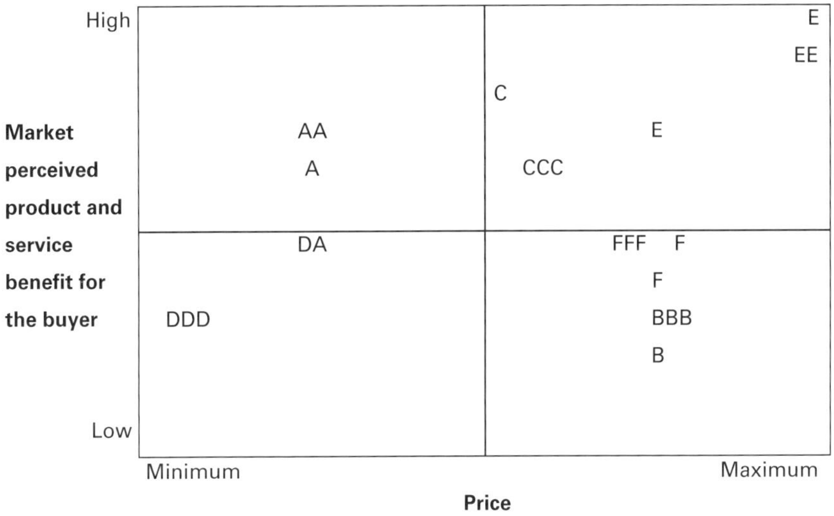


providing high buyer benefits. A is seen as low price but providing higher buyer benefits. Comparing these positions with the market shares being achieved prompts the questions for sellers:

1. Does the market want something different from what is being offered by the company?
2. Can the company increase the price for its product and service offer?
3. Can sellers change their positions in the matrix?

Market research can again provide an insight for answering these questions. Research to determine market perceptions of the future elasticity of price can be illustrated using the *market perception of product and service benefit fit versus price* matrix. This is illustrated in Figure 6.4.

Taking each product and service cocktail in turn:

A is perceived as providing high buyer benefits for a low price with the ability to increase its price for the same benefit fit or to increase its price significantly if it significantly improves the benefits it provides. It is a product and service with potential for further development.

B is perceived as highly priced for the benefits offered. It has limited ability to increase its price and would have to significantly increase its benefit to do so.

**FIGURE 6.4** Market perception of product and service benefit fit versus price matrix

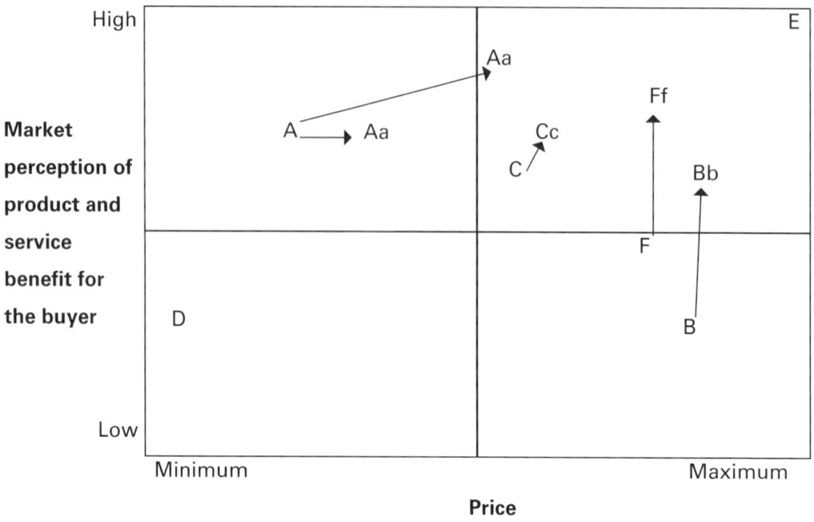


C is perceived as providing a good degree of benefits for an above-average market price. It is perceived as having limited ability to increase price or to increase its benefit fit.

D is perceived as providing few benefits for a low price without any scope to change these perceptions or price.

E is perceived as providing a high degree of benefits at the maximum price. It is not perceived as having the scope to increase the benefits offered and does not appear to need to reduce the price.

F is perceived as providing below average benefits with an above average price. It is perceived as having the ability to improve the benefit fit but not much scope to increase its price.

Answering the three questions posed above requires more data, particularly about market shares and the companies involved but generally:

**1** Does the market want something different from what is being offered by the company?

The matrix illustrates that A, B, C and F are perceived as having potential to increase their buyer benefits. Product and service A, however, has the biggest potential to increase its price. This difference in the potential to change the buyer benefits is often a reflection of the market's perception of the brand. It takes time and investment to change these perceptions and just making small adjustments to the product and service are not sufficient to achieve significant changes to these market perceptions.

**2** Can the company increase the price for its product and service offer?

B, C and F have some potential to increase their prices but would have to increase the market perception of the benefits offered. Product and service A has the biggest potential to increase its price both for the existing benefits and should it increase the benefits offered. In considering the price increase potential sellers have to consider the implications for sales volumes and profitability.

**3** Can sellers change their positions in the matrix?

D and E would find this difficult. B, C and F have some potential to change their positions but the biggest potential lies with product and service A. Changing position in the matrix often requires a significant investment in the product and service benefits offered and marketing.

It should be noted that a change of position by one competitor product and service can cause a competing product and service to seek to change its position, eg a reduction in price for one product and service can cause a price reduction in others to change the perception of the evaluation of buyer benefit versus price. Similarly a new entrant to the market can cause a re-evaluation of the existing competing products and services in the market, eg when Dyson entered the vacuum cleaner market.

The buyer benefit requirements for products and services can vary significantly between market segments. Sellers need to understand these differences to understand the products and services against which they are competing. The elasticity of pricing for different products and services varies and relates to the buyer and market perception of the buyer benefits and whether the buyer is in a *have to buy* or a *discretionary buy* situation. The potential to increase price is often very limited without significant changes to buyer perceptions. Changing these perceptions often requires significant time and investment. It is also the case that a change in price doesn't always correlate to an increase in profit.

The above illustrates that product and service strengths and weaknesses have to be identified from an external buyer perspective. History is littered with failed companies and managers that sought to impose their own evaluation of strengths and weaknesses to decide how products and services should be developed, offered and priced.

Creating buyer value is of prime importance and relates to the tangible and intangible contributions products and services make to meeting the needs of individuals consistent with Maslow's hierarchy of needs – tangible in the sense of physically changing something or being provided with something (eg a repair to a house) and intangible in the sense of changing the individual's emotions in terms of self-esteem, status, feeling of belonging, security or feeling that someone is interested and cares.

Try this test. Get two identical sweaters. Put a label in one from a high street retailer and in the other a label from a high-end fashion designer. Whilst the physical product is identical it is often the case that the buyer perceives the benefits offered by the two products as being very different. Ask those being tested which sweater they'd like to take home.

Buyers can believe that the perception of others about them being associated with wearing a high-end fashion label creates a *benefit edge*. Whilst there is no difference other than the label in the sweaters, the buyer perception of value enables the designer-branded product to charge a premium price. Sellers need to be aware that a *benefit edge* can be created by both the buyer's perception of the benefits provided by the product and service directly and from the buyer's perception of what others will think of them through acquisition of those benefits. Buyer benefit outcomes are both tangible and intangible.

> *A benefit edge can be created if buyers believe that brand association gives them intangible benefits through association with a particular product and service or brand.*

The importance of this *benefit edge* to buyers is further illustrated by the very fact that people will go to premium-brand stores and buy the most inexpensive of the products available just to get a bag that they can parade with in town!

The importance of brands is dealt with later. The key at this point is the recognition that buyers buy the benefits that products and services give them as well as the physical product. These benefits can be both functional and psychological. They can be associated with the buyer's perception of benefit, eg increase in self-esteem and their perception of the impact it will make on the perception of them by others, eg increasing the esteem of others for the buyer.

## Practitioner's tips

1 Ensure that your company understands what the benefits are that its products and services are seeking to satisfy.

2 Ensure that an evaluation of the benefits provided by the company's products and services and of the products and services of its competitors are undertaken from an external perspective based upon the benefit requirements of the buyers.

3 Challenge yourself and your colleagues to seek to understand the external perspectives of the strengths and weaknesses arising from (2) above.

4 Develop a 'Buyer Benefit Template' for the market and use it as a guide to identify what your company has to do to address the external perception of weaknesses and to protect/build upon its strengths.

5 Ensure that there is a shared understanding within your company of the relative positions of competing products and services in the market in terms of buyer benefit requirements.

6 Ensure that there is a shared understanding of whether the products and services are a *have to buy* or a *discretionary buy*.

7 Ensure that there is a shared understanding of the external perceptions about whether there is a difference between the *normal* and *absolute* price maximum for the products and services.

8 Ensure that the external perception of market perception of product and service benefits versus price is understood within the company.

9 Ensure that the external perception of the potential to change the market perception of product and services benefits versus price is understood within the company.

10 Identify what is required to change your company's product and service position on the market perception of product and service benefit versus price matrix to achieve the desired level of profit and competitive positioning required.

## Practitioner's questions

1 What are the benefits that willing and able buyers want from products and services and how are they prioritized?

2 How does your company ensure that it gets (and keeps track of changes to) market perceptions of the benefit requirements and their priorities?

3 How does your company identify and track price elasticity in the market and ensure that it understands the *have to buy* and *discretionary buy* dynamic?

4. How does your company ensure that it takes an external perception of the benefits that its products and services provide in the context of what the market requires?
5. How does your company ensure that an objective external evaluation of the relative strengths and weaknesses and market positions of competitor products and services within the market is achieved and is tracked for the future?
6. How will the results of the above be used within the company to evaluate the strengths and weaknesses of the company's products and services and to inform the objectives for those products and services?
7. Does the company wish to change the position of its products and services on the market perception of product and service benefit for the buyers versus price matrix?
8. Does the company have clarity of objectives in relation to the return it is seeking from its products and services now and in the future?
9. Does the company have access to the resources necessary to invest in the products and services and marketing to achieve its objectives for them?
10. Is the company clear about what it would do if competitors sought to change their positions on the market perception of product and service benefit for buyers versus price matrix?

# Market segmentation

07

## Introduction

Markets are not homogeneous. They can be segmented in a variety of ways to reflect the heterogeneous nature of them. The key is do so in a way that makes sense for buyers and which enables companies to develop their competitive strategies in a credible way. This chapter explores the segmentation of markets and how to develop the product and service benefit offer to attract the buyers within segments.

## Segmenting markets

There are many ways in which markets can be segmented. The key is for companies to define them in ways that will help them to achieve their competitive and corporate objectives. I have found that segmenting markets on the basis of products and services is often a reflection of internal company-focused thinking rather than market-oriented thinking. It is after all buyers who buy and sellers must understand buyers. Products and services have to be seen in the context of buyers.

Markets consist of willing and able buyers and willing and able sellers who seek to reach agreement on the buying and selling of products and services and price. Given the heterogeneous nature of the buyers it is useful to seek to identify whether or not the benefit requirements of buyers can be grouped together in some way. These groupings are known as *market segments* and the process of defining them is called *market segmentation*.

> *Market segmentation is the process by which willing and able buyers in a market with similar types of benefit requirements are categorized into groups, known as market segments.*

Market segmentation is not an end in itself but a means to an end. Segmenting a market enables companies to:

1. understand the requirements of groups of buyers in terms of the product and service benefits they require and how they trade off those requirements with price;
2. put the company's and its competitors' products and services in the context of the groups of buyers identified to facilitate the evaluation of relative strengths and weaknesses;
3. develop their product and service offer to meet the needs of specific groups of buyers;
4. identify and evaluate the market dynamic for those groups of buyers;
5. focus their marketing efforts and investments on the specific needs of those groups of buyers;
6. develop strategic options and choices for the market and its segments;
7. determine whether it is likely to be sufficiently profitable to target different segments of the market;
8. identify whether there are linkages and movement of buyers between different market segments and between markets.

## Marketing and market segments

There is often great concern about marketing spend and its effectiveness. If the marketing is not targeted at the needs and requirements of the buyers in specific market segments, it will not be regarded as relevant by those buyers. Whilst it may improve the general awareness of the brand of the product and service it is more likely in these circumstances to be a cost rather than an investment and not be effective in influencing buyers with the willingness and ability to buy.

> *The objectives and focus for segmenting a market need to be understood. A company that provides or markets one product and service offer to cover all market segments will underperform and confuse the market.*

Market segments of willing and able buyers should have:

1. definably similar benefit requirements;
2. definable differences from other groups of buyers;
3. similarity of reaction to external variables, eg marketing and the economy.

There are other ways in which companies seek to segment a market. These include:

- Segmentation by product and services.

  By only looking at products and services the company is more likely to be concentrating on what it believes the intrinsic values of the product should be rather than on what the buyers think is important. It could be ignoring other important intrinsic and extrinsic value benefits of the buyers, eg channel to market, the benefits both direct and referred (eg brand association) that the buyers rate highly. Segmentation based upon product and service features constrains competition to products and services rather than focusing on what it takes to win willing and able buyers to buy from the company.
- Segmentation by geography.

  The segmentation by geography assumes that willing and able buyers within a particular geographical area are susceptible to the same product and service marketing proposition. Whilst it is useful to target specific geographically defined markets, the likelihood of all willing and able buyers having the same benefit requirements and evaluation of the benefits offered by products and services is small. Geographically defined markets have different buyer market segments.
- Segmentation by demographics/B2Bographics.

  'B2Bographics' relates to the business-to-business market where the willing and able buyers are businesses. This approach assumes that willing and able buyers (whether individuals or businesses) can be grouped by criteria related to them, eg 20–30-year-old men or steel manufacturing companies. Whilst there are undoubtedly some common issues that can be ascribed to particular groups of individuals or companies, they are rarely sufficient to support the definition of a market segment in a meaningful way to inform the marketing proposition of sellers. Demographics/B2Bographics can play a role in identifying some of the characteristics of willing and able buyers in a market segment but cannot on their own define a market segment.

- Segmentation by channel.

  With the advent of the internet there is undoubtedly a channel shift by willing and able buyers in many markets. Segmenting a market, however, merely on the basis of the channel(s) used runs the risk of missing how willing and able buyers want to buy through a range of channels and the full range of benefits that they want to buy. Channel to market is but one of the benefits that willing and able buyers consider when making the 'buy' decision. Identifying the channel preferences of willing and able buyers can be useful in defining the characteristics within market segments. This should not be confused, however, with the need to have particular channel options available to meet the benefit requirements of buyers.

- Segmentation by psychographics.

  This seeks to divide buyers into different groups based upon lifestyle, social class or personality characteristics. It seeks to identify the internal drivers of willing and able buyers. It is akin to the different stages in the diffusion of innovation (Rogers 2003) where innovation is adopted by different people at different rates, eg innovators, early adopters, early majority, late majority and laggards. The buyers in each of these categories have different drivers for their buy decisions. Technology companies particularly are very alive to the different characteristics of buyers in the context of the diffusion of innovation and develop their marketing approaches accordingly. They do not, however, base their segmentation of the market solely upon these criteria. They identify the benefits from products and services that willing and able buyers in these categories desire and then look at how they can meet them and accelerate through these categories to get to the profitable higher volume market segments.

Elements of all of the above can be used to contribute to segmenting a market but should not be used individually to define a market segment. The process for segmenting a market starts by identifying some of the criteria drawn from the above to define the market. This process is called *identifying the locus for market segmentation.*

> *Market segmentation draws upon the criteria for making the buy decision to create a locus for market segmentation. This should not be confused with segmenting markets based upon the benefit requirements of willing and able buyers.*

Identifying the locus for market segmentation starts by seeking to answer the following questions:

1. What products and services relate to the market?

   Avoid developing a market definition that's too wide. Defining a market as consumer goods is extremely broad and could mean anything. It is not a useful basis for analysis. Markets are naturally segmented, eg footwear for leisure use is segmented into walking boots, mountaineering boots, cricket boots, football boots, basketball shoes, etc. Be more specific to identify a product and service type that forms a meaningful basis for segmentation. There are distinct markets for walking boots, cricket boots and football boots. Walking boots might be segmented into boots for ramblers, hikers, fell walkers, etc. Whilst there will be some common benefits required by all willing and able buyers of boots, eg waterproof, there will be distinct differences in the benefit requirements for different buyers for different types of boots. It is highly unlikely that a buyer of walking boots will have the same benefit requirements as buyers who want boots to play baseball in!

2. What is the geographical coverage of the market that is to be segmented ?

   There will often be significant differences between the buyer benefit requirements for the same product and services in different geographical markets due to cultural, economic, legislative, sociological and other reasons. A walking boot design and the benefits required by buyers in Mexico might have some commonality with those required by buyers in Ireland, for example, but are also likely to have some distinct differences.

   Even where the market is internet based there will often be distinct differences between the benefit requirements of buyers in different geographical locations using the internet-based market. The context of the buyers in terms of both their location and their proposed use of the product and services remains important.

> *Is it possible to identify common benefit requirements for all buyers and then distinct benefit requirements for different groups of buyers for the market selected?*

If buyers want to buy a watch it is likely that all buyers will require a common set of benefits (the core benefits), eg the watch keeps good time. Identify these core benefits and then identify what the different benefit requirements (differentiated benefits) are for different uses. Someone might want to buy a Cartier watch and require the differentiated benefits that it brings compared to buying another less expensive brand with fewer differentiated benefits. They both tell the time accurately and are waterproof, for example, but the Cartier has distinctly differentiated benefits for which a premium price can be achieved.

The groups of buyers for these products and services will 'weight' both the core benefits and the differentiated benefits differently. It is important that these weightings are identified, as they are fundamental to the segmentation of the market. In the watch example, having brand association and style will be very important for some, whilst for others being able to play sport with the watch on might be of utmost importance.

Narrowing it down further to watches, the process above will have identified what the core benefits for watches are in the market and it will also have identified the differentiated benefits required. It should then be possible to identify through the weighting process a hierarchy of differentiated benefits.

Each group of buyers will use this hierarchy to determine their *have to have* benefits and their *like to have* benefits. These are then traded off against price with the negotiation of price for sales being about the extent to which the *like to have* benefits can be secured for the price the buyer is willing and able to pay. If the *have to have* benefits are not part of the sales offer it is likely that the buyer will not be willing to buy and thus not be in the market. This is illustrated in Figure 7.1.

Figure 7.1 illustrates that different groups of buyers want different levels of *have to have* and *like to have* benefits. These groups are willing and able to pay different prices for these benefits. It is also likely that as price increases, the *have to have* benefits increase and could be more than the total requirement of a group of buyers with more modest requirements who are less willing and able to pay higher prices. This is illustrated in Figure 7.1 by comparing buyer groups D and A.

Another example could be the market for luxury cars. If a car hasn't got built-in satellite navigation, parking and distance control, cruise control, etc it will not be regarded as a competitor in certain market segments. Just having these levels of functionality, however, is not enough as buyers also want a brand representing the status desired. Brand is an often highly weighted buyer benefit. This is why Toyota developed the Lexus brand.

**FIGURE 7.1** Product and service buyer benefits versus price market segmentation

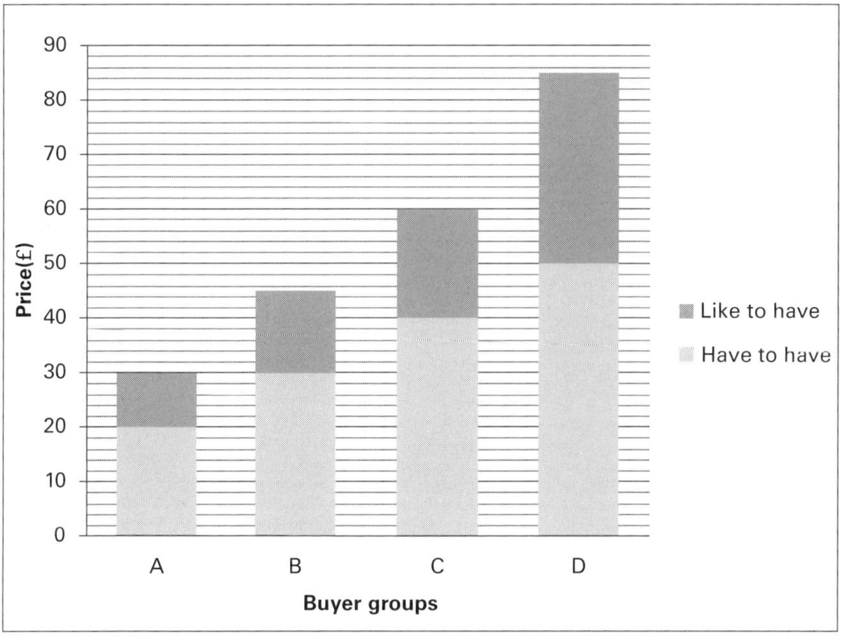


## CASE STUDY

### Toyota

Toyota had all of the functionality but not the perception of brand status required to compete successfully for willing and able buyers who wanted the total benefits associated with a luxury car. Lexus was consequently developed as a premium customer-oriented brand to overcome the limiting factors and perceptions about the Toyota brand.

The Lexus brand has been supported by it being awarded several J D Power and Associates' Customer Satisfaction Awards. These awards evaluate a product, utilizing four key criteria: vehicle quality and reliability; vehicle appeal; ownership costs; and service satisfaction from a dealer.

➔

This customer-focused orientation has led to innovations that have come to represent the Lexus brand. Lexus focuses on design to service quality, driving pleasure, environmental performance and safety. It has identified the core and differentiated benefits that buyers require and seeks to exceed the core benefits and continuously develop its differentiated benefits. This is supported by its marketing in order to create a well-known and strong premium brand distinct from Toyota.



Where brand is weighted particularly highly by willing and able buyers it is possible to get a premium price. In these cases the *have to have* requirements of the buyers are reduced with them being transferred into the *like to have* category.

This is illustrated by some 'luxury' branded cars. Some of these cars might only have the same functionality as standard as some of their rivals, or even less functionality, but they are able to achieve premium prices because their brand is weighted more highly by willing and able buyers.

> *Brand can distort buyer benefit requirement weightings to enable companies to get premium prices for the same or less functionality than their competitors. The key is to understand what benefits support the brand in the perception of the buyers.*

## Have to have, like to have and the economy

When the economy is buoyant the buyer benefit requirements often increase and so too does the price buyers are willing and able to pay. Buyers often want more but are prepared to pay more. Buyer benefit requirements see more benefits moving from the *like to have* category into the *have to have* category to create a new standard for the base product.

When the economy is heading towards recession buyers often want the same benefits but want them at a lower price. As the economy gets worse buyers become more willing to accept fewer benefits for a lower price and more benefits move from the *have to have* category to the *like to have* category; eg a Mercedes buyer might move down the model range of cars from an Avantgarde model to an SE model.

Sellers who have invested heavily in developing products and services want to retain buyers, to acquire new buyers, to increase cash flow and to grow market share. To enable them to do so profitably some sellers introduce new lower standard specifications for their products and services. This is illustrated by the value ranges of supermarkets and by the introduction of special edition cars.

## CASE STUDY

### The growing popularity of discount stores

The rise of discount retailers in Europe has been phenomenal, with Aldi and Lidl – the German discounters – leading the way. The business models that these two discounters have used have been based upon providing non-market-leading brands representing good quality at a low price with limited product ranges. This enables them to order in large volumes at low unit costs from suppliers.

Operating with low-cost limited size stores located to serve small communities ensures product turnover and freshness of products. This is supported by low-cost efficient distribution and logistics systems. Indeed the location of their stores seeks to mirror and serve the socio-economic profile of the communities within which they are located.

They have been particularly successful in product lines where the buyers have a low threshold for *have to have* rather than *like to have* product features.

Logic would dictate that Aldi and Lidl sales would be growing across the full product range but this is not the case. Take, for example, toiletries such as deodorant. Restricting the product range to mainly lesser-known brands has not led to buyers trying these brands in high numbers to challenge the dominance of the better-known brands. The lesser-known brands have not been able to surmount the *have to have* thresholds of the buyers.

Aldi and Lidl have sought to address the above in two ways. The first is through stocking more branded products where they can get reliable and sufficiently discounted access to the volume of supplies of them desired to support their →

low-cost offer. The second is to use external recognition for their lesser-known branded products to overcome the *have to have* product threshold of buyers.

If they are to increase their sales, lesser-known brands have to surmount two key challenges to convince buyers that they qualify to be considered as meeting their *have to have* product features. The first is brand awareness and the second is generating sufficient buyer confidence to entice buyers to try the products.

Winning awards is a way to overcome both of these challenges. Both Aldi and Lidl have been successful in stocking award-winning lesser-known brands in product areas such as wine and breakfast cereal that have overcome buyers' *have to have* requirements.

Through a combination of stocking more leading branded products where they are unable to overcome the buyers' *have to have* product requirements associated with the leading brands and stocking award-winning lesser-known brands Aldi and Lidl have continued their successful profitable capture of market share. Indeed, they are now attracting buyers from a higher socio-economic band, thus being able to overcome *have to have* buyer requirements and even being able to extend their offer into the *like to have* product requirements of buyers.

## Market segment research

The next stage in the market segmentation process is to identify who the buyers are and to find out as much about them as possible. Market research is about finding out about buyers and their willingness and ability to buy both now and in the future. Market research as a snapshot is looking backwards. Companies need to understand markets now and how they are likely to change in the future.

> *Market research provides a snapshot but needs to also provide a test of assumptions about the future.*

Investment decisions by companies, whether they be for the development of products and services or for the creation of capital-intensive facilities, require an understanding of how the market is likely to develop in the future. This is illustrated most clearly by clothes retailers planning next season's fashions and oil companies planning the location and nature of oil-refining facilities.

Market projections using market research are often portrayed as a science. They are not. Market research uses statistical techniques to provide data based upon both qualitative and quantitative research that are then evaluated subjectively and used to make subjective choices to develop market projections. No one can prophesy the future. Managers can only make assumptions about the future and hope that they are right. This is why market research needs to be ongoing and companies need the capability to understand changes in the market as the future unfolds.

Market research can usefully be used to create a profile of buyers. These profiles can then be used to create focus groups and a structured statistical population to use to gather data on which to base assumptions.

It is important when carrying out market research to identify the profiles for those buyers with the willingness and ability to buy but who choose not to buy. Whilst profit lies in the lifetime retention of buyers so too does it lie in converting those with the willingness and ability to buy but who choose not to buy from your company.

Different profiles are likely to be revealed for different market segments and internal assumptions about the *have to have* and the *like to have* buyer benefits need to be tested for now and for the future for each market segment along with the price elasticity of those buyers. There are often 'golden' differentiators (which are the key benefit requirements) for each market segment. Managers need to understand what they are for the segments that they wish to compete in or enter.

It is vitally important to seek to identify how the buyer profile might change over time and what is likely to affect the choices that they make. Chapter 8 looks at how to analyse markets. This analysis, which should be carried out for each market segment, should be used to identify how it affects buyers' benefit requirements and the choices that they are likely to make in the future.

At the end of the process for defining a market segment you should be able to:

1. identify the similar benefit requirements of willing and able buyers used to define the segment;
2. define the differences of those willing and able buyers in the chosen segment from other groups of willing and able buyers;
3. be confident of the similarity of reaction to external variables of those willing and able buyers in that segment.

Being clear about the segmentation of the market enables the company to then undertake an analysis and evaluation of the market and its segments to determine whether it is attractive for the company and what needs to be done to create a competitive and compelling marketing approach to it.

## Practitioner's tips

1. Make sure that there is a shared understanding of why the company needs to segment the market.
2. Make sure that the objectives for segmenting the market are identified and understood.
3. Make sure that the starting point for identifying the segmentation of the market is determined from an external perspective and not from an internal perspective.
4. Define the products and services to which the market relates and understand what benefits buyers with the willingness and ability to buy want in a defined geographical area.
5. Understand how buyers with the willingness and ability to buy weight the benefits they want and how they are categorized in terms of *have to have* and *like to have.*
6. Understand how the weightings in (5) above are traded off against price.
7. Understand the differences between different market segments.
8. Understand the relationship between the *have to have* benefits in each segment and how they change between segments.
9. Do not treat market research as a scientific snapshot but as part of the development of data-based subjective market assumptions and projections for the future evolution of buyer benefit requirements and volume of demand.
10. Companies need to make positive choices about the segments that they want to compete in, recognize how buyers can change segments over time and need to have product and service portfolios that evolve to meet the needs of buyers.

## Practitioner's questions

1. What are the company's objectives for segmenting the market?
2. Which products and services relate to the market to be segmented?
3. Which geographical area is covered by the market to be segmented?
4. How are buyer benefits categorized into *have to have* and *like to have* benefits for each segment?
5. How are the product and service buyer benefit requirements traded off against price for each segment?
6. How will the company test its assumptions about the buyer's views of benefit requirements against the external perceptions of buyers?
7. Over what time period will assumptions be made about the market segments for the future?
8. What will the company do with the results of the segmentation of the market?
9. How will the company keep in contact with the changing requirements of buyers in each market segment in which the company competes or wishes to enter?
10. How will the company plan its investment and continue to evolve its product and service benefit offer to meet the evolving needs of the market segments?

# How to analyse markets

08

## Introduction

This chapter deals with how to analyse markets and challenges some of the taken-for-granted assumptions about strategic analysis. It sounds like an oxymoron but the definition of a market is crucial to the analysis of markets. Defining a market enables you to identify both the buyers and the strategic variables that are likely to affect the demand they create in the market.

A step-by-step guide is provided that enables both key variables to be identified and for them to be evaluated to enable managers to understand the market dynamic and the key strategic market issues that provide a context for the company and the development of its competitive strategy for the market.

## Starting with the market

Many companies do not adequately define their markets and indeed do not define (or have a shared understanding of) the business that their company is in. Is Rolex in the watch business, for example? Does Rolex compete in the watch market?

As with the definition of a market the definition of what business the company is in has to be focused externally. A company might manufacture and sell watches but may not be in the watch business or compete in the watch market. Against which products and services does a Rolex watch compete?

I have found that companies that focus internally often talk about the industry that they are in and the companies against which they compete. Companies that focus externally often talk about the markets in which they compete and the products and services against which their company's products and services compete.

It is vital that companies focus externally first before they focus internally. Their products and services have to be put into an external context. Analysis of a market requires a clear definition of a market and a clear understanding of what business the company is in.

*Market analysis starts from an external perspective of the definition of the market.*

## Variables in markets

Having defined the market it is important to understand the segments within it. Different segments can be affected differently by the same variables. It is important to understand what common variables apply to all segments and what individual variables are required to be identified and analysed for different segments of the market.

Take for example the housing market in London. Access to capital is a key variable affecting demand in the housing market. It could be that access to capital is a variable that affects demand for houses up to £300,000; significantly less so for houses between £300,000 and £1 million; even less so for houses between £1 million and £3 million and not at all for houses above £3 million.

When seeking to analyse the market it is important to identify the variables that are affecting demand now before seeking to identify the variables that are likely to affect demand in the future. A market analysis should be not only a snapshot at a point in time but also an assessment of the future.

In this context the definition of 'now' and 'the future' needs to be clear. It is for those undertaking the analysis to choose based upon their understanding of the market context. In many markets for analysis purposes, 'now' is often defined as 'in the next three to six months', with 'the future' being one to three years. Clearly the longer the time frame, the more speculative the assumptions that have to be made and the more important it is to review whether or not those assumptions have become reality as the future unfolds.

To enable the assessment of the current market to be undertaken the following model has been developed over a number of years, working with a wide range of companies operating in different businesses and markets.

The starting point for the analysis is to answer the question:

**1** What business is the company in and how is the market defined?

The answer to both parts of this question should be very closely linked. How would managers in Rolex answer the two parts to this question? Would they state that they are in the watch business and the market is defined as buyers who want to buy a high-quality high-cost watch? Unlikely!

Imagine that you are doing some consultancy for a multinational company where managers from different parts of the company answered the two parts of the question differently. One answer is that the company is in the manufacture of meters business and that the market is defined in terms of anyone wanting to buy a meter. The second answer is that the company is in the metered solutions business and that the market is defined as buyers needing a metering solution. Whilst the common factor of meters is present, the role that they play in the business and the markets the company is in are very different. The implications of the two sets of answers are huge.

One definition provides a narrow focus based upon a core manufacturing competence and the other a much broader definition encompassing a portfolio of services and providing a wider context for the role of the physical product in creating value for buyers. The first results from a historical manufacturing competence-based paradigm and the second from a buyer-focused services paradigm requiring the development of a much wider set of competencies. Where there are such divergent views, decisions on strategy and on priorities for the investment of resources are likely to lack coherence and consistency.

> *Having a shared understanding of the definition of the business the company is in and the definition of the market are vital if analysis of the market is to be possible and lead to the development of a strategy capable of being implemented.*

It is not unusual for managers in the same company to answer the two elements of the question differently. If this is the case, work needs to be done to get an agreement on the answers to be used for the market analysis and a clear understanding of them. It is hard to climb to the top of the same mountain if the climbers are starting from different base camps and looking at different peaks to climb!

There should be a shared understanding of who the willing and able buyers are within the market; the product and service mix required by buyers; the role and/or business of the company in meeting the needs of buyers; who the competitors in the market are; and where the market to be analysed exists.

**2** How is the market segmented and what impact does this have?

As we saw in Chapter 7, markets can be segmented by reference to the benefit requirements of buyers. The demand in different market segments will have a significant impact on both the attractiveness of those market segments for sellers and for competition within them.

Falling demand in a market segment that has been attractive in the past is likely to increase competition as existing competitors fight harder for sales. Growing demand in a market segment may result in reduced competition, as the competitors are satisfied with the returns that they are receiving.

In both cases the competitive dynamic will depend upon the competitive strategies of the competitors. For example, a competitor that cannot afford the cost of exiting the market segment might fight very hard and introduce a price war whereas a competitor exiting the market segment might reduce competition, even in a market segment where demand is falling as the remaining competitors are able to increase their sales and to make acceptable returns.

It is also important to understand the linkages between different market segments. It may be that it is important for sellers to be able to compete in all market segments or just compete in some market segments. Take, for example, the market for cycles.

The market for cycles can be segmented for illustrative purposes by reference to the uses for which cycles are purchased, for example on-road leisure, racing, off-road leisure and commuting and for age groups, such as adult, teenager and child. The benefit requirements of each of these segments are linked by core requirements but have important differences. All buyers will want reliability, safety, strength and the like as a basic benefit requirement (although perhaps to different technical specifications) but will want some importantly different benefits depending upon the market segment.

Cycling as a social activity is often subject to a concept known as *progression*. Progression is where a buyer moves through different market segments. I buy an on-road leisure cycle for a child; I then buy a bigger on-road leisure cycle as the child grows and then an off-road leisure cycle and then a racing cycle. I progress through the market segments as the benefit requirements change for my child.

It is also the case that I don't just buy a cycle for one child. As a social activity I want my family to cycle together and with others and so I not only buy my youngest child a cycle, I buy the rest of my family cycles. My family consists of my wife and two children and each has different benefit requirements. This buying covers a number of market segments. Am I likely to go to a specialist cycle shop for each type of cycle required or to a cycle store selling cycles to meet the needs of all of my family?

There are clear linkages between the different market segments. To get my business, and to retain it through the progression process, sellers need to offer cycles in each of the market segments in which I want to buy, now and in the future.

In this case, sellers need to decide whether they want and are able to offer buyers products and services to meet their requirements for different market segments or to specialize in cycles to meet the requirements of specific buyers, eg racing cycles. The decision is often based upon the assessment of the attractiveness of the market segment and whether or not the linkages between market segments and the benefit requirements of buyers is so strong that having product and service offers for those market segments is regarded by the seller as being absolutely necessary.

This raises the issue of *specialization*. Buyers in some market segments for specific products and services require a specialist approach to the sale and support of products and services. I am unlikely to buy a specialist road racing cycle with a high technical specification, carbon frame, etc from a general cycle store. I want access to expertise and confidence that the seller knows the products and services required.

In this case as a buyer I do not want to see linkages between market segments but a distinct separation. I want the reassurance and status of specialization.

Understanding how the market is segmented is an important element in the analysis of markets. What affects one market segment may, or may not, affect what affects another. Managers need to understand and respond to this buyer requirement.

> *Be clear about how the market is segmented and whether or not there are linkages between segments.*

It is important and useful to use the first two questions as a team development tool and to seek to gain a shared understanding of these most fundamental issues. Do not be surprised at the variation in answers that are given to these questions. Use this variation as an opportunity to have an informed team-building exercise that will provide benefits for both individuals and the team.

**3** What are the key marketing, economic, sociological, technological and supply drivers affecting current demand in the market?

It is important to use these headings to identify the key variables that are affecting demand now. It is also important to remember that demand relates to willing and able buyers. If buyers do not have both willingness and ability to buy they are not part of the market and consequently not part of demand.

Taking each in turn:

- *Marketing* – Buyers are bombarded by marketing. Sellers are desperate to get profile for their products and services and to create a desire and need for buyers to buy them. Whether it's product placement in a James Bond film, sponsorship of popular television programmes or advertising, marketing can create an increase in demand. It can also maintain a level of demand in a market.

  Although marketing is largely specific to a particular branded product and service portfolio it also acts to create awareness and demand within the market more generally. Marketing for a particular brand of biological washing powder will raise awareness of the power and properties of all biological washing powders. Demand in the whole market segment may therefore rise because of a product and service-specific marketing. What impact is marketing currently having on demand in the market segment as a whole rather than just on a specific brand?
- *Economic* – Demand in different market segments is affected differently where the income of buyers and/or access to money changes. Uncertainty about employment, reducing income and a reduction in access to credit finance or loans have affected the ability of buyers to buy and taken many out of the market. This has inevitably meant a reduction in demand in many markets.

  This has particularly been the case in relation to demand in a wide variety of market segments for discretionary buy products and services. It has, however, been responsible for an increase in demand for lower-cost lower-quality discretionary buy products and services, eg demand for own-brand supermarket products and services has increased whilst demand for higher-cost branded food and non-food products and services has reduced. In better economic times I might have bought a Harley–Davidson motorcycle as a discretionary buy but in a recession I would either not buy a motorcycle or buy a less high-status brand with a lower specification. Similarly, when people cannot afford to move house, the demand for curtains and soft furnishings reduces.

- *Sociological* – Changes in lifestyle and peer pressure can affect demand: 'I need to be seen as a member of the club, therefore I must own a pair of Hunter wellingtons or own a smartphone or own a Barbour jacket.' 'My family is not complete unless I have three children.' Changes in household formation due to marriages ending in divorce have increased the demand for particular types of housing. Demand can fluctuate due to changing sociological contexts.
- *Technological* – Technology affects demand in the way that people no longer need to own a desktop computer or indeed possess a standalone camera. The demand for the physical delivery of post has been decimated by the advent of e-mail. Conversely new technological developments create a demand, eg Dyson vacuum cleaners.
- *Supply* – The relationship between supply and demand is a fundamental economic concept. A market is said to be in equilibrium where supply and demand are equal. Fluctuations in supply and demand therefore can create disequilibrium so that supply and demand are not equal. This can be created by excess supply or the price being too high and the demand thus falls or excess demand where the price is too low. It is also the case that where companies have excess stock or wish to enter a market they may artificially reduce prices to seek to increase demand for their products and services. Whilst this can increase the demand for a specific company it is likely that competitors will reduce their prices and thus a price war will result, which will increase demand in the market overall.

  Demand is also linked to access to supply. Increasing the accessibility of products and services through improved or new channels to market can increase demand. The internet has been a key player in this respect as willing and able buyers are now able to shop from their sofas and not have to go to the physical shops. The supply is now physically capable of being delivered to the buyer and this increased accessibility to supply can increase demand. A barrier to converting interest to demand has been removed.

## Keep it simple

I have found that many managers produce long lists of issues under each of these headings and then get lost in complexity and volume. The key is to identify which of these issues is really having an effect (both positive and negative) on demand now. The managerial value-adding competence lies in evaluating the list to identify which are the ones that need to be understood and which are having the biggest impact on demand.

> *Keep it simple and ensure that you and your colleagues understand the impact of each variable on demand.*

Anyone producing these lists should be able to state what the impact on demand in the market is now. Again discussing these issues and their relationship with demand is a useful team-building exercise and produces greater shared understanding of markets. Do not produce long lists under each heading but take each heading, identify the three to five key issues and their impact on demand and then input the net impact in the *Key Issue Impact on Demand Matrix* below:

**FIGURE 8.1** Key issue impact on demand matrix

The demand for granite for the manufacture of kitchen work surfaces.

| Key issue | Net impact on demand |
|---|---|
| Marketing | + |
| Economic | – |
| Sociological | + |
| Technological | + |
| Supply | + |

The above illustrates four positives and one negative. This exercise is not a science but a subjective analysis of the issues. The important task now is to determine the weighting given to these impacts. In the example above the economic impact could be having a disproportionate impact on demand. The overall net impact on demand could therefore be that it is negative. Demand is going down.

The above provides an understanding of what is happening in the market. Understanding these issues and the impact they have on demand enables the company to identify what needs to change if the market is to increase in its attractiveness and demand is to increase.

**4** What is the nature of competition in the market?

Analysis and evaluation have to be in an agreed and defined market context as different markets and market segments can have very different contexts with the same variables having very different impacts. As has been seen, demand in different market segments can have a significant impact on the competitors and the relationships between buyers and between buyers and sellers. It is important to understand these impacts and to use them as part of the analysis and evaluation of the competitive dynamic within the market or market segment.

If the buyers are few in number and they account for a significant proportion of the total demand in the market segment they can have a significant power over sellers, for example large supermarket chains over their suppliers. These buyers can also 'crowd out' other buyers, eg small retailers, as they can buy most or all of the entire current and planned stock or capacity of the sellers, leaving little for anyone else to buy or use. They can also use their buying power to negotiate a price that gives them a significant competitive advantage in the market segment that others cannot match.

Where sellers are few in number and buyers are large in number with no buyer having a dominant position the power is in the hands of the sellers, eg diamonds and oil. It is important to understand the power dynamic between sellers and buyers in markets. A dominant seller in a market with few sellers and many buyers can control the market.

Where sellers believe that they are at risk of having to leave the market and that the costs of doing so (both economic and reputational/brand) are prohibitive they may adopt aggressive competitive strategies aimed at either seeking to force others to leave the market or to acquire market share to try to give them economies of scale benefits or to make them more attractive as either a takeover target or as a partner.

Where the number of competitors and the basis of competition are stable in a market segment, a new entrant can change the competitive dynamic significantly. A new entrant may believe that it can profitably win a proportion of the demand or sales that currently exist in an acceptable timescale or that demand will grow over time and its profitability will increase in the future (eg Samsung and smartphones). A new entrant may believe that it needs, for portfolio reasons, to meet the requirements of important buyers in other markets or segments in order to enter the market or segment and to keep its sellers in those other markets or segments. An example could be financial institutions creating subsidiaries worldwide for global clients to operate internationally and locally or telecoms companies providing communications technology worldwide for international clients. Similarly where existing competitors believe that an existing competitor will be leaving (or can be forced to leave) a market or segment, the competitive dynamic can change. The threat of a competitor leaving the market or segment can result in a price war to make it more necessary or attractive for the competitor to leave.

It is important to recognize the barriers to market or segment entry and exit. Where barriers to entry and exit exist they affect the competitive dynamic within markets. Barriers to market entry include:

- the ability to develop, secure and offer products and services that attract and meet the needs of willing and able buyers;
- access to flexible capacity to respond to buyer volume requirements under time pressure;
- having access to the research and development capacity and skills necessary for product development;
- having access to raw materials;
- having control over intellectual property;
- having access to the necessary channels to market;
- having access to the capital to invest in manufacturing, logistics, etc and the revenue to build the brand, cash flow the business and to provide confidence in the delivery of the product and service to meet buyer needs;
- having the ability to compete as demand and the competitive dynamic change;
- having the ability to be unprofitable in the market or segment until the brand is established;
- having the ability to weather a price war created as a barrier by existing competitors.

Establishing a branded presence in some markets or segments is of key competitive significance with buyers and often takes a significant time. Companies wishing to enter markets or segments have to have not only the resources to invest until successful but also the support of their key stakeholders. Stakeholder requirements regarding cumulative company risk profile and the timeliness, as well as extent of returns, can be internal company barriers to entry.

Barriers to exit which create a pressure to stay in a market or segment and thus affect the competitive dynamic include:

- the ability to realize the value of capital assets;
- the extent of previous capital investment in specialized capital assets and the ability to use them for other purposes;
- the portfolio effect, where not having a presence in some markets or segments can affect the ability to compete in other markets or segments;
- contractual commitments with high penalties for termination;
- the cost of reducing headcount;
- the impact on the ability to spread corporate overhead;
- the belief that the acquisition of a competitor will become possible;
- the inability to change the core competencies of the company to enable it to compete in another market;
- hope and commitment that the demand in the market or segment will increase and the company will be able to transform its performance or return on investment;
- lack of managerial confidence that the company can compete successfully in an alternative market or segment to the current market or segment.

> *Recognize that the evaluation of options is subject to subconscious screening. You cannot choose options until you've evaluated them.*

It is interesting to note that when doing an evaluation of strategic options with senior managers, I have found that the option that is often least considered is that of exit from the market or segment. This is not because of the inability of those managers to analyse the market but rather the impact of the company's history, leadership and their vested interests. It is as if considering exit from a market or segment is personal both in terms of the company and the managers involved. It is sometimes viewed as a corporate and managerial loss of face or an admission that performance has not been adequate or that there are corporate or managerial weakness and inability to compete.

I have also found that some managers do not want to be seen to challenge the desire or requirements and personal allegiance of the leader of the company. Whilst the analysis of the market or segment needs to be undertaken with the leader of the company, their leadership style sometimes inhibits the process. This inhibition can prevent managers from saying what they really think and to acknowledge self-evident truths about the attractiveness of the market and their views on how the company can compete within it.

Regrettably some leaders do see a difference of view as a challenge to *their* existing strategy and *their* evaluation of the market and as a challenge to *them* personally. It is a brave manager that is prepared to accept or to create that challenge. The skill of the facilitator of this process is in identifying and addressing this challenge before the process commences and during it should it arise. The analysis and evaluation of the market or segment are about the market or segment and not about personalities – that comes later!

Considering exit from a market or segment needs to move from being viewed by leaders and managers in some companies as an admission of failure rather than as a strategic evaluation of the market or segment and the ability, within the current competitive market dynamic, to compete. Unless this is the case it will be difficult to identify and to respond to the likely competitive challenges identified for the future.

Many of the most senior managers have specific career paths to the top based upon a professional discipline or association with a particular business or market. Although their senior role may be termed strategic, they often find it difficult to take a dispassionate strategic view of those disciplines and businesses as part of a strategic review. Regrettably, this can lead to those companies staying in markets or segments far longer than they should. Managerial utility and organizational culture can be barriers to exit.

*It is vital that managers can divorce their own vested interests from the analysis of the market.*

There are often taken-for-granted assumptions about competition, competing products and services and competing companies. These taken-for-granted assumptions, known as the *current nature of competition in markets*, constrain the analysis that is undertaken. It is important that the opportunity is taken to identify and challenge these taken-for-granted assumptions to ensure that the foundations for the analysis are sound.

In some sectors the existing competitors are all constrained by the current nature of competition and assumptions, eg Tesco will always be the largest competitor by market share, Japanese cars will always have greater levels of specification and reliability, Apple will always have a pipeline of innovative commercially successful products, Hoover will always be the market leader and synonymous with vacuum cleaners, Kodak will always be the leading photography company. Competition and assumptions can change!

It often takes a new entrant to the market to challenge and shatter this current nature of competition. A new entrant that is not constrained by the past and is able to develop new rules of the competitive game, eg budget airlines making mass airline travel possible; e-mail; pre-prepared fruit ready for eating; and smoothies as a convenience drink.

A new leader of a competitor in a market from outside the sector can also change the current nature of competition. Unconstrained by the current nature of competition they are able to see the market differently and to challenge and change how their company relates to it. Richard Branson has made a career and fortune out of entering markets and looking afresh at (and changing) the current nature of competition, whether it's flying the Atlantic, music or train travel.

*Don't allow yourself to be limited by the current nature of competition in the market. Think like a new entrant to the market.*

It is interesting however, that the current nature of competition in markets without new entrants or new leadership is often self-reinforcing. The assumptions that underpin the current nature of competition become unwritten rules of competition that are subconsciously followed. Competitors become almost self-regulating. I have experienced first-hand managers in competing companies stating that one company will do something and then the rest will follow. There is a leader in the market and the rest are followers.

## Shared understanding

Combining the outcomes from the Key Issue Impact on Demand Matrix output with the current nature of competition in the market and the power of buyers, the power of sellers in the market and the risks of new entrants to and/or exits from the market should enable a shared understanding of the current market dynamic to be identified. This shared understanding is vital if the company is to be able to put itself and its products and services into the context of the market.

Again this is not a science and attempts to assign scores to each of these elements to two decimal places are not credible. Evaluation is based upon gaining a shared subjective view, supported where possible by quantitative data, of the key current strategic issues for the market.

> *An analysis of the market should mean that you and your colleagues have a shared understanding of the current market dynamic in terms of:*
>
> 1. *what the current nature of competition in the market is and why;*
> 2. *what power buyers of products and services in the market have and why;*
> 3. *what power sellers of products and services to the market have and why;*
> 4. what *the potential for new entrants to and exits from the market is and why;*
> 5. *the current nature of demand in the market and of the future key strategic market issues.*

The above is illustrated in Figure 8.2. (See also Porter (1980).)

Managers should be able to state and understand what the current market dynamic is and what the current strategic issues underpinning that dynamic are within the market. This should mean that the discussion within the company moves from being anecdotal and disjointed with different levels and types of understanding in different parts of the company to a shared understanding of the key current strategic issues in the market. This is often a big step forward for many managers and companies.

Having reached a position of understanding the current market dynamic managers will want to be able to test assumptions about the future and to

**FIGURE 8.2** The current market dynamic and key current strategic market issues matrix

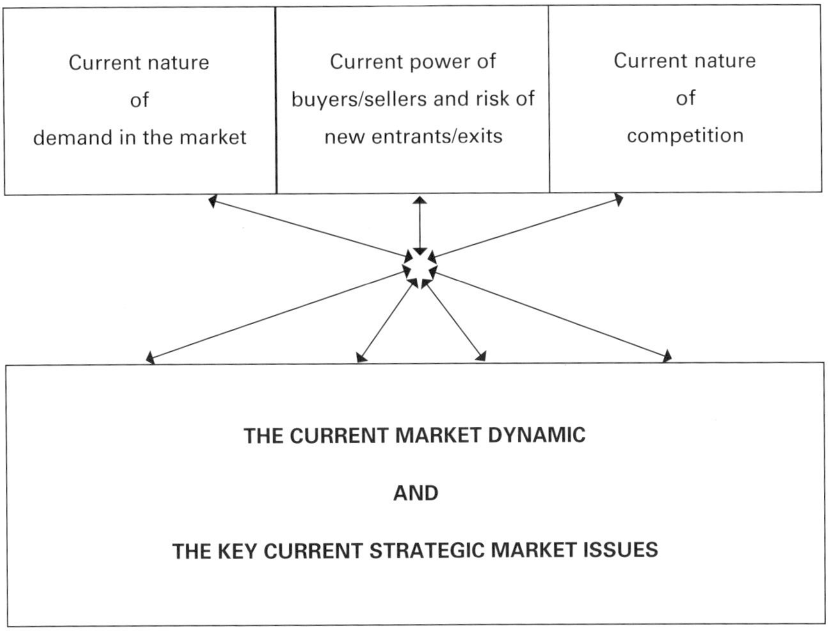


understand their impact. This is accomplished by developing market scenarios, which is dealt with in Chapter 9.

## Practitioner's tips

1. Ensure that there's a shared understanding of the business that the company is in and a shared understanding of how the market is defined.
2. Ensure that there's a shared understanding of how the market is segmented and the linkages between different market segments.
3. Ensure that there's a shared understanding of what 'now' means as the time frame for the analysis of the current market.
4. Be clear about the drivers of demand in the market or segment and the impact that they have on demand.
5. Recognize what the current paradigm of competition in the market is and the impact that it is having on the nature of competition.

6. Be clear about the power of buyers and sellers and the impact that this has on competition.
7. Be clear about the risk of new entrants and exits from the market and the impact that this is having on the market.
8. Recognize that market analysis has to be undertaken from an external perspective and not from the vested interest perspectives of the leader and managers in the company.
9. Remember that market analysis is a subjective process, supported by data wherever possible, and not an objective mathematical process to two decimal places.
10. Ensure that there's a shared understanding of what the key current strategic issues are in the market before moving on to consider market analysis for the future.

## Practitioner's questions

1. What business is the company in, how is the market defined and how is it segmented?
2. Is there a shared understanding in the company of the answers from (1) above?
3. What are the linkages between market segments and what impact do they have on competition?
4. How is 'now' defined for the purposes of the market analysis?
5. What are the key current drivers of demand in the market segments?
6. What is the current paradigm of competition in the market segments?
7. What is the current power of buyers and sellers in the market and what impact is this having on competition?
8. What is the current risk of new entrants to the market and exit from it and what impact is this having on competition?
9. How is the process of analysis used to ensure that vested interests don't influence the analysis?
10. What are the key current strategic issues to be drawn from the market analysis?

# How to develop market scenarios – demand

09

## Introduction

This chapter deals with identifying the current strategic market issues and current market dynamic and testing different scenarios for the market on them in order to ascertain their impact. A step-by-step guide is provided to enable managers to test a shared understanding of what the key variables are likely to be in the future and what their impacts are likely to be. It also enables different scenarios with different likelihoods of occurrence and different levels of impacts to be tested. In this way managers can provide a foundation for the development of the company's competitive strategy and prepare for the future.

## Scenarios

Developing market scenarios enables managers to identify and evaluate what impact different assumptions about the future will have on the current strategic market issues and current market dynamic. This then enables managers to put their own companies in context and to identify and evaluate what they need to do to prepare their companies for that future.

It must be stressed of course that scenarios are based upon assumptions. The future is uncertain, as are the impacts and reactions of different companies to them. Events change history and can change both the competitive dynamic within markets and the companies that seek to compete within them. It is a brave (or some would argue foolhardy) manager that just lets the future unfold without any thought about it and how the company might prepare for it.

Whilst scenario building cannot foretell the future it can play an important role in helping managers collectively to seek to identify and evaluate options for the future. The key is not to treat scenario building as a science but as part of the development of the strategic competence of the company and its managers.

Collective learning, its dissemination and its use are important issues in the development of the strategic competence of both managers and companies. This important issue is dealt with in Chapter 16.

It is pointless if scenarios are developed as just theoretical exercises. Whilst this approach can help with team building it is likely to undermine credibility. Too often so-called strategic exercises or activities just lead to the production of documents to which no one subsequently refers. Scenario building can support companies in making key strategic decisions for the future. They can only do so, however, if they are credible and are kept under review as the future unfolds.

In developing credibility, three issues need to be considered. The first is the shared confidence within the company in the identification of the assumptions to be used in the analysis about the future. The second issue is the shared confidence in the identification of the impact of those assumptions on the market and the third is the shared confidence in the evaluation of how the scenario will affect the market overall.

Shared confidence is vital. Credible scenario building that improves the company's ability to prepare for the future requires a shared confidence being generated throughout the company in the scenarios. Without this they will remain theoretical. Scenario building should not be a one-person exercise but part of the development of the strategic competence of the company and its managers.

Similarly it is important to recognize the difference between analysis and evaluation. Analysis is about identifying and categorizing data. Evaluation is about identifying what that analysis actually means within a defined context.

Analysis answers the questions: How many? What type? Evaluation seeks to answer the questions: So what? What does this mean? Managers need to consistently challenge themselves and their colleagues to answer the evaluation questions. Evaluation leads to the identification of the issues to be addressed, the options to be considered and the choices that need to be made for action.

## CASE STUDY

### The effect of downloading on the music industry

#### *Analysis*

In 2009 the International Federation of the Phonographic Industry (IFPI) identified that approximately 95 per cent of all music downloaded from the internet was done so illegally.

#### *Evaluation*

The market for music had changed due to the ability of individuals and others to download music from the internet resulting in the following strategic market issues:

- The intellectual property and income of the artists were being seriously eroded and needed to be protected more effectively.
- The ability of companies to profitably publish music and to invest in new artists was being destroyed.
- The market for music was being fundamentally changed with existing authorized and legitimate channels to market being increasingly seen as part of the marketing mix rather than as profitable income streams in their own right.
- The importance of touring would need to increase as a major revenue source.
- The number of new artists 'breaking through' and receiving music company support would reduce and would increasingly depend upon the ability to tour.
- The dominant paradigm of competition was changing with the risk of music company (seller) exits from the market increasing without it resulting in more power for the remaining competitors as the risk of new entrants (sellers) to the market would increase based upon a radically different business model from the existing competitors in the market.

#### *Action required*

The action required to address the strategic market issues included:

- Improve coordinated government approaches to international law-making to create a more effective legislative framework for the protection of intellectual →

property and to reduce the risk of new entrants to the market using illegal channels to the market.

- Improve the effective enforcement of the law internationally.
- Improve the security of the intellectual property.
- Achieve the cooperation of internet search engines and other internet-based channels to market to protect intellectual property.
- Improve the cost and access of buyers to legal music downloads.
- Recognize and respond positively to the changing benefit requirements of buyers.

Note that there is nothing in the above analysis, evaluation and action that relates to an individual company. The issues relate to the market context. It is not until the market context has been analysed and evaluated with the action required to address the strategic market issues identified that a consideration of individual companies should take place.

*Managers need to be able to undertake market analysis and evaluation and to identify what action is needed to address the strategic market issues concluded from the analysis and evaluation.*

## Context is all

Analysis requires a context within which to undertake evaluation. Without this context evaluation is not possible and analysis remains theoretical and of little use. Evaluation:

1. Requires preceding context-based analysis if the manager is to understand what it is that is being evaluated. Using only implicit analysis runs the risk of merely reinforcing existing assumptions and jumping to conclusions. These conclusions are often consistent with the existing nature of competition and the

taken-for-granted assumptions that have influenced past managerial decision-making.

2 Should be seen as an opportunity to test the analysis explicitly, individually and collectively with colleagues. In this way not only is it more likely that taken-for-granted assumptions will be challenged but that differences in assumptions within the team will be surfaced and addressed.
3 Should not be without challenge. If all managers immediately reach the same conclusions arising out of the analysis it is important to identify why this is the case. My experience is that some managerial teams understand the market and have developed an externally focused, strategic competence. Regrettably, more managerial teams need to do so and their rapid drawing of evaluation conclusions relate more to the desire to be seen to be consistent with the leader and the desire to resist external challenges to existing strategies and roles.
4 Without action remains theoretical. Managers must constantly ask themselves: What am I going to do? What is going to make a difference? What is best for the company? How can we influence the market? How can the company address the strategic market issues and compete more successfully?

The options for action and the management of strategic change are covered in Chapter 15. Understanding markets and exploiting them have to be grounded in practical action based upon an evaluation of the analysis of the market.

> *The development of scenarios for markets should be grounded in the practical and move from analysis through evaluation to action.*

## Keep it real

In seeking to ground scenarios in the practical, managers need to identify the relevant issues for each scenario to be considered, build them into the relevant scenarios and be clear about the timescale for each of the scenarios. Timescales are an important part of the context and vary between markets.

In financial markets the timescale for scenarios can be very short whereas in capital-intensive industries such as oil it can be years. The pace of change is such, however, that taking a 20-year or even 10-year timescale as the basis for scenario development is increasingly less credible.

The identification of issues to be used in scenarios can be achieved using the *Likelihood and Impact Matrix* below:

**FIGURE 9.1** Likelihood and impact matrix

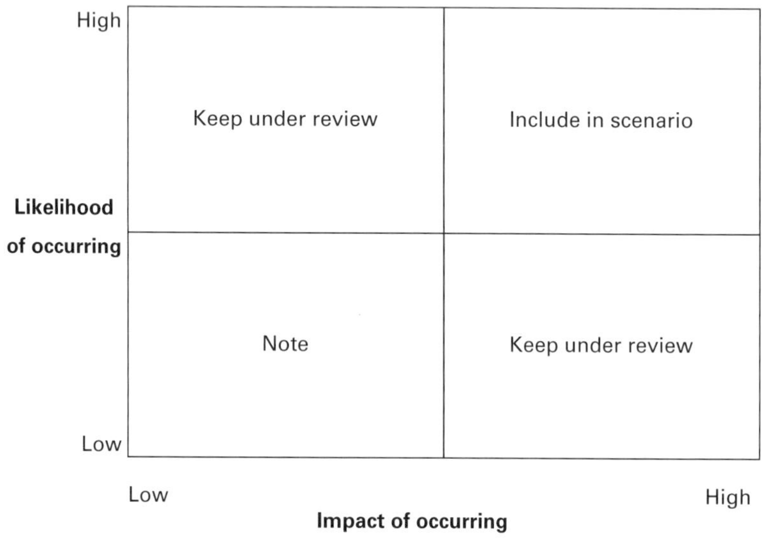


Managers often produce long lists of issues. The matrix provides a means to reduce these to those that are likely to be relevant for the analysis and evaluation at this time. Remember, however, that context changes over time and it may be that issues identified today may not be in the quadrant identifying them for greater consideration at this time but they might become so as the future unfolds. It is beneficial to record all of the issues raised and to revisit them periodically to determine whether they should be included in the refinement of the scenarios developed for the future.

The Likelihood and Impact Matrix should be used by managers individually and then as part of a group exercise. There are often some distinct differences in how managers assess what is likely to happen and what its impact is likely to be. These differences provide the opportunity to uncover different perceptions about the market and to ensure that a single person-based scenario isn't developed. Shared credibility and confidence arise from shared understanding.

Whilst there is often a temptation, arising out of either external pressures or the training of managers, to adopt a particular time frame for the scenarios, the time frame needs to be determined by the market context and not the company's. It is always possible to break down the impact of the scenario into different time horizons but constricting its development artificially to a company's time frame runs the risk of missing key issues. Remember that the context is the market and not the company. How the company seeks to influence and/or respond to the market scenario in future is another issue. Market first, company second. Understand the macro to put the micro in context.

In times of market and economic stability it might be possible to adopt a longer timescale than in times of less market stability and more economic turbulence. As you have to be clear about the definition of the market for which the development, analysis and evaluation of scenarios are to be undertaken, so too you have to be clear about the time frame over which you are seeking to identify and assess the future strategic market issues.

Having chosen the time frame for the development of the scenarios, likelihood and impact matrices for the different elements of the scenarios need to be developed for the future. The process of developing scenarios for the market or segment can now really start by populating the likelihood and impact matrices by looking at future demand in the market.

Identifying the issues affecting future demand to be used in scenarios can be achieved by using the categories of marketing, sociological, economic, access to scientific and technological change and supply which were covered in Chapter 08 for the current market dynamic and current key strategic issues. These now need to be put into the future scenario context and whilst other categories can additionally also be used, these issues provide a focus and guide the thought processes of managers. Taking each in turn:

## *Marketing*

Markets consist of willing and able buyers and willing and able sellers. Marketing seeks to influence demand, ie to increase the willingness of able buyers to buy.

In looking at future demand managers need to form a view about the likelihood and impact overall of marketing on demand. This can be done by taking a view in aggregate as to whether marketing overall is going to have a high, medium or low impact on current demand and whether this is positive or negative. Whilst it is possible to assess the impact as neutral this should be used with real care as it is sometimes used to avoid taking a view.

# Practitioner question

What nature and level of marketing are likely in the market or segment and what impact will they have overall on demand in the market or segment?

## *Economic*

In general terms there is a direct correlation between buyer income and demand. This relationship, however, differs for products and services that are perceived by buyers to provide benefits that are average, below average or above average for the market.

In the case of market-average products and services, an increase in buyer income leads to a higher demand for those products and services. In the case of market below-average products and services, a reduction in buyer income leads to a higher demand for those products and services. In the case of above-market-average products and services, an increase in buyer income leads to a higher demand for those products and services.

In the increasingly linked international world in which companies compete, what happens in one economy often impacts on the economy for the market being considered. This has been seen particularly in relation to the international banking crisis and its effect on the confidence of buyers and sellers in markets and access to capital. This has a direct impact on demand and it is important therefore to recognize these impacts in the development of the scenario.

In developing scenarios managers need to take a view on how the economy relevant to the market or segment being considered will develop within the time frame being considered and what impact overall it will have on demand in the market or segment. This can be done by taking a view in aggregate as to whether economic issues overall are going to have a high, medium or low impact on current demand and whether this is positive or negative. Whilst it is possible to assess the impact as neutral this should be used with real care as it is sometimes used to avoid taking a view.

# Practitioner question

What economic issues are likely to occur and what impact will they have overall on future demand in the market or segment?

### *Sociological*

Society continues to change and this results in changes in the nature and level of demand for products and services. Increases in household formation through the increased prevalence of the breakdown of relationships result in higher demand for housing and for the furnishings and so on required. Increased life expectancy increases the demand for nursing and/or social care. Gap years for young people prior to going to university are now the norm with the demand for flights to South America and Asia increasing as a result.

Everyone now expects to own a mobile phone and to change it for an upgraded model every 18–24 months. Communication is increasingly through social media. People want products and services now and not tomorrow.

In developing scenarios managers need to identify what changes in lifestyle or society are likely to occur and what impact they are likely to have overall on current demand in the market or segment. This can be done by taking a view in aggregate as to whether sociological issues overall are going to have a high, medium or low impact on current demand and whether this is positive or negative. Whilst it is possible to assess the impact as neutral this should be used with real care as it is sometimes used to avoid taking a view.

## Practitioner question

What sociological changes are likely to occur and what impact are they likely to have on current demand in the market or segment?

### *Access to scientific and technological change*

The pace and extent of scientific and technological change have been, and continue to be, extraordinary. Things not conceived of, never mind possible, even in the recent past have become possible. Whether it's breeding cereal crops resistant to disease, crops capable of growing in the most arid of climates, the generation of electricity from solar panels, the creation of bulletproof materials, the creation of intelligent materials that remember and return to 'memorized' shapes, information technology enabling you to call home from a desert halfway around the world, being able to analyse unimaginably huge data sets in the blink of an eye or the development of drugs that prolong the life of those with HIV, scientific and technological change has been huge.

Demand, however, is not affected by these scientific and technological advances unless buyers with the willingness and ability to buy them want and can gain access to them. Scenarios need to consider the likelihood and impact on demand of buyers being able to get access to scientific and technological changes.

Take for example the human genome. A decade ago it cost $3 billion per person to sequence the human genome. Today it costs $3,000 and is getting cheaper. This means that far more people have access to this technology and it is more likely that drugs will be developed to treat and cure specific human illnesses.

Many technology companies have brilliant technically gifted people working for them. The technological discoveries and developments for which they have been responsible have been impressive. They have created large amounts of intellectual property but too often they have failed to fulfil the commercial potential of their discoveries and developments.

In developing scenarios and assessing the impact of scientific and technological change on demand the key consideration is the access buyers will have to the advances achieved. Managers need to consider what buyers will be able to do or achieve as a result of gaining access to the scientific and/or technological change that they can't currently do or achieve now and how this in aggregate will consequently affect current demand in the market or segment. This can be done by taking a view in aggregate as to whether access to scientific and technological change issues overall is going to have a high, medium or low impact on current demand and whether this is positive or negative. Whilst it is possible to assess the impact as neutral this should be used with real care as it is sometimes used to avoid taking a view.

## Practitioner question

What scientific and technological changes are likely to become accessible to buyers and what impact will they have on demand in the market or segment?

### *Supply*

An increase in supply generally causes a reduction in price and an increase in demand and vice versa. Companies increase supply where they have excess capacity and stock and where they wish to enter a market, gain market share or to put pressure on competitors with a view to forcing them to exit the market. They also increase supply where there is increased demand and where it is beneficial for them to do so.

Oversupply to a market can distort pricing and competition. This is why, for example, The World Trade Organization and many countries throughout the world have anti-dumping laws. These laws enable the statutory bodies to undertake investigations into allegations that imports are sold at less than fair value ('dumped') or that they benefit from subsidies provided through foreign government programmes to provide an unfair competitive advantage, which may cause – or threaten to cause – damage to the competitors within the markets in which the products and services are being dumped.

An example of this use of these laws to address a market distortion and unfair competition within markets is provided by the case example below in relation to solar panels.

## CASE STUDY

### Solar panels

In September 2012 an anti-dumping investigation was launched by the European Union (EU) following a complaint from EU ProSun, an association representing more than 20 European companies producing solar panels. The collective output of these companies represented more than 25 per cent of the EU's production: a key criterion for a complaint. The complaint demonstrated a possible subsidization by the government of China, injury suffered by the EU industry and a possible causal link between the subsidized imports and the injury suffered by the EU industry.

China is the world's largest producer of solar panels with approximately 65 per cent of the world's panels being produced there. The EU is the main export market for solar panels and accounts for approximately 80 per cent of all Chinese export sales of the products.

In June 2013 the EU imposed provisional anti-dumping duties on solar panels and key components (ie cells and wafers) from China. The EU investigation revealed that Chinese solar panels were sold far below the normal market value in the European market and should have been 88 per cent higher in price. In some cases the panels should have been 112.6 per cent higher. This action had resulted in material injury being caused to the EU industry in the form of loss of profitability and the insolvency of a number of companies.

On the basis of these findings the EU imposed provisional anti-dumping duty tariffs in stages – initially an 11.8 per cent duty with a subsequent duty on the panels of between 37.3 per cent to 67.9 per cent, with an average duty of 47.6 per cent.

In 2012 Chinese production capacity of solar panels was over 55 gigawatts representing approximately 150 per cent of the global consumption of panels. Excess Chinese production capacity represented almost double the entire EU demand in 2012. This overcapacity was the result of a massive government-supported investment boom. Interestingly Chinese production capacity in 2009 was only 6.5 gigawatts!

The USA has also taken action against the dumping of solar panels in US markets. Governments are prepared to act where unfair competitive advantage is being gained that is distorting the market.

Supply within markets is a key issue that can have a significant impact on the market dynamic and is a key strategic issue within markets. Managers need to be able to understand where, why and how supply is becoming an issue and legislatures need to have both the market intelligence and willingness to act to prevent market distortion and the competitive dynamic being unfairly changed through non-competitive supply.

Companies make commercial decisions on the levels of supply to which they commit. If they make capital investment decisions based upon an overly optimistic view of demand in the market and their ability to compete successfully to meet that demand they are likely to have excess stock and capacity. This may lead to price reductions to either achieve a greater market share from the existing level of demand or to stimulate increased demand. They are under pressure to sell their overcapacity until either they reduce that capacity to be in equilibrium with the market demand (and their ability to fulfil it) or they see a sustainable increase in demand to justify the capacity that they retain. This is different from 'dumping'.

Demand is increasingly subject to change where sellers need to respond to what is selling and what is not. This means that the capacity to supply the market is not just about volume of supply but about the flexibility of supply. Sellers have to get what is in demand quickly into the market or segment in the volumes required if they are to take advantage of the demand.

Whilst sellers want to 'push' what they supply in the market or segment, buyers 'pull' what they want from the market. This tension between 'push' and 'pull', supply and demand, is an increasingly important issue in the competitive dynamic of markets.

Supply issues are also affected by access to raw materials. The transformation of China's economic approach to trade has led to a hugely increased demand for metals. This has led in turn to an increase in prices and vertical integration to control access to raw materials. Supply of manufactured products to markets/segments is dependent upon access to the materials necessary to undertake manufacture. Markets along the supply chain are linked and managers need to be aware of supply issues not only in the market for finished products and services but in the markets that enable those products and services to be supplied to the market at the end of the supply chain.

In developing scenarios managers need to take a view on how the supply issues relevant to the market or segment being considered will develop within the time frame being considered and what impact overall it will have on current demand in the market or segment. This can be done by taking a view in aggregate as to whether supply issues overall are going to have a high, medium or low impact on current demand and whether this is positive or negative. Whilst it is possible to assess the impact as neutral this should be used with real care as it is sometimes used to avoid taking a view.

## Practitioner question

What supply issues are likely to arise in the market or segment and what impact will they have on demand?

### *Evaluating the impact on future demand*

By discussing the issues from the above categories and agreeing which ones should be used in the development of scenarios, managers are able to address differences of view and to develop a shared understanding of those issues. It is of course possible that over time or due to events the position of these issues in the likelihood and impact matrix could change and managers need to remain alive to this potential.

This potential for movement in the matrix is important and should not be underestimated by managers. The future is uncertain and managers can only know, and make assumptions about, what they currently know or believe will happen. As has been seen on many occasions, events such as wars, natural disasters and the banking crisis can have a significant impact on demand in markets.

Having focused on the high impact/high likelihood issues to consider each category of issues affecting demand, agreement then has to be reached on what this actually means for demand in aggregate – the process of evaluation. Managers need to agree on how they project that the nature and level of demand will change over the period of the scenario.

Different demand scenarios can be developed by putting the issues in different positions in the matrix and by changing the evaluation of them to produce different characteristics of future demand. Given this potential for different outcomes from the evaluations it is vital that it is undertaken jointly to ensure that there is a shared understanding of the outcomes of the evaluation and most importantly a shared commitment to use what is agreed in the development of the company's competitive strategy and how it makes decisions, allocates resources and seeks to perform in the future.

## Putting the elements together

Having looked at each of the elements likely to have an impact on current demand in the timescale identified for the scenario, it is important to put them together to evaluate what the aggregated impact on current demand is likely to be to enable a view of the future demand to be gained. The *Future Key Issue Impact on Current Demand Matrix* (illustrated in Figure 9.2 below) can be used for this purpose.

The impact on current demand can be identified in terms of high/medium/low positive or negative impact or neutral. The last is less likely as the scenario chosen relates to the issues likely to have an impact, although theoretically the net impact can be neutral due to different elements of the issue cancelling each other out.

**FIGURE 9.2** Future key issue impact on current demand matrix

| Future key issue | Net impact on current demand high/medium/low positive/negative |
|---|---|
| Marketing | |
| Economic | |
| Sociological | |
| Access to scientific/ technological change | |
| Supply | |

Once populated, the matrix above illustrates how the overall future demand is projected to be impacted by marketing, sociological, economic, access to scientific and technological change and supply issues. Based upon the rationale for drawing these conclusions managers should be able to illustrate what future demand will look like and why it is likely to look like that. They should also, if they have carried this analysis and evaluation out jointly, have a shared understanding within the company of what is likely to have an impact on current demand and what that impact is projected to be. If asked what the key issues in relation to future demand will be they should be able to give a credible answer supported by a rationale from which confidence can be drawn.

## Practitioner's tips

1. Ensure that the concepts of analysis and evaluation are understood before trying to analyse and evaluate the future demand in the market.
2. Do the preparatory work to ensure that you and your colleagues understand why you are going to look at the key issues affecting demand before you start the analysis and evaluation.
3. Ensure that the focus of the analysis and evaluation to be undertaken is the market and not the company.
4. Be clear about the time frame over which the analysis and evaluation are to be carried out and whether or not milestones are required to be considered at particular points in time.
5. Ensure that you understand current demand so that you can understand what the issues being identified will have an impact on.
6. Ensure that the issues of marketing, economic, sociological, access to scientific and technological change and supply are understood before undertaking the analysis and evaluation.
7. Don't restrict thinking about demand but use the likelihood/impact matrix to identify what the analysis and evaluation should focus on.
8. Remember that you need to understand not only what you think the impact on current demand is but why that impact is likely to occur.
9. Always remember that thinking about the future is not a science but should be informed by data where they exist.

10 Remember that if you don't have confidence in the conclusions drawn from the analysis and evaluation it will be difficult for you to be able to inspire confidence in others in those conclusions.

## Practitioner's questions

1. How would you explain the differences between analysis and evaluation?
2. What time frame is to be used to assess how demand might change and are there any time milestones that need to be considered in this period?
3. What are the key issues to be considered in the categories of marketing, economic, sociological, access to scientific and technological change and supply relevant to future demand?
4. What nature and level of marketing are likely in the market or segment and what impact will they have overall on demand in the market or segment?
5. What economic issues are likely to occur and what impact will they have overall on future demand in the market or segment?
6. What sociological changes are likely to occur and what impact are they likely to have on current demand in the market or segment?
7. What scientific and technological changes are likely to become accessible to buyers and what impact will they have on demand in the market or segment?
8. What supply issues are likely to arise in the market or segment and what impact will they have on demand in the market or segment?
9. What is the aggregate impact of the key issues likely to affect current demand and what are the projected characteristics of future demand in the market or segment likely to be?
10. How is the company going to keep its assumptions about demand in the future under review and to ensure that variances from its assumptions are recognized and used by the company?

# How to develop market scenarios – competition

10

## Introduction

This chapter looks at how the development of scenarios affects competition and how to understand how that effect can be identified and evaluated. It focuses on the issues of geo-political changes, intellectual property, innovation, mergers and acquisitions and the regulatory environment.

## Market scenarios and what affects competition

The next stage in market scenario development is to identify what issues will affect competition in the market or segment and what impact these issues will have on it. This is done by following a similar process to that we used in the previous chapter for demand and also looks at the categories of geo-political, intellectual property, innovation, mergers and acquisitions and regulatory environment.

It is important, however, to be clear that competition is defined by reference to the current nature of competition, the power of buyers, the power of sellers and the risk of new entrants to and/or exits from the market. In developing scenarios, managers have to be clear about the impact that the issues above will have on these different elements of competition.

The first step is to identify the issues to be included in the scenario for each of the categories (geo-political, intellectual property, innovation, mergers and acquisitions and regulatory environment). The first scenario generally includes the issues thought likely to occur with a high impact as per Figure 9.1.

This is an important step and can again be used to surface different understanding and views within the managerial team. It is often the case that whilst there is agreement on some issues there is often significant disagreement on others. Getting to an agreed set of issues is an important first step.

Taking each of the categories in turn:

## Geo-political

Managers frequently define markets by reference to geography, eg 'the US market', 'the UK market'. In doing so there is a temptation to only consider political issues that are generated within those geographical limits. This is inadequate.

Geographically defined markets, never mind virtually based markets, are rarely immune from what happens outside those geographical boundaries. For example, the change of political policy in China in relation to allowing elements of capitalism to be introduced has resulted in China producing huge trade deficits and the creation of a wealthy 'middle class' demanding Western products and services. This has changed competition both within the Chinese market and in the markets of supplying countries. The demand for meat, raw materials and luxury products in China has led in some cases to a shortage of supply in producer countries, which has affected competition in markets within them. The competitive dynamic in other countries has even been affected by the demand for shipping to carry raw materials to China, reducing the availability of shipping to transport raw materials and products to those other countries.

Political decisions in the European Union (EU) can affect markets throughout Europe. Germany's desire to ensure the survival of the EU and the European Monetary System has led to conditions being applied to the operation of both, which have affected competition within both the domestic markets within the EU and the ability of companies in EU states to compete outside the EU.

A change of president in the United States, resulting in a change of policy in relation to world trade agreement negotiations, can affect markets worldwide. If a political decision was taken to change the focus of the North American Free Trade Agreement NAFTA (United States, Canada and Mexico) this could have significant implications for competition in international markets.

Managers must be aware of geo-political issues and how they might affect competition within the markets in which their companies compete and those in which they might wish to compete in future.

## CASE STUDY

### Oil market

Access to oil supplies is seen politically as a key strategic issue, as the economy and security of countries are still significantly dependent upon access to oil, its refinement into many products and their distribution. Civil unrest, never mind military impotency, results if oil is not available in the forms and volumes required when they are required. Given this strategic importance, access to supplies of oil has long been subject to geo-political considerations. Control over the access to oil can have a significant impact on competition in the market. If members of the Organization of Petroleum Exporting Countries (OPEC) increase or decrease their output, the dynamic in the market changes.

A result of conflict in Libya has been a collapse in its oil production. Stability in Libya resulting in a significant increase in oil production would have an impact on access to oil supplies and consequently the price in the market.

International sanctions applied to an oil-producing country, such as Iran, prohibiting the sale of oil can reduce access to supplies and consequently affect the market and so can the lifting of such sanctions.

In November 2013 a deal was made whereby Iran agreed to a temporary suspension of its uranium enrichment programme in return for a lifting of sanctions in part associated with the sale of oil. Iran sits on approximately 9 per cent of the world's proven oil reserves but its crude oil output has been languishing at a 20-year low due to the imposition of sanctions.

Announcement of the lifting of the sanctions led immediately to a reduction in the price of crude oil in anticipation of the rising Iranian oil production. The price subsequently recovered as Reed reported in the *New York Times* (2013). The main benefit of the sanctions being lifted may have been the psychological impact on the market which has been propped up by fears of a supply disruption. Any diffusion of these fears will lead to energy markets more fully reflecting supply and demand issues and the global search for alternative energy sources.

In the USA there has been an aggressive approach to developing oil and gas supplies from shale rock. This increase in supply has almost compensated for the Iranian reduction in supply to the market. Oil from shale rock in other parts

➔

of the world is being proposed but is being challenged for political and technical reasons that could affect the production of oil.

New oil supplies are being exploited off the coast of Brazil, with technical difficulties being resolved in other parts of the world such as Kazakhstan. If these new supplies are realized and not subject to disruption, whether political or technical, they will have an impact on the market dynamic.

Politics within the geographically defined area should, of course, not be overlooked. A change of government with a change of policy, whether in relation to the economy or the investment of public monies in physical infrastructure or in outsourcing services or in making significant cuts to public sector employment can have significant implications for competition in markets. Managers developing scenarios need to agree what political issues relevant to competition, wherever they are initiated, are likely to occur and what impact they are likely to have on competition in the market or segment for which scenarios are being developed.

## Practitioner question

What are the geo-political issues that are likely to occur relevant to the market or segment that are likely to have a significant impact on competition in the market or segment?

### *Intellectual property*

The importance of intellectual property continues to grow and provides the companies controlling it with the ability to compete successfully and in some cases to dominate markets. In the past, a company's value was determined largely by the tangible and physical assets it possessed. Increasingly companies are now valued by the intellectual property they control. Intellectual property is a core strategic asset that needs to be protected, enhanced and exploited for competitive success in markets.

Intellectual property is the product of human intellect and can relate to ideas, products and services and processes. Whilst some intellectual property exists without protection, in the commercial world companies generally seek to protect it as a key component of their competitive advantage through patents, trademarks, copyrights and trade secrets. An extensive and complex framework of legislation has been created and individuals and companies invest huge amounts of money to both register and protect their intellectual property rights internationally.

Regrettably the legal framework to protect intellectual property is not global in its consistency or in its enforcement. This means that intellectual property can have a variable impact on competition in different markets. Fast-to-market copies of products and services can distort competition in markets where intellectual property rights cannot be adequately protected.

In many markets and/or segments in the future, access to, control of and exploitation of intellectual property will become an increasingly important issue for competition. The immediacy of communication and the ever-increasing demands of buyers for new, higher-quality, smaller, more flexible, personalized, cheaper and timely products and services mean that the evolution, creation and control of intellectual property will continue to grow as a key competitive issue for companies. Markets will be increasingly created – and competition within them shaped – by intellectual property.

The creation of intellectual property is a particular competence that requires the support of a particular organizational culture. A number of large companies have recognized this and have changed their business models whereby they have separated the research and development required for the creation of intellectual property from its commercial exploitation.

This is sometimes achieved through the creation of separate companies within a group, supporting independent companies undertaking research with an agreement to buy the intellectual property created or in some cases to just buy the companies that have developed the intellectual property. An example of the latter is Merck, the world's largest maker of liquid crystals used in television, tablet and smartphone screens, agreeing to buy Britain's AZ Electronic Materials for £1.6 billion to expand its range of specialist chemicals for hi-tech equipment.

This change in the model for the creation of intellectual property means that managers need to be aware of both the demands of buyers in the market and how competitors are developing their strategies for the acquisition of intellectual property to satisfy it and to gain competitive advantage. It is no longer a case of just seeking to know what a competitor is developing but what others, who may not be competitors in the market, are developing that may change the competitive dynamic in the market.

Access to and control over intellectual property means that managers can decide when it is exploited. Exploitation could be in the form of being first to market, creating competitive turmoil, or in delaying its introduction because of an existing competitive advantage. Managers may not want to undermine an existing competitive advantage where there is still the scope for significant commercial returns. The timing of the exploitation of the intellectual property in the market can have a significant impact on competition within it.

Preventing intellectual property being exploited by competitors can provide competitive advantage. Some competitors seek to stop a competitor or delay them from achieving a technical breakthrough by buying the rights to a key part of a process or recruiting the people involved in the process.

Competition in a market can also be affected by the legal protection of intellectual property ending, eg patent protection for a pharmaceutical product going out of patent and becoming available as a generic. Many pharmaceutical companies have faced the 'cliff' due to the pipeline for the development of intellectual property not delivering sufficient new products to replace those going out of patent. This has led in some cases to acquisitions and mergers to ensure that there is ongoing access to intellectual property and the rewards that go with being able to exploit it.

Access to, control of and exploitation of intellectual property can play an important role in the competitive dynamic in markets as long as they are not deemed to be anti-competitive by the laws applicable to the market. Some companies are leaders and some are followers. Irrespective of what business the company is in, managers need to understand the intellectual property context within the market and how it is likely to affect competition within it in future.

## Practitioner question

What intellectual property advances or changes are likely to occur relevant to the market or segment that are likely to have a significant impact on competition in the market or segment?

### *Innovation*

Intellectual property is the product of innovation but not all innovation leads to the creation of intellectual property. Intellectual property is capable of being patented and protected by law whereas innovation may only lead to changes in what is done and how it is done that is not capable of being so protected.

Innovation is a process that leads to a discovery of something not previously known and/or the further development of existing knowledge, products and services and/or developing new ways of doing things. Take for example retailers with large investments in bricks-and-mortar retail outlets innovating to facilitate buyers ordering via the internet and collecting what they have bought from the seller's shops. A win–win as some buyers don't want to wait for delivery and the retailer gets buyers into the store with an opportunity to sell more to them.

In the context of markets, innovation is about finding new ways to create value for buyers. It is also about finding new ways to create and sustain competitive advantage for sellers, eg transforming efficiency to enable the seller to be the lowest-cost provider of products and services.

It is important to recognize that competition in markets is dynamic and maintaining competitive advantage or relative competitive position requires innovation. As the company's competitors change their offer to buyers the company needs to change just to 'stand still'. Improving competitive advantage or competitive position often requires a transformational innovation rather than one that achieves incremental change.

A key corporate objective of a company should be 'to achieve more from the company's innovation processes than its competitors'. The link between innovation within companies and competitive success is too frequently ignored in evaluating competition within markets.

The willingness and ability to innovate within companies or to adopt and adapt to the innovation of others often reflect the organizational culture of the company. Being a fast follower can be less risky than being an innovation pioneer as long as the innovation is not protected as intellectual property and is capable of being adopted and/or adapted to get an acceptable share of the first mover's advantage. Managers need to understand innovation in the market and how it is affecting competition.

Competitive advantage in markets created through innovation can be nullified if that innovation is capable of being copied quickly. The key is to have an organizational culture that sustains ongoing innovation and its exploitation. Innovation without the ability to exploit it merely causes frustration within the company rather than supports the achievement of competitive advantage.

I have seen many corporate policy statements about innovation, eg: Our mission is to innovate for the benefit of our customers; Our success relies upon our ability to innovate.

Regrettably, when I have sought to gain evidence of how these statements have been converted into action I have found that they are more to do with marketing slogans than practice. To demonstrate whether this is the case for your company try the following quick test:

## Innovation test

1. How many people in the company have to authorize any proposed innovation before it can be actioned?
2. What was the most recent innovation that made a significant difference to the competitive success of the company?
3. Is any reward system in the company reliant on or relevant to innovation?
4. Is any profile in the company given to innovations produced by the people in the company?
5. How quickly is innovation in one part of the company communicated, accepted and used in another part of the company?
6. Does the company constantly scan competitors for any innovations that they have introduced?
7. Do buyers have any role in innovation in the company?
8. Do buyers regard your company as innovative?
9. Do your company's competitors regard your company as innovative and able to implement innovation to achieve competitive advantage?
10. Do you know what the next transformational innovation is that your company wants or needs to achieve?

People in a truly innovative company will answer the questions above very easily and differently from those in a company that talks in slogans about innovation but doesn't have an organizational culture that supports it.

Innovation, particularly where it involves invention and entrepreneurship, requires an organizational culture to sustain it. Large companies sometimes find it difficult to provide the culture necessary to support innovation and entrepreneurship. This results in innovators and entrepreneurs not feeling as if they 'fit' with those companies and innovation and entrepreneurship being inhibited.

How often has it been seen that larger companies acquiring smaller companies because of their innovation and entrepreneurship soon lose the leaders of the innovation in those acquired companies because of a clash of organizational cultures? How often have the acquiring companies not been able to realize a sustained competitive advantage that they had hoped from the acquisition?

Innovation can have a significant impact on competition within markets. New entrants to markets are often associated with innovation that enables those new entrants to change the current dominant paradigm of competition. How many competitors in the market identified that the innovative technology associated with Dyson vacuum cleaners would make such a huge impact on the market and the competitors within it?

## Practitioner question

What innovations are likely to reach the market or segment that are likely to have a significant impact on competition within the market or segment?

### *Mergers or acquisitions*

Mergers and acquisitions can have a significant impact on competition hence there is law to prevent them where it is believed that this impact would be deleterious for buyers and the ability to compete within the market.

Competitors pursue mergers and acquisitions for a wide range of reasons. These include:

1. to achieve market entry;
2. to achieve increased market share;
3. to achieve greater economies of scale and cost reduction;
4. to gain access to physical assets, products and services, innovation and intellectual property, eg brand;
5. to gain access to distribution channels;
6. to save time as acquisition is faster than organic growth;
7. to achieve synergy from the combination of assets;
8. to achieve a diversification of risk;
9. to achieve better returns from the capital employed;

10 to increase competitive power in the market;
11 to achieve a critical mass and/or geographical coverage to enable them to compete for buyers with large and geographically dispersed requirements.

Mergers and acquisitions can change the current dominant paradigm of competition in the market and the market dynamic. If the number two and three competitors in the market merge so that they become significantly bigger in market share terms than the former number one competitor, they may be able to get significant economies of scale benefits that enable them to compete more effectively on price or to invest in product and service development to provide a competitive advantage over the former number one competitor. The whole competitive dynamic in the market can change.

Similarly if a company not currently competing in the market acquires an existing competitor and the acquiring company has significant resources available to invest in product and service development, marketing and an aggressive competitive strategy, the current dominant paradigm of competition and market dynamic can change.

It is also the case that where the merger or acquisition relates to buyers in the market, the power of the buyers can change relative to the sellers. Consolidation of buying power in the market changes the market dynamic.

# Practitioner question

What mergers or acquisitions are likely to take place relevant to the market or segment that are likely to have a significant impact on competition in the market or segment?

## *Regulatory*

As mentioned above, legislation exists to prevent anti-competitive behaviour by companies. This is designed to prevent companies gaining a position where it would be possible for them, should they choose, to pursue a strategy that was to the detriment of the buyers. Whether through the aggregation of power in the market due to the removal of competitors or through becoming a dominant controller of inputs to enable competitors to supply the market, anti-competitive behaviour is legislated against.

Anti-competitive behaviour is illustrated by:

1 Creating cartels and collusion where competitors agree to act in unison to exercise power over suppliers or other competitors or to fix

prices in the market. Cartels and collusion can also seek to erect barriers to entry to protect the existing competitors in the market.

2 Restrictive practices where dominant companies use their power to prevent other competitors from gaining access to resource inputs, to prevent other competitors gaining access to technology that could undermine the cartel member's current offer and to control channels to market and to the best promotional opportunities.

3 Holding buyers captive by creating switching barriers, reducing choice and the ability of buyers to gain improved value for money.

The legislation concerning anti-competitive behaviour provides a range of sanctions against those found to be guilty of such behaviour, ranging from fines to requirements to dispose of parts of the companies to reduce the dominant position, eg the sale of Gatwick and Stansted Airports in the UK was as a direct consequence of a Competition Commission ruling on the acquisition of the British Airports Authority (BAA) by Ferrovial, the Spanish infrastructure group.

In addition to legislation in countries where markets have been liberalized for monopoly providers of products and services such as utilities (water, gas and electricity), the legislatures have created industry or market Regulators. These Regulators have wide-ranging powers.

A Regulator may require regulated persons and companies to provide the Regulator with information to enable them to monitor compliance with its and other legal requirements and can undertake investigations for suspected breaches of the law and its requirements. They have a wide range of sanctions available to them and can determine the maximum by which prices may rise. The Regulator can provide conditions that encourage competition and enable new entrants to enter the market by requiring existing competitors to provide access to infrastructure.

In addition to the above regulatory requirements and powers relevant to competition, market legislatures can also legislate to protect health and safety. These wide-ranging requirements can create barriers to entry and exit to markets.

The barriers to entry relate to the need to have access to expertise and the proof that products and services are safe and will not harm health, eg the Food and Drug Administration (FDA) requirements in the United States. Access to clinical trials and the time taken between initiating research and being able to supply a medicine to market can be years and require access to huge amounts of money.

The requirement for investment in research and capital investment can create barriers to exit. The past investment and prospect of losing huge amounts of money if the company was to exit the market might mean seeking to stay in the market.

These legislative or regulatory requirements can have a significant impact on competition in markets.

## Practitioner question

What changes in the regulatory environment relevant to the market or segment are likely to take place and likely to have a significant impact on competition in the market or segment?

### *Evaluating the impact on future competition*

Having identified the issues to be considered for the scenario in each of the categories of geo-political, intellectual property, innovation, mergers and acquisitions and regulatory environment within the defined timescale for the scenario these have to be evaluated in terms of their impact on future competition. This is done using the following *Future Competition Matrix*:

**FIGURE 10.1** Future competition matrix

| | Current nature of competition | Current power of buyers | Current power of sellers | Current risk of new market entrants | Current risk of market exits |
|---|---|---|---|---|---|
| Geo-political | | | | | |
| Intellectual property | | | | | |
| Innovation | | | | | |
| Mergers/acquisitions | | | | | |
| Regulatory | | | | | |
| Future competition | | | | | |

Remember this isn't a science and the 'scoring' for each box can be in terms of high/medium/low positive or negative change or no impact. The last is more unlikely as the scenario development will most likely choose issues that will have an effect on the market. The key is for there to be a discussion of the differences in view and to come to an agreed view of what the issues in the scenario should be and what their impact on competition will be. It is then possible to identify how competition overall will change in future.

Managers in some cases have sought to use a precise scoring mechanism to one decimal place. This has generated a lot of time-consuming discussion with total scores being formulated, with the differences between a score of eight and nine being discussed and argued over.

Whilst discussing these differences is often useful and important, these discussions in my experience have sometimes been less about the assumptions about the future impact of issues on elements of competition and more to do with power plays and status within the managerial cadre.

It is important that the strategic management process and the development of scenarios are not used as part of 'managerial game-playing' but as part of the strategic development of both managers and the company. The more the process is used by individual managers to further their own agendas the less likely it is that scenario building will be effective and that the products of it will lead to the development of strategies that will lead to strategic change.

Generally more than one scenario is developed for a market. In developing different scenarios, not only differences of view within companies can be highlighted but also the lack of knowledge about competitors and the market within the company. Research is often required as part of the preparation for the development of scenarios. Without this research, which should be actively challenged by those undertaking the scenario development to ensure that they understand its implications and can have confidence in its evaluation, the relevance and robustness of scenarios may not be sufficient to build the company's future strategy upon.

Different issues and different impacts for the same issues can be used to develop different scenarios. The development of different scenarios can highlight the significantly different competition challenges that may be present in the market in the future. This underlines the importance of the robustness of the research necessary to support the development of the scenarios.

Identifying the future competition challenges in the market is not like betting on a one-horse race! Different scenarios need to be developed and, as in racing, the form needs to be studied before the race. It is also the case that managers need to be mindful that races don't always go according to plan and that existing competitors can do the unexpected.

Developing different scenarios can be a challenge to the current dominant managerial paradigm within the company. Some managers find it very difficult to contemplate that what they have invested in, built a career around and used as the foundation for their ongoing status and role may be challenged by the implications arising from different scenarios. It is important that this is recognized and not allowed to influence the development of the scenarios.

Scenario development and identifying the impact on competition are not an academic exercise. As with intellectual property, managers need to understand how they are to use the scenarios developed.

## Practitioner's tips

1. Before embarking upon scenario development for future competition in markets, remember that this is not a science but a subjective process supported by data where possible.
2. Use the opportunity to get a shared understanding of the probable issues most likely to affect competition in the market.
3. Think externally in terms of the market and not just internally in terms of 'industry' or company.
4. Recognize that the knowledge within the company may be inadequate and that research may be required to inform the development of the scenarios.
5. Before managers can understand the challenges in the market in the future they need a shared understanding of competition in the market now.
6. Don't overcomplicate the process through the volume of the issues identified; ensure that managers focus on the most important issues and their net impact on the different elements of current competition.
7. Ensure when developing scenarios that the linkages between different issues are identified and fed into the process consistently.
8. In thinking about competition in the market in the future, remember that existing competitor actions can have a significant impact on the market.
9. Take the opportunity to develop a range of scenarios to test managerial thinking and the willingness and ability to address

challenges to the dominant managerial paradigm within the company.

10 Remember that as the future unfolds it is important to revisit assumptions in the analysis and to identify whether this changes the thinking about the market going forward.

## Practitioner's questions

1. What are the current nature and level of competition in the market?
2. In evaluating the issues that could have an impact on competition in the market in the future, how is agreement to be reached in the company on the two or three key issues for each category of issue to be used and on the net impact on competition in the market?
3. What timescales are to be used for developing and testing different scenarios for the variables affecting the market?
4. What are the geo-political issues that are likely to occur relevant to the market or segment that could have a significant impact on competition in the market or segment?
5. What intellectual property advances or changes are likely to occur relevant to the market or segment that could have a significant impact on competition in the market or segment?
6. What innovations are likely to reach the market or segment that could have a significant impact on competition within the market or segment?
7. What mergers and acquisitions are likely to take place relevant to the market or segment that could have a significant impact on competition in the market or segment?
8. What changes in the regulatory environment relevant to the market or segment are likely to take place and likely to have a significant impact on competition in the market or segment?
9. How is the company going to ensure that it challenges its thinking and gets differing views within it surfaced and addressed in a constructive way?
10. How is the company going to keep its assumptions about competition in the future under review and ensure that variances from its assumptions are recognized and used by the company?

# Market scenarios – future strategic market issues

11

## Introduction

In the previous two chapters scenarios using key issues affecting demand and competition in the market were developed. We now need to bring these together to enable us to identify the future strategic market issues that will form the context for the company's development of its strategies for the market.

## The future scenario market matrix

The identification of future strategic market issues is done through using the *Future Scenario Market Matrix* illustrated in Figure 11.1. Using the scenarios developed for geo-political, intellectual property, innovation, mergers and acquisitions, regulatory environment and demand, the overall impact on the current nature of competition, current power of buyers, current power of sellers, current risk of new entrants to the market and current risk of exits from the market are evaluated. This enables the future strategic market issues to be identified.

Populating the matrix will enable the impact on the current nature of competition, the power of buyers, the power of sellers, the risk of new entrants to the market and the risk of exits from the market to be identified for the chosen scenarios. The result of this impact will represent the projected future market dynamic and in each case, the key issues arising from these differences between the current market dynamic and the future market dynamic will be able to be identified.

**FIGURE 11.1** The future scenario market matrix

| Future scenarios ↓ | Current nature of competition | Current power of buyers | Current power of sellers | Current risk of new entrants to the market | Current risk of exits from the market |
|---|---|---|---|---|---|
| Geo-political | | | | | |
| Intellectual property | | | | | |
| Innovation | | | | | |
| Mergers/ acquisitions | | | | | |
| Regulatory environment | | | | | |
| Future demand | | | | | |
| Future market dynamic → | | | | | |

As before the 'scoring' will be in terms of high/medium/low positive or negative impact. Again, this is not a science where scores can be allocated to two decimal places. The key is through discussion to get to an agreement within the team of what the impacts are believed likely to be. The first scenario tested is often the 'best guess' scenario. The scenario that the managers collectively agree is most likely to happen.

The evaluation of the 'scores' in each column needs to assess the overall impact of the different scenario issues on the current nature of competition, the power of buyers, the power of sellers, the risk of new entrants to the market and the risk of exits from the market. Will, for example, the change in the power of buyers be high/medium/low positive or negative overall? What are the key issues in these changes?

For each scenario developed managers should ask themselves the following questions (example answers are given as an illustration):

## *Future nature of competition*

**What are the key issues that competitors in the market need to address?**
**Example answer:** The current nature of competition will change. This change will be high and negative as the competitive stability in the market will be disrupted by buyers becoming more 'promiscuous' with increasing willingness to change sellers to get better deals. Competition will increase as competitors seek to protect market share where demand overall is not increasing significantly. An undermining of brand loyalty will reduce switching costs and economy of scale benefits will become more difficult to achieve.

## *Future power of buyers*

**What are the key issues that competitors in the market need to address?**
**Example answer:** The current power of buyers will change. This change will be high and negative as mergers and acquisitions of buyers will result in fewer larger buyers controlling more of the demand in the market giving them increased purchasing power. Competition will increase to secure the larger buyers with pressure on prices and margins.

## *Future power of sellers*

**What are the key issues that competitors in the market need to address?**
**Example answer:** Increased competition based on price will create pressure on margins and increase the importance of binding large buyers to sellers. Achieving economies of scale and reducing unit cost whilst increasing the value added for buyers increase in importance but will become increasingly difficult to achieve. The likelihood of mergers and acquisition of sellers increases to give access to volume benefits and to increase competitive power in the market.

## *Future risk of new entrants to the market*

**What are the key issues that competitors in the market need to address?**
**Example answer:** A reduction in brand loyalty and a concentration of the power of buyers will increase the attractiveness of the market to new entrants that can service the market using existing productive capacity from outside it to get economies of scale and low unit costs and therefore prices. Existing competitors will need to review the barriers to entry and to consider how new entrants can be inhibited or how they will have to respond to new entrants. An increase in the number of competitors in the market is likely to lead to a significant increase in competition, pressure on prices and more power to the buyers. Smaller, weaker competitors may become attractive to new entrants as takeover targets as a means to enter the market.

## *Future risk of exits from the market*

**What are the key issues that competitors in the market need to address?**
**Example answer:** Increasing competition and pressure on margins will increase the pressure on the smaller, weaker competitors to exit the market. However, given the barriers to exit, eg difficulty in being able to realize the value of previous capital investment in assets, competitors will fight hard to stay in the market, providing further pressure on prices and margins. Competition is likely to increase and focus on securing volume buyers and seeking to increase switching costs between sellers. There will be opportunities for stronger competitors to acquire weaker competitors.

## *Overall*

Having identified the key issues for each of the above it is now possible to take an overview of the market in terms of the scenario developed. This overall evaluation provides another opportunity for managers to develop and test their shared understanding of how the scenario is likely to affect the market. It should encapsulate the key issues that the company will need to address to put itself in the context of the future market dynamic. This forms the bedrock for putting the company in the context of the market for the development of its future strategies.

This can be illustrated as in Figure 11.2:

**FIGURE 11.2** The future market dynamic and key future strategic market issues matrix

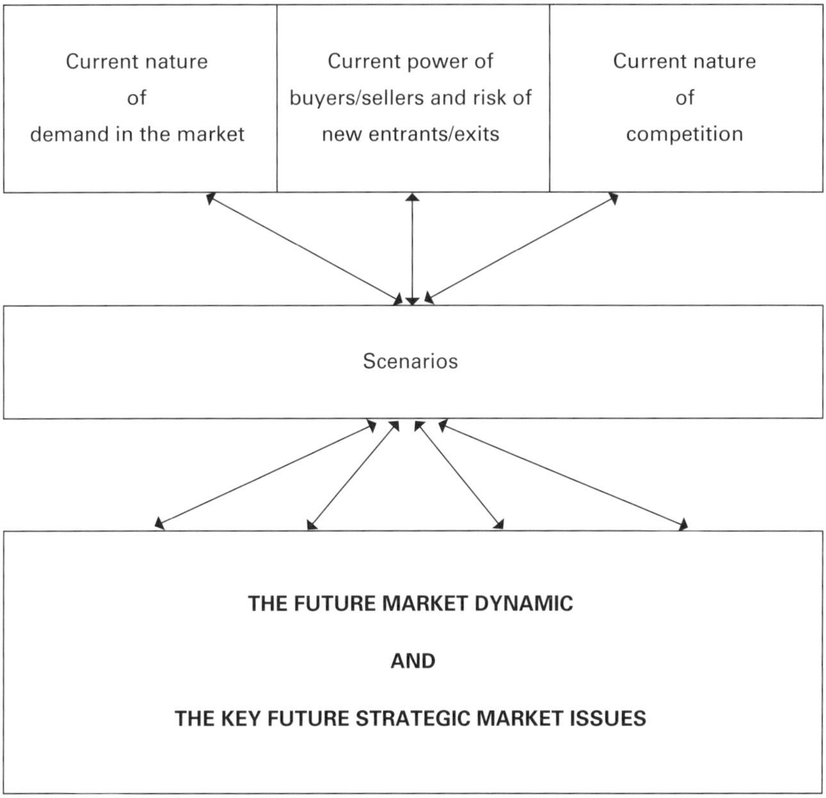


In Chapter 2 the attractiveness of markets was explored. The overall evaluation of the impact of a scenario on the current market dynamic should enable managers to start to develop a view and rationale for whether a market is likely to be attractive or not in the future. The final determination of attractiveness, however, will be whether or not the company can respond to and/or influence the future strategic market issues better than those against which it will be competing profitably.

If asked about the current market dynamic and the future market dynamic based upon the scenario developed, managers should be able to state succinctly what the key issues are and are likely to be and why they believe this to be the case. Without this level of understanding it is hard to see how the company can develop and implement a coherent and relevant strategy for the future.

## Don't bet the company

It is sometimes the case that through managerial laziness or arrogance companies only develop one scenario. This means that they are effectively stating that they can predict the future. In doing so they run the risk of 'betting the company' on the basis of their projections and assumptions being right. This scenario is the 'best guess' scenario. It represents what the managers really think is likely to happen and what the implications of those events will be on the current market dynamic.

The world, however, is unpredictable and companies need to develop between three and five scenarios. The number developed has to be consistent with the context of the market. It also has to be consistent with the capacity of the company not only to develop them but to track them and to evolve them over time. Scenario development is not a once-a-year, one-off process that is done and then frozen.

The criteria to be chosen for the development of differing scenarios relate to optimism and pessimism – optimism in terms of the variables for the issues being more optimistic than the 'best guess' scenario developed and pessimism in terms of the variables for the issues being worse than the 'best guess'.

Using the starting point of the current market dynamic, assumptions about the impact of different scenarios on that market dynamic can be tested. This is likely to lead to some similar key strategic market issues being identified for the future but also some different important ones.

In a scenario where the outcome of a national election will change the appointment of Commissioners of the European Union or an election in a state in the United States affects the regulatory requirements for a market for which the scenario is being developed, it would be necessary to identify under geo-political assumptions what the changes in policy might be after the election and what impact they would have on the future competition matrix. It would also be necessary to identify the impact of the changes on the future scenario market matrix and the strategic market issues arising from it.

It should also be noted that changing assumptions for one issue can have an impact on another issue. An assumption about a change of government is likely to have an impact on economic policy that might have an impact on demand or have an impact on the regulatory environment and therefore affect competition or the threat of new entrants to the market.

When developing a number of scenarios, do not overcomplicate the process by changing too many elements of the issues. Develop focused scenarios that will have relevance and credibility. This is more likely to enable managers to engage with the process and work together to identify and test what they believe is likely to happen in the market.

It is possible, however, to test less predictable scenarios. This is best undertaken when the team is experienced in scenario building and the individuals within it have mutual respect and trust.

In asking the 'What if?' question the company can develop scenarios and plans for the future, eg what if Apple takes over Google or vice versa?

Predicting the future is neither easy nor straightforward. It is important that as the future becomes the present the assumptions made in the analysis are revisited to determine whether or not the conclusions drawn are still accurate and relevant. Analysis of the market should be part of the ongoing management process. It is also important that this isn't an academic exercise and that the company uses the analysis and evaluation in the development of its competitive strategy, its understanding of the evolving benefit requirements of buyers and its product and service development.

When issues affecting markets change, so too does the need for managers to share the understanding of that change and the implications for the market. If this isn't the case then decision-making by those managers becomes inconsistent. Scenarios and the ongoing analysis and evaluation that should accompany them should be used as a means to improve the understanding of markets, the competence of the managerial process, the consistency of decision-making and communication with the company.

## Triggers of change

As important as identifying changes in the issues affecting markets is the understanding of the triggers for those changes. Understanding why things change enables managers to look for the triggers of change that might give an edge in being ahead of the competitive game. Those who had a greater understanding of the technology market recognized that the price bubble was unsustainable and withdrew from it or weren't tempted to pay hugely inflated prices for businesses that hadn't made profits and which were never likely to do so. Those that didn't either went out of business or paid too much for acquisitions, destroying shareholder value whilst incurring huge debts, or struggled to survive with the value of assets written down massively on their balance sheets.

In developing scenarios it's also important to recognize not just what might happen but what needs to happen to make the scenario occur. What events or milestones need to be in place to make the scenario a reality? Can the company influence them to make them happen or to prevent them happening as appropriate?

Identifying these triggers and milestones is a good way to keep track of how the future is unfolding relative to the scenario developed. It also identifies what the company needs to influence if it can. A discussion by managers of what needs to happen to make a scenario a reality is also a useful reality check on the development of the scenario.

Changing the managerial view of the world can be extremely challenging. As Chapter 16 on making strategic choices explores later, issues of power, status, security and paradigms come into play. Scenario development can be a useful part of the process of getting managers to think differently and to constructively challenge taken-for-granted assumptions about the market.

Where companies do not develop scenarios they are bystanders. They wait for things to happen or change and then seek to respond to them. At best they make investment decisions based upon less than robust information and evaluation. I have often heard it argued that a manager has an implicit knowledge of the market and knows what's required. Is one person's view of the future really adequate?

Whilst in stable markets a responsive approach to markets may be adequate, the more unstable a market the more a shared evaluation of the market is required to support decision-making. The more intense the competitive pressure the more the necessity to seek to understand how the market is likely to develop and to have alternative options evaluated for different scenarios.

So what are the strategic issues affecting your market now and how are they likely to change in the future?

## Practitioner's tips

1. Unless you have developed a shared understanding of the current market dynamic you cannot develop a scenario about the future.
2. Start by developing the 'best guess' scenario as this will encourage the engagement of those less committed to scenario development.
3. Developing more radical scenarios often requires a higher level of experience and confidence in the team doing so.

4 Remember that evaluation is subjective.
5 In developing scenarios remember that whilst many events and issues can affect the market, you are choosing the ones that are consistent with the scenario being developed.
6 Remember that it is the net effect of the events and issues that you have selected that you are seeking to evaluate.
7 Try to identify the linkages between the effects of events and issues on the different strategic market issues.
8 Different events and issues can have very different levels of impact and it could be that a particular event or issue can outweigh all others in a scenario.
9 Having identified the future strategic market issues it is important to try to identify the triggers and milestones relative to them so that the scenarios and their underpinning events and issues can be tracked.
10 Not developing scenarios means that the company is a bystander in the market and less likely to be able to plan effectively for the future.

## Practitioner's questions

1 Does the team have a shared understanding of the current market dynamic and the current strategic issues in the market?
2 Is there a shared view within the team developing scenarios of the 'best guess' events and issues that will form the basis of the first scenario to be developed?
3 How will differences of view within the team about the events and issues for the 'best guess' scenario be resolved?
4 What is the net effect of the events and issues identified to be used in the scenario on each of the elements creating the future market dynamic?
5 How many scenarios will be developed and what will be the criteria for their selection?
6 Does the company have sufficient available data to inform the scenario development process?
7 Are there sufficient confidence and trust within the team to develop more radical scenarios?

8. What are the future strategic issues in the market that the company needs to understand?
9. How will the scenarios developed be tracked and the milestones and trigger points for them be identified and used?
10. If scenarios are not to be developed, on what basis will the company seek to identify and prepare for competing in the market in the future?

# Putting the company and its competitors in the context of the market

12

## Introduction

Putting the company and its competitors in the context of the market has to be undertaken for both the present and the future. The previous chapters provide a means of developing an understanding of the current and future market dynamic and the current and future strategic issues in the market. This chapter enables managers to put the company in the context of the current and future strategic market issues and market dynamic as a bedrock on which to build competitive and corporate strategies.

## Looking from the outside in

Key to being able to put the company and its competitors in these contexts is the ability to take an objective view not only of the market but also of the company and its competitors. This is an obvious statement but one that causes real difficulties for some managers.

Companies must be able to take an external view of their competitors as well as the way in which the company itself and its products and services are perceived in the market – by buyers, by other sellers and by those from whom they may wish to raise finance. Too often, companies fail to resist the temptation to form an unrealistic internal view of their competitive position in the market and their attractiveness for investment. This disconnection between external and internal reality can lead to a distorted view of the market with dangerous consequences for the future success (and even for the survival) of the company. This internally created disconnection is illustrated very clearly by the use of the most basic of analytical tools taught on every management course: the SWOT.

As all managers who have been on a management course will have seen, a two-by-two matrix is created with managers having to identify the strengths and weakness of the company and the opportunities and threats they observe. It is an exercise that managers approach with relish and find easy to complete.

In the dash to complete the matrix, regrettably (as with the dash to implementation in the strategy process that we'll discuss in Chapter 14) lists are formed without first thinking of the context. You can't identify strengths and weaknesses until you understand the context in which you are seeking to identify them. Similarly, opportunities and threats relate to a context and to the company within it.

In Chapters 8 to 11, a methodology has been provided for identifying the current and future market dynamic and the current and future strategic market issues. This methodology illustrates the challenges of creating an external context and recognizes that different scenarios will create different contexts. This means inevitably that the strengths and weaknesses of a company and the opportunities and threats in markets will differ with the scenarios being developed.

In the absence of identifying and understanding the current and future market dynamic and the current and future strategic market issues, what tends to happen is that the perspectives of individuals from their own vested interest positions prevail. This after all, in the absence of the development of a credible strategic market context, is the only context that such an approach leaves for the managers in which to identify strengths and weaknesses, opportunities and threats.

Too often in-company strategy processes and courses for managers (and for those aspiring to be managers) start with a SWOT. Such SWOTs often do not have the benefit of a clear definition of the market or indeed of the timescales to which they relate. A SWOT in the context of the current market dynamic and the current strategic market issues could look very different from a SWOT in the context of the future market dynamic and the future strategic market issues.

In the absence of a clearly defined and understood market-focused strategic context, it is perhaps of no surprise that the list of strengths is often longer than the list of weaknesses and that the list of opportunities is longer than the list of threats. The justification of such differences is frequently not as resilient as companies require them to be to enable them to develop credible competitive and corporate strategies.

## Whose strength or weakness is it?

Strengths and weaknesses are relative terms and products and services have to be put into the evolving context of buyers' needs and the offer of competitor products and services in the market. Companies and their products and services only have strengths if the buyers believe them to be so when compared to the competitors' products and services.

> *Products and services only have strengths if potential buyers believe that they do so when compared with other competing products and services. Danger lies where internal perceptions are different from those of the buyers in the market.*

A company can be known for its ability to innovate and to produce technically leading products and services. If, however, those products and services are not seen by buyers as relevant to their needs and/or are too far in front of the buyer's willingness and ability to buy them, an internally perceived strength might actually be an externally perceived weakness.

Managers need to be really clear about what is being evaluated in terms of strengths and weaknesses and by whom. They must relate directly to the market issues identified. Being good at something that is not relevant to the market will not be a strength in the market! Against what are buyers evaluating the strengths and weaknesses of competitors? Is it:

- products and/or services;
- technical expertise;
- innovation process;
- ability to develop products and services relevant to the needs of buyers both now and for the future;

- ability to convince buyers to buy the products and services it creates;
- ability to develop, launch and support products and services for the market;
- ability to exit markets and/or products and services that they are no longer able to service or support to the quality and cost required;
- ability to develop new channels to market;
- ability to work collaboratively and in partnership with other products and services/brands;
- brand?

Buyers are rarely interested in the internal processes of companies. They are interested in what competing products and services give them. A company might have a great innovation process but if it isn't delivering the products and services the buyer wants it will not be a strength.

## CASE STUDY

### Creating a strength from innovation

A multinational telecoms company produced a huge amount of intellectual property. It had many talented people who were technically brilliant. The potential of such innovation was massive and the company believed that not only was its innovation process a strength but that it was world class. Indeed, few of the company's competitors could produce the volume of innovation or the technical brilliance of it. The problem was that this brilliant innovation was not being commercially exploited.

The company had built up a huge repository of intellectual property that was admired internally, jealously protected but not exploited. It was as if the innovation process had become an end in itself rather than as a means to produce world-beating products and services focused on the needs of buyers.

An internally perceived strength was actually a weakness as the innovation process consumed large resources that could have been used to generate value for the company, was frustrating the ability of the company to compete in the market to its full potential and was actually undermining the brand by creating a disconnection between the marketing message about being an innovative company and the conversion of that innovation into products and services valued by buyers.

To address this disconnection the balance between innovation and commercialization was changed. Innovators were paired with commercial managers and incentivized not just to innovate but to use innovation to create commercially viable products and services. Business process and resource allocations were changed to ensure that commercialization and innovation were equal partners. An internally perceived strength but externally perceived weakness was converted into an externally perceived strength and an internally perceived strength. A significant organizational cultural change as well as a significant strategic change was pursued that required high levels of leadership vision, commitment and skill.

Buyers in different markets look at products and services in different ways. The distribution curve for the adoption of innovation in different markets has different profiles. In one market the buyers may want a constant flow of new products and services whereas in another, the buyers may want to be fast followers seeking reassurance that the products and services work and have reliability. In yet another, the buyers might want not only proof of the product and service but lower prices and will be well behind the fast followers. This isn't just about segments of the same market having different rates of adoption but different markets having different approaches to the market.

Where a company's investment in marketing is not sufficiently connected to its ability to identify what the market will buy, when it will buy it, the price at which it will buy and creates buyer expectations that are not capable of being met by the products and services then the company's marketing, despite internally held views of its strength, will be perceived externally as a weakness.

Marketing professionals, by the very nature of their roles, are confident, positive and articulate people. They are often able to create positive perceptions internally. The acid test of marketing, however, is buyer perception and behaviour. Regrettably there are many examples where internal confidence in the strength of the marketing role is not supported by the external perception and behaviour of buyers. This is no better illustrated than by some of the disastrous advertising campaigns that have highlighted a total lack of understanding of buyers.

Opportunities and threats have to be considered in the same way. One competitor's threat may be another's opportunity. If, for example, it is believed that a new entrant to a market is likely to change the competitive dynamic, challenge the dominance of the competitor with the largest market share and weaken the current power of brand loyalty this might be viewed as an opportunity rather than a threat by some competitors. Similarly, a shift in channel to the market where buyers increasingly use the internet might be seen as a threat by competitors with a heavy investment in retail premises but an opportunity to others without such a physical infrastructure.

As with scenarios the key lies in the evaluation of the strengths and weaknesses, opportunities and threats to form a net position. They are not discrete lists to be created hoping that numerically there are more strengths than weaknesses or more opportunities than threats. One strength can outweigh several weaknesses as one threat can outweigh several opportunities. A current net position where strengths outweigh weaknesses or opportunities outweigh threats, however, does not mean that the weaknesses and threats can be ignored. Weaknesses and threats still have an impact on buyer perceptions. It should be clearly understood that context is all and that as the context changes so too do the relative strengths and weaknesses of companies and their products and services and the opportunities and threats with which they are faced.

> *Danger lies where internal perceptions are different from those of the buyers in the market and are allowed to dominate the strategy process and the investment of resources in innovation, product and service development and marketing.*

## Convincing others of your SWOT

A SWOT should only be undertaken after the current strategic market issues have been identified to create a context for the SWOT. The company and its competitors' products and services need to be put into the context of the market.

As we all know competing in a market requires access to finance, particularly if the company is to accelerate the rate of its growth. The company decided to explore the venture capital route.

Venture capitalists seek to reduce risks and need to be convinced that the company seeking to raise money has the leadership, the products and services necessary to compete in the market, the cost base to be profitable and the ability to create value from the investment so that they can get a multiple return on their investment within a defined timescale. Venture capitalists take great care in understanding the market, competitors and the prospects for the company in which they are considering investing.

The due diligence and research processes of venture capitalists will produce detailed and insightful dispassionate assessments of markets, products and services, competition, etc. These will be tested against the owner or manager assessments. In doing this, the venture capitalists are not only checking the owner or manager's market knowledge and understanding but whether or not they are able to take an external view of organizational strengths and weaknesses and market opportunities and threats.

If venture capitalists see an internally focused SWOT that is not based upon an objective and robust view of the market now and for the future and on the position of the company relative to competitors within it, they will have serious doubts about the credibility of the leadership and management of the company. Confidence in the leadership and management and in its ability to recognize the reality of markets and the role of the company's products and services within them is a very important part of the key assessments for determining the investment potential of venture capitalists.

*If your company is looking to raise money from venture capitalists it is vital that it can illustrate an externally focused, credible view of the market, the opportunities and threats within it and the strengths and weaknesses of the company and its products and services.*

In putting the company's and competitors' products and services in the context of the current key strategic market issues the following tool in Figure 12.1 can be used:

**FIGURE 12.1** Relative strengths and weaknesses matrix

| | Current key strategic market issues A | B | C | D | E | Average ranking |
|---|---|---|---|---|---|---|
| Comp. 1 | | | | | | |
| Comp. 2 | | | | | | |
| Comp. 3 | | | | | | |
| Comp. 4 | | | | | | |
| Comp. 5 | | | | | | |
| Strength/ weakness | | | | | | |

For each of the current key strategic market issues identified from the market analysis and evaluation the competitors are ranked from a buyer's perspective. It is always interesting to compare the different rankings of managers. There is often a difference in the rankings between managers and these differences frequently relate to the roles that managers play within the company. This raises a question mark over whether the company has a managerial team that faces the market as a team rather than as a group of individual functionally focused managers.

It can be particularly interesting to compare internally generated rankings with rankings gained from independent external research based upon buyer feedback. Successful companies are those that are the most self-aware, that understand the buyer's perspectives of their own and competitors' strengths and weaknesses and have management teams that collectively understand and act upon these buyer realities.

> *Understand why differences exist in internal assessments of strengths and weaknesses and test internal assessments of strengths and weaknesses against independent external buyer research. Ensure that the differences are understood and acted upon internally and addressed externally.*

## Knowing your competitors

Evaluation of the rankings for each of the current key strategic market issues (vertically in the columns of Figure 12.1, opposite) will put the company in context for each current strategic market issue in terms of whether the company, when compared to its competitors, has a strength or weakness. Calculating the average rankings for each competitor horizontally across the columns in the table and evaluating them will indicate whether the company has a strength or weakness overall for the current key strategic market issues in the market and identify its position in the market currently.

These evaluations, for each current key strategic market issue and for them overall, will enable the managers to identify the issues that the company needs to address if it is to build upon its strengths and to address its weaknesses and change its position in the market. These issues are likely to be significantly different from an internal approach to a SWOT not grounded in a clearly understood and agreed context based upon an analysis and evaluation of the market.

Having undertaken the analysis and evaluation above helps managers as a team to understand why their company has performed in the market as it has to date. It also, sometimes for the first time, enables a real debate about the company's approach to the market, its performance and how it invests its resources to be undertaken focused externally rather than internally.

This approach requires knowledge of competitors as well as their products and services – a knowledge that is more than apocryphal. It is sometimes surprising how little research is done on competitors and how little the research done is shared within companies.

Whilst strengths and weaknesses assessed from a buyer's perspective will enable rankings to be made for products and services, managers will want to understand as much as they can about the competitors' ability and intent to act to improve their competitive position. This is particularly important when looking to the future and seeking to identify relative strengths and weaknesses in the context of how it is believed the market might change in the future.

Understanding current strengths and weaknesses is important but leaders and managers need to prepare the company for the future. As has been seen in the previous chapters the development of scenarios, which can make differing assumptions (including about the actions of competitors), can result in different future key strategic market issues being identified. Companies need to put themselves in the context of those future issues. This can be done by using Figure 12.2 overleaf.

**FIGURE 12.2** Ranking and future strategic market issues matrix

| | Future key strategic market issues* A | B | C | D | E | Average ranking |
|---|---|---|---|---|---|---|
| Comp. 1 | | | | | | |
| Comp. 2 | | | | | | |
| Comp. 3 | | | | | | |
| Comp. 4 | | | | | | |
| Comp. 5 | | | | | | |
| Strength/ weakness | | | | | | |

* These are derived from scenarios.

Competitors are ranked, from an external buyer perspective, for each of the future key strategic market issues. Analysis and evaluation of the rankings for each future key strategic market issue (vertically for each column in the matrix above) illustrate whether the company is projected to have a strength or weakness for that issue. Averaging the rankings for the future key strategic market issues (horizontally across the columns) and then comparing the average rankings for each competitor enable the company to put itself in the context of its projected position in the market overall.

Repeating the above for different scenarios will illustrate the projected strengths and weaknesses of the company for individual future key strategic market issues and will enable managers to project the company's position in the market for those scenarios. Key to this analysis and evaluation are an understanding of and assumptions about the intent and likely actions of competitors.

An understanding of the market and the ability to place competitors within it add to the context for the company to enable it to clarify its objectives, identify and evaluate its options and to make choices for its strategy and to analyse and evaluate its performance. How will it convince the market if it does not understand itself in the external reality in the market?

It is sometimes naively stated by internal company literature that the company will be 'the best' or world class in all of its activities. Such statements being made without any reference to where it is compared to its competitors in the market now and what the gap is and is likely to be in future in the context of the key strategic market issues and market dynamic lack credibility. It is also the case that companies find it very difficult to even identify what 'the best' or world class is in the context of the market.

Such statements are more likely to undermine credibility and confidence rather than instil confidence and inspire people both internally and externally. Understanding the market and the relative strengths and weaknesses of the competitors within it is a precursor to considering any strategic and/or positioning statements for the company. Realistic (as well as credibly stretching) objectives can only be set if they are based upon an understanding of the market and the competitors within it. Aspiration has to be supported by an understanding of the market context, a shared intent to act, action and confidence in the ability to deliver the aspiration in practice.

## Practitioner's tips

1. Putting the company and its competitors in the context of the market requires an understanding of the market in which it is to be positioned.
2. The understanding of the market for putting the company and its competitors in context needs to be shared and actively used by the managers in the company.
3. Always ensure that the identification and evaluation of strengths and weaknesses of the company and its competitors are focused on the buyer's perceptions in the market rather than internal perceptions.
4. Always ensure that the identification and evaluation of opportunities and threats are relevant to the key strategic market issues for the market and the competitive dynamic within it.
5. Recognize that different scenarios can result in different future key strategic market issues to provide different contexts for a SWOT.
6. Identify whether there is a disconnection between internal views of strengths and weaknesses and an external view of them.
7. Try to base assessments of the company and its competitors – as far as you are able – on fact and independent research.

8. Recognize that competitor action and intent can be part of scenario development and can change relative strengths and weaknesses.
9. Use the understanding of the company and its competitors in the market context as a foundation for the development of the company's objectives, option evaluation and choices.
10. Use an understanding of the company and its competitors in the market context in internal and external statements about the company, as this will improve confidence, credibility and understanding of what the company is seeking to achieve.

## Practitioner's questions

1. Is there a clearly understood and agreed market context for the evaluation of strengths, weaknesses, opportunities and threats?
2. Is the context consistent with and derived from the analysis and evaluation of the current key strategic market issues and the future key strategic market issues resulting from scenario development?
3. What are the strengths and weaknesses of both the company and its competitors now and what are they likely to be in future?
4. What are the opportunities and threats now for the company and its competitors and what are they likely to be in future?
5. How are scenarios to be used to inform the assessment of SWOTs?
6. How is the consistency of understanding about the market context and the strengths and weaknesses of the company and its competitors to be tested?
7. How will the strengths and weaknesses be evaluated to create a net assessment?
8. How are opportunities and threats to be evaluated to create a net assessment?
9. How are the relative strengths, weaknesses, opportunities and threats identified to be used consistently within the company?
10. How are the relative strengths, weaknesses, opportunities and threats identified to be used consistently outside the company?

# What is success? 13

## Introduction

Managers want success for themselves and for their companies. This chapter explores what success is and who needs to define it in the context of the markets the company wants to be successful in. It also covers the relationship between the definition of success and the power and willingness to use it within the companies to guide the strategy process.

## Getting the terms right

There is sometimes confusion about the terms 'objective', 'strategy' and 'strategic'. *Objectives* are what the company is seeking to achieve. *Strategy* is how it intends to achieve its objectives and *strategic* relates to issues that are fundamental to the survival and success of the company.

A strategic objective therefore is what the company is seeking to achieve that is fundamental to its survival and success. Most people understand the concept of survival, which in some contexts can in fact be regarded as a success. Success, however, is much broader and more complex than survival and needs to be understood as another important part of building a context for the development of objectives and strategies for a company.

Success for some companies is often defined simplistically in terms of maximizing profitability. It is surprising, therefore, that in many such companies there often does not appear to be a widely shared understanding of the company's margin levels at different price and volume points in the market segments in which it seeks to compete; neither does it often understand the relationship between fixed and variable costs or show evidence of a consideration of the timescales for the achievement of different levels of profitability in the constantly changing market context.

A low profit level on a large turnover in one market context may be regarded as a success but a failure in another market context. A profit level may represent a low return on investment and be deemed less successful than the same level of profit representing a higher level of return on investment.

The same level of profit for one company may be regarded as a success but for another company may be regarded as a failure in the context of previous returns on investment. Similarly the time taken to generate the same level of profit for two companies may be regarded very differently if one company has taken four years and the other has taken 10 years.

Similarly if the projected key strategic market issues indicate that competitors will be faced with a prolonged price war, a company with a low level of profitability now may be regarded as less successful than one with a higher profitability with more resilience and scope to reduce prices.

## Success is more than market share

Companies frequently define success in terms of market share and are driven by a desire to have a particular market share. There appears in some companies to be an assumption that market share equates to success. Whilst one company's market share means that other competitors don't have a bigger market share at its expense, it doesn't necessarily equate to that company being profitable or indeed successful.

To change market shares requires an investment in innovation, product and service development, marketing, channel to market, etc and overcoming barriers to switching such as brand loyalty. Buyers need to choose to buy the company's products and services rather than those of its competitors. These investments take time to deliver market share and ongoing investment to maintain it. They are also likely to initiate a response from competitors.

Companies need to be clear about what they are seeking to achieve in seeking to gain market share and what they need to do to achieve it. Market share is a means to an end and not an end in itself and success should be defined in relation to the end and not the means to an end.

Indeed it is the case that wildly optimistic assumptions made and published about the future success of companies in terms of the market share that managers believe they can achieve, and which are either subsequently not achieved or which actually dilute the returns the company delivers, merely undermine confidence in the company internally and externally. It is often better to predict less and to deliver more. Is the company more successful with a large market share making a small profit and small return on investment or a smaller market share making a larger profit and larger return on investment?

> *Success is about the outcome and not the process for achieving the outcome.*

Many practical examples exist where those within companies lose sight of what success means or confuse their personal success with success for the company.

## CASE STUDY

### More than turnover

'My company has the biggest turnover we've ever had' was the proud statement made by the owner of a supplier of machine parts, as part of a discussion of the company's future strategy. It was clear that he had a fixation about the turnover figure, which had become his proxy for the definition of success. Indeed, he incentivized the company's salesforce on sales volume and value rather than margin and contribution to profit. Turnover was growing, as was market share. The company had been a success in his eyes but it was at risk of failing!

It was found that the salesforce was selling focused on their volume and value-related commission rather than the financial contribution to the profit of the company. They shared the owner's definition of success and it was paying them handsomely for doing so. Every quarter, the salesmen received large commission payments and they were happy. They found selling easy because they were offering a comparable product and service to their competitors but at a lower price.

Regrettably the company did not know the relationship between the fixed and variable costs of the product and service and the contribution to profit. The product was being sold at a price to cover variable costs and a margin was being made because of the low fixed costs. As variable costs increased the company was selling product at a smaller and smaller margin and continuing to reward the salesforce generously! As the need for new investment in fixed costs grew so too was the likelihood that the profitability of the company would disappear altogether.

➔

Challenging taken-for-granted assumptions about the definition of success is often not easy. A journey has to be embarked upon, as the challenge of the definition is often perceived as a challenge to the individual. Loss of face can be a powerful barrier to recognizing when a definition of success needs to change.

When the owner of the business suddenly understood that his definition of success had to change and what was happening because of the current definition of success he was naturally very unhappy about it. He was faced with a dilemma as the buyers in the market now associated his company's products and services with low prices and he had a salesforce that had become accustomed to a way of selling and a level of reward that were unsustainable. If he were to increase prices significantly to generate the profitability required for future investment in the company he would lose buyers and change perceptions about his company. He knew that if his competitors reduced their prices he would not be able to sustain his prices and would lose money. He also knew that his salesforce had been encouraged to develop relationships with key buyers and if they left and went to a competitor so might his buyers. The definition of success had led to a situation that put the whole company at risk.

Defining success is not straightforward and getting it wrong can have significant implications for the company. It is often the case, however, that the definition of success is a taken-for-granted assumption within companies. Defining success needs to be on the managerial agenda.

In Chapter 12 it was seen that strengths and weaknesses were relative terms that had to be put into the context of competition and the key strategic market issues. It was also seen that strengths and weaknesses were defined by the buyers in the market. Managers might think that the company has strengths and weaknesses but unless buyers buy, the company will struggle.

## Success and stakeholders

Success is also a relative term and managers need to be clear about how different stakeholders define success. Managers need to be aware of these different stakeholders, their definitions of success, which might be very different from their own definition, the power they have to impose their definition of success and their willingness to use that power.

The *Stakeholder Power and Willingness-to-use-power Matrix* is a means by which managers can assess where stakeholders are in terms of their power and their willingness to use it. It also recognizes that different approaches are required for different stakeholders. This is illustrated below in Figure 13.1:

**FIGURE 13.1** The stakeholder power and willingness-to-use-power matrix

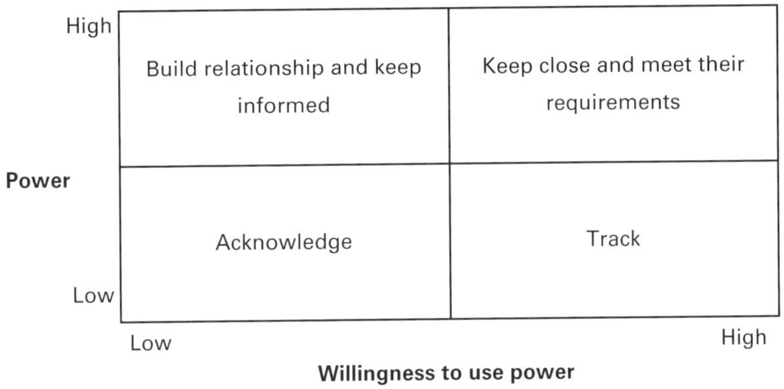


The first step is to identify and agree who the stakeholders are and where they fit into the matrix. The position in the matrix will determine the approach to them. Those with low power and low willingness to use it will only have to be acknowledged (eg individual buyers in a highly fragmented stable or growing market). Those with low power but a high willingness to use it need to be tracked (eg pressure groups). Those with high power but low willingness to use it need to be kept informed and have time invested in building a relationship with them (eg large shareholders receiving the returns that they regard as acceptable). Those with high power and high willingness to use it need to be kept close to the company, need to be kept informed of issues and performance and their needs should be met (eg buyers with large buying power where the market is concentrated in the hands of a small number of buyers).

The *Stakeholder Power and Willingness-to-use-power Matrix* provides a snapshot of stakeholders at a point in time. As markets and companies change over time, however, so too can the position of stakeholders in terms of both the power that they have and their willingness to use it. It could be, for example, that a financial institution with large outstanding loans to a company may currently be in the high-power, low-willingness-to-use-power quadrant, as it is receiving the returns that it wants, it is content that the company is performing well and it is confident that its loans are secure.

It has a relationship with the company and is content not to interfere in the management of the company.

Over a period of months, however, what if the performance of the company deteriorates, the market changes or the competitive dynamic changes due to the merger or acquisition of a competitor? What if confidence in the company's management reduces, key senior managers leave, communication from the company becomes patchy and concern grows about the security of the outstanding loans? It is likely that the stakeholder will move its position to high power and high willingness to use that power.

This movement is seen where companies get into trouble and financial institutions or investors, major buyers or regulators who have been passive become active and move quadrant in the Stakeholder Power and Willingness-to-use-power Matrix. They force a change in the company's leadership, force a change in company strategy and may even force a sale of the company.

The international banking crisis saw a number of high-profile chief executives being replaced. Whilst many announcements are made about chief executives leaving to pursue other interests, there is often a coincidence with difficulties occurring with stakeholders with high power and the willingness to use it arising out of company performance or lack of confidence in interpersonal relationships.

It is also the case that 'underperforming' companies can be seen as a target for investors who, through their share acquisitions, put themselves directly into the high-power with high-willingness-to-use-power quadrant of the Stakeholder Power and Willingness-to-use-power Matrix. Such investors are active and have a significant impact on those companies. They impose their definitions of success and seek to achieve the changes that they believe are necessary to achieve it.

## CASE STUDY

### Cevian Capital

Cevian Capital, the Scandinavian fund with $12 billion under management, is Europe's largest activist investor and has successfully pushed for radical changes in strategy at a number of companies, including the ceramics maker Cookson and the building material supplier, Wolseley. It has taken a significant stake in G4S the world's largest security contractor with 630,000 employees in 125 countries and £7.3 billion in annual sales and in companies like truckmaker Volvo and Germany's ThyssenKrupp.

As Helstom and Shanley reported (2013) it has been a prime mover in ousting boards or forcing corporate break-ups in recent years in the United States and Europe at companies such as Yahoo!, Canadian Pacific Railway and F&C Asset Management. It is an active investor.

The mere fact that a stake is taken by Cevian in companies creates a market reaction and anticipation of change. It looks for companies in markets that are 'overlooked' or 'misunderstood' in countries with strong corporate governance. It then looks to increase value over a three- to five-year period.

Cevian acquires large stakes in companies so that it can take seats on their boards. It uses these seats to push through change, to shake up management and to achieve the divestment of non-core businesses. Prior to the acquisition of a stake it undertakes detailed research of the market, of the competitors within it and of the target company. It has a clear view of how profitability and value can be enhanced and regards itself, through its hands-on approach, as the catalyst for corporate change and value enhancement. It puts itself into the high-power and high-willingness-to-use-power quadrant of the Stakeholder Power and Willingness-to-use-power Matrix.

Stakeholders can also change position due to changes in the law giving stakeholders with low power higher power and empowering them to action their willingness to use the power. Changes in the law can also reduce the power of stakeholders, eg competition law.

These potential changes in position in the Stakeholder Power and Willingness-to-use-power Matrix need to be identified consistently with the development of scenarios. It is part of putting the company in the context of the market and creating the context for the development of objectives and the evaluation of options for the choice of strategy.

*Managers need to track the movements of stakeholders in the Stakeholder Power and Willingness-to-use-power Matrix to ensure that they understand their power and their willingness to use that power.*

## Understanding 'acceptable'

Key to the above is the identification of what 'acceptable' means to the different stakeholders. Acceptable to a pension fund might be defined by reference to a minimum rate of return on investment in terms of annual dividend payments and capital appreciation. A venture capitalist might define acceptable in terms of not only annual return on investment but the ability to exit the investment on a multiple value basis within three to five years. A buyer might define acceptable by reference to price, quality and reliability and timeliness of supply. One set of shareholders will define acceptable by reference to ethical standards whilst others might not. Managers might define acceptable in terms very different from other employees of the company.

Some stakeholders will have an absolute standard for the definition of acceptable. If something is present it will be unacceptable or something has to be achieved to be acceptable. Generally stakeholders have few absolutes and will be prepared to review what is acceptable in the context in which they are making the judgement. Take for example a pension fund that normally requires *x* per cent level of return on investment in annual dividends. It could be that given the state of the market, a lower level of return than would normally be acceptable is acceptable for a period of time.

It is also the case that a definition of acceptable often relates to a number of criteria. As with the assessment of strengths and weaknesses it is the net effect of the different criteria used to define acceptable that is used unless there is an overriding issue which cancels out the others; for example, performance on safety could be regarded by an investor in a construction company as being of paramount importance and a death caused by a failure of health and safety processes will cancel out all other criteria that would have otherwise led to an assessment that the company's performance had been acceptable.

It is important for managers to understand how stakeholders define acceptable and how they might influence that definition. Communication between the company and its key stakeholders is vital so that those stakeholders can take an informed view of performance and the managers of the company can identify what they need to pay particular attention to in seeking to meet the stakeholder's definition of acceptable and how they need to communicate performance.

Understanding the key stakeholder's definition of acceptable is particularly important when objectives for the company are being set and when different strategic options are being considered. As an example, if a key stakeholder defines acceptable in terms of a minimum level of annual return on investment in the form of dividends then the option of acquiring a competitor (or diversifying where such an acquisition or diversification will, whilst promising improved earnings at some point in the future, reduce return on investment below the minimum level defined as acceptable by the stakeholder in the next two years whilst increasing the risk profile of the company) might not be acceptable to that stakeholder.

How stakeholders define acceptable can be illustrated as follows in Figure 13.2:

**FIGURE 13.2** Stakeholder definition of 'acceptable' diagram

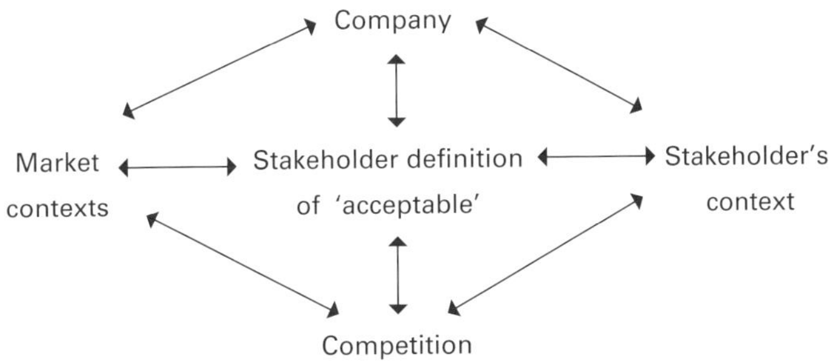


Stakeholders put the company's offer and the company's competitors' offers into their context and then look at what other market contexts offer. Stakeholders determine what they are likely to get from the company and its competitors and what they could get from other markets. They then decide whether what they are being offered is acceptable to them. In the case of investors, where they decide that what they are getting from the company in which they have invested is inferior to what a competitor can offer then they may regard what they are being offered as not acceptable and either move their investment to a competitor or use their willingness to use their power to change what the company offers. If the investor believes that neither the company nor its competitors can offer what an investment in another market can offer it may be that the investor does not regard any of the options for the market as being acceptable and withdraws from it and invests in an alternative market.

It is also important to recognize that timescales are relevant to stakeholder contexts. Some stakeholders have invested at a price in the past that, even when averaged out for different prices paid over time, can mean that the cost of exit could result in them losing too much money. This then leads to the stakeholder definition of acceptable annual return being reduced until such time that they can exit at a price value they believe to be acceptable.

Some stakeholders are willing and able to reduce their definition of acceptable in the belief that they will get greater returns later. This represents a vote of confidence in the company's managers. Where the managers don't deliver what the stakeholders believe should have been delivered then these stakeholders often act decisively and quickly in moving quadrant in the Stakeholder Power and Willingness-to-use-power Matrix and increasing their willingness to use their power.

It is the willingness to exercise the power that the stakeholder has that is important. Stakeholders might believe that performance is unacceptable and have the power to do something about it but unless they are willing to exercise the power that they have or to support others with the willingness to act their concerns remain academic. Failure to deliver promises of returns and crises often create the willingness to exercise the power that stakeholders possess. How many times have the most senior managers in a company in crisis or that is underperforming against the stakeholders' definition of acceptable been removed by stakeholder actions?

Managers cannot seek to understand and to respond to all of the stakeholders. It is important that the Stakeholder Power and Willingness-to-use-power Matrix is used to focus managers' attention and to develop an effective stakeholder management process. Managers need to understand how to position the company with stakeholders in terms of their power and to understand the trigger points for their willingness to use that power now and in the future.

This is not a science and reinforces the need for managers to understand the motivations and requirements of people. Managers need to understand how 'success' and 'acceptable' are defined from the stakeholders' perspective and not just from their own perspective.

## Getting beyond market share

As we have seen above, success is sometimes defined by reference to market share and a company regarded as a success because it has the largest market share. This might be important to managers but is it important to buyers and other stakeholders? Will it encourage buyers to buy and other stakeholders to invest in the company?

Market share can only act as a proxy for success if it delivers the stakeholders' definition of success. Being market leader in volume of sales terms might be great from a promotional point of view but if the margins and profits in achieving it do not enable the company to deliver the returns on investment that shareholders deem acceptable will they believe it equates to success?

If market share is to be used as a proxy for success managers need to test this against the requirements of stakeholders and be clear about what market share can deliver for them. A company's aspirations about market share require buyers to understand the benefits for them so that they make choices in favour of the company rather than its competitors.

Market share requires managers to put buyers at the centre of their focus and to understand the 'Buyer 3Cs': company, competitors and context. This is illustrated below in Figure 13.3:

**FIGURE 13.3** Buyers and the 3Cs

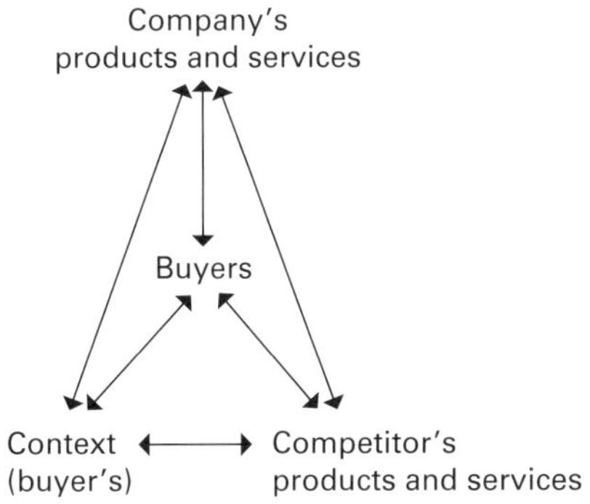


Understanding this 'Buyer 3Cs' dynamic is vital to understanding how the market share aspirations for the company's products and services might be achieved. It is also vital to managers being able to change the company's market share.

Market share relates to the aggregate buyer's perception of where the company and its products and services are compared to competitors for the issues that the buyers regard as important in their context. These perceptions influence them in deciding whether or not to convert their *ability* to buy into a *willingness* to buy decision. A company may seek to position its products and services in the market as being the price leader to increase market share but if buyers want low prices (not necessarily the lowest price) but with high quality where does this leave the company that positions itself as the lowest-price competitor but whose quality is not that required by the buyers?

It could be that the returns on investment required by the company's key stakeholders with high power and high willingness to use that power cannot be met through seeking to have the largest market share. This could be because the company:

- can't adjust its cost base sufficiently (past investment in premises, plant and machinery have created high fixed costs);
- can't gain access to the supplies that it needs (manufacturing capacity or raw materials);
- hasn't got access to the channels necessary (eg an internet channel to buyers);
- hasn't got access to the innovation necessary (ongoing intellectual property creation);
- requires a large marketing spend;
- needs to invest in breaking down switching barriers to become market leader in the prevailing market competition context whilst achieving profit margins and returns at a level acceptable to those stakeholders.

Companies need to understand the relationship between market share and profitability. Market share is not an end in itself but a means to an end. Whilst a large market share can crowd out existing competitors and inhibit new competitors entering the market it has to meet the acceptable definition test (eg return on investment) of key stakeholders.

It is sometimes found that company mission statements state things such as: 'The company aims to be the number one in the market.' Experience has shown that such statements are sometimes not understood (What does 'number one' relate to?) and do not reflect what the company actually wants to achieve. They are more promotional statement than strategic statement.

Indeed, understanding the above can lead to a recognition that the company does not have (and is unlikely to secure access to) the resources (financial, intellectual property or operational) or does not have the risk appetite to seek to be the number one in the market for specific key strategic market issues (or for them overall) and in fact does not aspire to be so. The worst position for companies to be in is where such statements create a buyer and other stakeholder expectations that the company cannot, and has no intention to, fulfil.

Whose success is it? How this question is answered states a lot about the company. In seeking to answer it, always have regard to the Stakeholder Power and Willingness-to-use-power Matrix and the willingness and ability of stakeholders to move within it. Managers need to understand the key stakeholders' definitions of success and of acceptable. Managers who believe that their personal success is a proxy for the definition of success by key stakeholders often find out the hard way that stakeholders can move and act decisively and quickly to impose their definition.

## Practitioner's tips

1 Stakeholders are many and varied. Ensure that you understand where they sit in the Stakeholder Power and Willingness-to-use-power Matrix.

2 Have a clearly understood approach within the company to different stakeholders in the Stakeholder Power and Willingness-to-use-power Matrix.

3 Understand what the trigger points are for stakeholders to move quadrant in the Stakeholder Power and Willingness-to-use-power Matrix.

4 Understand the linkages between stakeholders and whether a stakeholder with a high willingness to use their power but low power can influence a stakeholder with high power but low willingness to use that power to increase the latter's willingness to use that power.

5 Understand how different stakeholders define 'acceptable'.

6 Review how the company is performing against key stakeholders' definitions of acceptable.

7 Communicate proactively with key stakeholders to ensure that they understand how the company is meeting their definition of acceptable or what they are doing if they currently are not doing so.

8 If market share is being used as a proxy for success, question why this is so and recognize that to achieve a particular market share is a means to an end and not an end in itself.

9 Be clear about the objective for the achievement of market share to avoid it becoming just a position stated as a marketing ploy.

10 Be clear about whose success it is and avoid confusing personal success with stakeholder success.

# Practitioner's questions

1. Who are the company's current stakeholders and where do they sit in the Stakeholder Power and Willingness-to-use-power Matrix?
2. How is the company going to identify the willingness of stakeholders to use the power that they have?
3. How is the company going to track stakeholders in the Stakeholder Power and Willingness-to-use-power Matrix?
4. How is the company going to understand and track the trigger points for stakeholders with high power but low willingness to use that power to decide to increase their willingness to use their power?
5. Does the company know how 'acceptable' is defined by key stakeholders?
6. Does the company know how the company is performing against the definition of acceptable by key stakeholders?
7. How does the company proactively communicate with key stakeholders to influence their willingness to use their power?
8. If market share is to be used as a proxy for success what will it achieve for key stakeholders?
9. Can the company achieve its aspirations for market share and still meet the key stakeholders' definition of acceptable?
10. Is the personal success of senior managers seen in the context of key stakeholders' definitions of success?

# What is strategy and why is the strategy process important?

14

## Introduction

This chapter deals with what is actually meant by the much-abused term, 'strategy'. It then goes on to look at why the strategy process is important.

The strategy process is often portrayed as a scientific rational process. This chapter challenges this concept and looks at the strategy process in practice. It recognizes that the strategy process is only as good as those using it and implementing it. It also recognizes that the strategy process, and thus the strategy, has to be a living dynamic process that responds to (and seeks to influence) what is happening in the market.

## Defining 'strategy'

I have often asked senior managers the question: 'So, what is strategy?'

Not to be used as an icebreaker at parties but it can be a useful way to get to what senior managers actually think. I have had a wide range of answers to this question but one type of answer sticks out: 'Surely everyone knows what strategy is? It's what senior managers do.'

Regrettably this is not a spoof answer but what some senior managers actually believe. When pressed about what this means the answers go along the lines of:

- Strategy is what the company is going to do to beat the competition.
- It's the direction that we decide the company is going to take.
- It's how we're going to invest.
- It's how we're going to structure the company.
- It's how we're going to sell our products.
- It's how we're going to diversify.
- It's how we're going to be successful.

The list goes on.

A number of issues arise out of the above. The first is that strategy is the preserve of senior managers. The second is that strategy is what senior managers do and the third is that strategy relates to activities (invest, structure, sell, diversify, etc).

Strategy that is exclusively the preserve of senior managers remains with senior managers and will not be understood by, never mind have the commitment of, those who have responsibility for implementing it in practice. If all senior managers do is 'strategize' then they do not understand the role of senior management. Activities may be a product of a strategy but they are not a substitute for it.

> *So what is strategy?*
>
> *Strategy is the expression of how the company is to achieve its objectives and an expression of its intent to achieve those objectives.*

Unless the objectives and intent to achieve them are clear, there can be no credible strategy. Objectives without intent to achieve them are like balloons released from the hand of a child. After the initial excitement of their release all you can do is watch as they are blown in different directions depending upon the prevailing air current at the time, landing at their unplanned destination when they have either burst, got snagged on an obstacle or run out of helium.

Objectives relate to a context. The context is created at the interface of the buyers in the market, the competitors within the market and the company's stakeholders. As we have seen in previous chapters, contexts change over time, as do the definitions of success, the definitions of acceptable, the willingness and ability of buyers to buy and the willingness and ability of companies to compete. A strategy has to recognize and be able to respond to the changing context. A strategy is not a statement fixed in time but creates a living dynamic framework that puts the objectives and intent of the company in the context of the market as it changes.

Unless there's an intent to implement a strategy, the process for its production is merely academic and the strategy produced is unlikely to be implemented. In such cases the lack of intent is evidenced very quickly by a disconnection between the statements in the strategy and the strategy in action illustrated by the decision-making, resource investments, performance and behaviours within the company. An intent to implement a strategy does not mean that the strategy is a fixed position, immune from events and to be implemented without deviation. It does mean, however, that it will provide a meaningful framework in which to put those events as part of the strategic approach of the company to the market and its stakeholders.

Strategy is sometimes described as a route map of what the company will do, the way the company will react to events, the way the company will do things, the positioning of the company in the market and how the company will compete in the market. All of these things can be important but strategies without objectives, context and intent are just promotional literature. It is like seeking to assess a company's success without being clear about how success is defined.

As we saw in the Chapter 13, we need to understand whose success it is, then to define it and to use it as part of the strategy process. Too frequently the way in which success is defined and what strategies are seeking to achieve are not understood and made explicit. Too often strategies are created by the few based upon their vested interests and not understood by the many! Regrettably, both within companies and outside them there is scepticism about the strategies that are produced and the intent to implement the strategy because of this lack of understanding. This undermines confidence not only in the strategy but in those with whom the ownership of the strategy sits.

## Understanding the strategy process

It is vital that the strategy process is understood and that it creates the ability to deliver a credible strategy in terms of the context in which the company seeks to achieve its objectives as well as the confidence within the company and its stakeholders to support it through their actions. This strategy process should embody the intent to achieve the company's objectives, provide a framework for action as assumptions about the future are tested against the reality of the present and relate to the key stakeholder's definition of success.

There is a danger, however, that the strategy process is credited with a rationality that is not present in practice. The strategy process is about people, their personal agendas, their definitions of success, how they perceive the market, how they perceive competitors and how they perceive the strengths and weaknesses of their own organizations. It is also a reflection of their competence, their power and their willingness to use that power.

People impact the strategy process at every stage, from identifying what needs to be analysed and evaluated, identifying the context in which this is to take place, identifying the data relevant to what needs to be analysed and evaluated, identifying and evaluating options, making choices, making decisions and behaving consistently with the choices made, undertaking performance review and developing and tracking scenarios for the future. The strategy process can only be as rational as the people within it and the external context within which it is being operated.

In understanding the strategy process the following have to be recognized:

1. The strategy process reflects the power and the willingness to use the power of those involved in it.
2. There can be an official planned strategy and an unofficial planned strategy.
3. Planned events can influence and change strategies in unplanned ways.
4. Unplanned events, the impact of changes in power and the willingness to use it, changing definitions of success and acceptable, learning and actions becoming the norm cumulatively over time can lead to changes in strategy.
5. The strategy in action can be very different from that originally intended and is the realized strategy at that time.

The above will be dealt with in turn but are illustrated by Figure 14.1:

**FIGURE 14.1** The strategy process

The strategy process reflects the power and the willingness to use the power of those involved in it. See Mintzberg (1994) for the schools of thought for strategy processes. The strategy process starts with the stakeholders with high power and high willingness to use the power and their definition of success and acceptable along with their interpretation of the key current and future strategic market issues and key company issues. It is important to state that these definitions are sometimes implicitly rather than explicitly communicated and managers sometimes make assumptions about these definitions. It is also the case that many stakeholders will not understand or have access to the knowledge and information necessary to enable them to understand the key current and future strategic market and company issues. Knowledge is sometimes used to protect or gain power.

This asymmetry of knowledge within companies between senior managers and other stakeholders enables the senior managers to exercise power over and in the strategy process. This power and the willingness to use it are important ingredients in the strategy process. Unless non-senior manager stakeholders have clear definitions of 'success' and 'acceptable' and the knowledge, ability and power to interpret the key current and future strategic market and company issues it is only the senior managers who really are in a position to have both the power and the willingness to use that power in the strategy process.

This affects the nature of the strategy process itself and can be illustrated as follows in Figure 14.2:

**FIGURE 14.2** The nature of the strategy process matrix

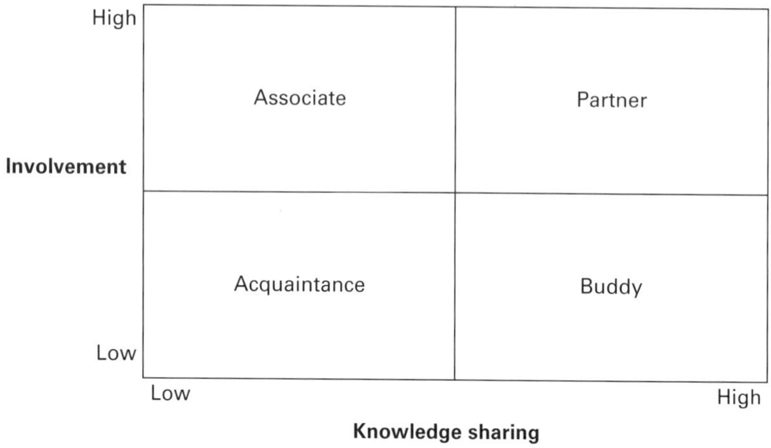


The *nature of the strategy process* matrix identifies the different levels of knowledge sharing and involvement in the strategy process. Those with high knowledge sharing and high involvement are real *Partners* in the strategy process. Partners are co-producers of the strategy, with each playing a role in developing ideas and testing them out together based upon mutual trust and confidence.

*Associates* at work might have high involvement but their knowledge is restricted until you have confidence in their ability to contribute more widely and that you can really trust them. They are often involved because they have to be, whether because of their position in the stakeholder power and willingness-to-use-power matrix or they hold information about the market or they're part of the company that is useful to the strategy being developed. Associates can become Partners.

You test things out and develop ideas with your *Buddies* at work. These are people whom you can trust and know that they will not share with others what you many not want to be known yet within the company. They will not know the whole context for the strategy development and may not have the ability to contribute strategically to it but there is high knowledge sharing with low involvement in the strategy process. Their usefulness is because they are external to the strategy process (as long as the knowledge sharing is secure). Buddies can become Partners.

There are others within the company who have neither the willingness nor the ability to contribute to the strategy process. There are also those who might have the willingness and ability to contribute but where such a contribution is not appropriate at that time. These are *Acquaintances* whose knowledge and involvement are limited. Where and when it becomes necessary and appropriate for them to have increased knowledge and involvement they move to other quadrants. This is generally not straight to Partner but to either Associate or Buddy, as trust and confidence in their contribution have to grow first.

As the company's context changes and/or the trust and confidence in individuals changes, so too can the position of those involved in the strategy process in the opposite direction. Partners can move to become Associates. Buddies can become Acquaintances. Associates can become Acquaintances. Associates can become Buddies where roles change but trust and confidence increase. Buddies similarly can become Associates where the role changes and where trust and confidence in the individual change.

It is useful to put those involved in the strategy process in the nature of the strategy process matrix to illustrate the approach to them in the strategy process as per Figure 14.3 below:

**FIGURE 14.3** The approaches in the nature of the strategy process

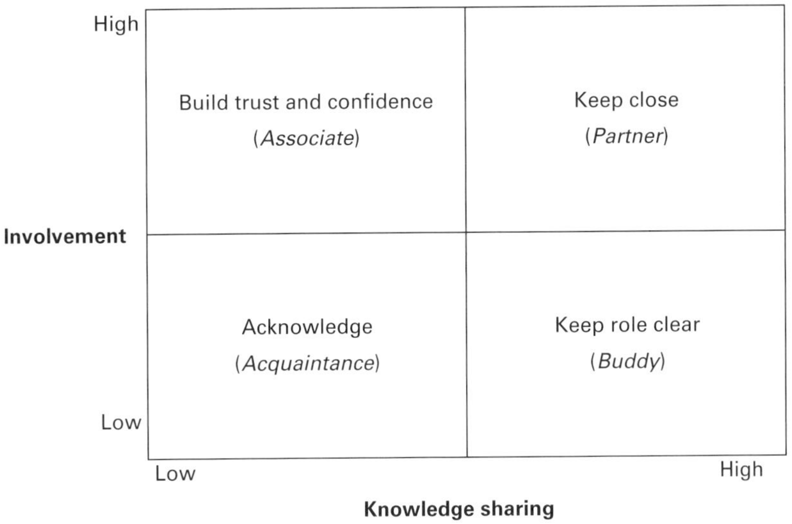


It is also important to recognize that whilst those leading the strategy process might want certain stakeholders to be in certain positions in the matrix those stakeholders might have different ideas. If those stakeholders don't have the ability to impose their requirements for their role in the strategy process this situation can be contained. Where, however, the stakeholder has the power and the willingness to use that power to impose the position that they want this can cause conflict in the strategy process.

Be clear about the roles individuals will play within the strategy process and be consistent with how you approach them in those roles. If you treat Partners like Acquaintances you may come to regret it when the strategy is challenged by events and you need their support.

Some might argue that it is the role of senior managers to set the strategy for the company and to be the custodians of the strategy process. Indeed, shareholders are often content for this to be the case as long as their definition of success is met. As we have seen from the Stakeholder Power and Willingness-to-use-power Matrix, some stakeholders with high power will only have the willingness to use it when their definitions of success are not met and are content in other circumstances to leave the senior managers to set the strategy.

To illustrate this point, too often it has been found that non-executive directors, who have been appointed to the boards of companies to represent and safeguard the interests of shareholders, have been only marginally involved in making decisions about future strategy as part of the strategy process. They have not sought, or been given, sufficient knowledge and have merely supported the senior managers' propositions.

Action to remove the senior managers and to exert influence over the strategy process only occurs where the results of the senior managers' strategies do not meet the expectations of shareholders. Too often non-executive directors act like (or allow themselves to be treated like) Associates or Acquaintances rather than Partners.

Stakeholders can achieve a change in chief executive where they lose confidence in the individual because of the results produced or the strategy that is being pursued. There have been many instances of this occurring.

## CASE STUDY

### Change at the top

In July 2013 the chief executive of Siemens was replaced by the chief financial officer of the company after a series of profit warnings and reported concerns about deteriorating profit margins and the slow pace of cost cutting. Siemens, an international diversified company with revenues from energy, products and services to industry, infrastructure and healthcare of 78 billion euros in 2012, has a two-board governance structure with a supervisory board and a managing board.

The managing board has responsibility for managing the company whilst the supervisory board advises the managing board on the management of the company and monitors the activities of the managing board. Power generally rests in the hands of the chief executive and the executive team in the managing board with an overview being taken by the supervisory board. The supervisory board consists of 20 members, 10 elected by the shareholders meeting and 10 elected in accordance with the provisions of the German Codetermination Act. It was the supervisory board that changed the leadership of the company.

In what could have been a direct reference to the Nature of the Strategy Process Matrix, Bryant (2013) reported the challenge of the new chief executive Mr Kaeser:

> Although Mr Kaeser is seen as a friend of the capital markets, he must operate within the constraints of any Siemens chief by retaining the support of workers, whose representatives make up half of the Siemens supervisory board. Siemens' workforce is upset about the cost-cutting, which is set to cause thousands of job cuts. Mr Kaeser was careful to emphasise that he valued both margins and Siemens' 370,000 workers and argued that the best recipe for success was value-creating growth. 'I will not try to reinvent Siemens,' he vowed.

Those with the greatest power and willingness to use it prevail in the strategy process in getting their definitions of success and acceptable and their interpretation of the key current and future strategic market or company issues to provide the context for the official planned objectives and strategy of the company. This is important to recognize as it is the official planned objectives and strategy resulting from this strategy process that get published internally and externally as appropriate. It is also these objectives and strategy that should guide decision-making, resource allocations, performance, performance review, behaviours and communication.

Shareholders have to have the opportunity to use their power but they often do not know what they don't know and consequently do not have that opportunity. In many companies shareholders, unless they have a significant shareholding that gives them representation on the board or influence with the board, have limited opportunities to find out what is happening and to challenge it. Shareholder meetings may only occur once or twice a year with their agendas being tightly controlled by the board. At these meetings the nature of the company's official strategy is only outlined in general terms under the cloak of competitive secrecy with decisions required from shareholders being specific and limited. Discussions, such as they are, tend to be about results rather than strategy.

The strategy process reflects the vested interests of, and is controlled by, those with power and the willingness to use it in companies. The nature and operation of the strategy process are not only a symbol of the competence and power within a company but of its organizational culture. So too is the official strategy that results from it.

## 1. There can be an official planned strategy and an unofficial planned strategy

The official strategy process results in the official planned strategy. The board agrees the official planned strategy for the company, a glossy generalized document is often produced for public consumption supported by detailed internal strategy documents (not for public consumption) and the company's future approach to the market is laid out. As we will all have seen, however, the official planned strategy is rarely implemented as per that espoused and agreed.

Where a senior manager or a group of senior managers disagrees with the official planned strategy or does not wish to comply with the requirements of a powerful stakeholder that is using their power to impose their requirements on the official planned strategy they will plan their own unofficial strategy. The degree to which this unofficial planned strategy is planned will be a factor of the willingness and ability of those involved to overtly or covertly plan their strategy and implement it systematically rather than respond to events opportunistically within a general strategic direction. Developing an unofficial planned strategy is not without its risks!

It is also the case that in some companies the official planned strategy is seen as merely a promotional tool to keep the market or stakeholders happy. The strategy states one thing but the intention is another. As has been seen from the definition of strategy, it is the intent and not just the words that are important.

The official planned strategy may state that the company will seek limited international expansion within a defined fiscal risk framework whilst maintaining its market position and profitability in its home country. The unofficial planned strategy and intent of the chief executive may be to make this their principal focus and to accept significant risks trying to expand internationally. Many UK companies have sought to expand into the United States and in doing so have suffered back in the UK by losing focus on their home market, by underestimating the investment required to do so, by not understanding the key current and future strategic market issues in the US markets and by mistakenly believing that the successful business model in the home market can be replicated in another market.

The degree by which the unofficial planned strategy varies from the official planned strategy depends upon the power of the senior managers and their willingness to use that power. This is dependent upon their perception of risk and their willingness to accept that risk.

In large companies and particularly diversified companies there can be opportunities for the development of unofficial planned strategies. The group board may agree a strategy for the company overall and for the divisions within it but such is the headquarters' 'distance' from the divisions that the divisional senior managers have sufficient scope to develop, plan and pursue their own unofficial planned strategies.

How often is it seen that a powerful divisional manager is left to 'get on with managing' their division? The key for corporate headquarters and the board is the delivery of acceptable results. The definition of 'acceptable' is crucial and powerful divisional managers often have significant influence over this definition as it gives them the scope to pursue their own strategies.

## Strategic turmoil

Whilst results are acceptable the dissonance between the official planned strategy and the unofficial planned strategy is not challenged or officially recognized. Where results fall below the definition of acceptable and the confidence that they will improve to acceptable levels is lost, strategic turmoil occurs. Strategic turmoil is generally triggered by some event of strategic significance that highlights the difference between the official planned and unofficial planned strategies. These *trigger events* illustrated on the diagram of the strategy process are often linked to the power and status of a senior manager or stakeholder being put at risk forcing a response to protect that power and status.

Where these trigger events are sufficient individually or cumulatively to create a risk to the power or status of an individual or a company, strategic turmoil is created resulting in the official and unofficial planned strategies colliding. This strategic turmoil becomes a test of power and the willingness to use that power.

These trigger events can cause stakeholders with high power but low willingness to use that power to move in the Stakeholder Power and

Willingness-to-use-power Matrix (see Chapter 13) to the high-power, high-willingness-to-use-that-power quadrant. There can consequently be collateral damage through individuals being held to account and political manoeuvring within the company leading to the 'sacrifice' of individuals. *In extremis* whole divisions or companies can be sold off.

Strategic turmoil creates confusion and uncertainty about what the strategy is and who has power within the company. Some individuals see this as an opportunity to seize power by seeking to remove competitors in the senior management cadre and to be seen as the 'saviour' through providing the promise of a solution. Some stakeholders see it as an opportunity to introduce new people with new skills into the company.

Strategic turmoil – if serious enough – can put the whole company at risk from predators. The key is to remove the turmoil, to provide stakeholders with confidence about the future and to determine what the strategy will be for the future. This may be through confirmation of the official planned strategy with the unofficial planned strategy becoming an aborted strategy or through the adoption of the unofficial planned strategy with the official planned strategy becoming an aborted strategy.

In practice the strategic turmoil often leads to a *hybrid strategy* being agreed, taking the best bits from both the official and unofficial planned strategies. The hybrid strategy becomes the new official planned strategy. This results from a compromise between those with power within the organization. Compromises that seek wherever expedient to do so to remove instability, to retain the experience and skills required within the company, to post-rationalize positively the reasons for the unofficial planned strategy (particularly where the official planned strategy was inadequate or defective) and to also recognize that where through the unofficial planned strategy significant capital and revenue investment has been made, it can often be difficult to extricate the company from it without significant loss. In these circumstances the strategy may seek to accommodate the use of this investment.

## 2. *Planned events can influence and change strategies in unplanned ways*

Many strategies include planned events, for example the launch of a new car, a new range of clothing or a new phone, a new production process or a new technology. Assumptions are made about the impact of these events on the market and on competitors. Such assumptions by their very nature are not certain. Impacts assumed and planned for may not be realized – a new clothing range does not sell 1,000 cashmere sweaters per day for the first month after launch. This can mean that contracts entered into with suppliers create a large liability and disruption to the supply chain.

It could also be that a new phone is so popular that all assumptions about its adoption and purchase by the market are exceeded and supply cannot keep up with demand. In an effort to meet this burgeoning demand through accelerated manufacturing quality suffers, which undermines confidence in the product and ultimately the demand for it and other products and services in the company's portfolio.

The successful launch of a new product can affect the competitive dynamic in the market significantly. If competitors cannot match the new product and service launched it can force them to discount their products and services heavily and even force them out of the market if there is no prospect of them being able to compete with the new product and service. Where this is the case the planned new product and service launch can have an impact on the competitive dynamic far in excess of the assumed impact.

It is also the case that companies, in planning events such as new product launches, make assumptions about the impact of them on the other parts of their product and service portfolio that can prove wildly inaccurate. Škoda has successfully seen the launch of new cars such as the Octavia and through investment from its parent company Volkswagen, a series of upgrades and new models. Demand has increased across the product and service range and so too has the need to accelerate capital investment in manufacturing.

The ability to flex capital-intensive capacity is limited. The ability of the supply chain to satisfy increases in demand to short timescales can be challenging and access to raw materials can be a limiting factor. Whilst demand outstripping supply can lead to increases in pricing and an increase in brand value, a consistent inability to meet demand can have a negative impact on perceptions about the product and service which reduces demand and provides opportunities for competitors. This can lead to capital investment delivering capacity after the demand has reduced or where the competitive dynamic has changed requiring a unit cost of production below that for which the capacity was designed.

The success of a planned launch of a new product and service can be such that the company's strategy changes to focus on that new product and service to the exclusion of its other products and services as a planned strategy to have a diverse range of products and services. The company's business becomes redefined by the success of a single product and service.

A planned strategy of diversification can lead to the whole company being put at risk through a drain on resources, incurring unsustainable debt levels and undermining confidence. Diversification can lead to the company changing to become a very different type of company from that planned. A strategy planned to redefine the business the company is in can also lead to failure.

## CASE STUDY

### Marconi

Marconi employed a strategy of moving from a company known as GEC, a diversified company but largely involved in defence contracting with a strategy that was risk averse and a cash mountain in 1996 of £2 billion, into a telecoms equipment manufacturer. This planned change of strategy came about through a change of leadership in the company and from a strategic review.

The defence business was sold and the proceeds, along with the cash mountain and debt, used to buy expensive telecoms assets as a rebranded company to be known as Marconi. As Marconi was expanding into the market, a combination of overcapacity and a worldwide slowdown affecting telecoms operating companies having to pay for third-generation mobile phone licences meant that the buyers for Marconi's products and services cut back severely on their equipment expenditure.

The official planned strategy was a 'bet the company' strategy that went spectacularly wrong. The bet was lost and so too was the company. The new leadership of the company left and it is estimated that the shareholders lost £3.7 billion of market value in just 18 months.

Planned events can influence strategies in unexpected unplanned ways both positively and negatively.

## *3. Unplanned events, learning, changes in power and the willingness to use it, etc. cumulatively over time can change strategies*

Nothing in life is certain. There is no such thing as perfect knowledge and a perfect strategy process. There are too many variables in play, too many people interpreting those variables and too many ways for people internally and externally to react to them to be able to predict the future. As we have seen, people have different levels of power and different levels of willingness to use the power that they have available or can influence and events can change both their power and their willingness to use that power.

Different stakeholders have different definitions of success and acceptable and consequently react to events differently. The best that we can do is to learn as the future unfolds and apply that learning in the context of the market and the company within it.

Former British prime minister, Harold Macmillan, is often quoted in response to a question from a journalist about what blows governments off course:

'Events, dear boy, events.'

The same is equally relevant to companies.

Whether these events are natural disasters, such as the 2004 tsunami, or man-made disasters, like the 2011 Fukushima nuclear meltdown, or wars, for example Iraq, or civil unrest as seen in Egypt, or biological disasters such as avian flu, or food chain disasters (eg foot and mouth disease) or economic disasters (eg the banking crisis) or corporate events (eg the fall of Enron) or a major shareholder selling their equity to a venture capital fund looking for rapidly ramped-up earnings, enabling them to exit in three years with a multiple capital yield rather than a long-term hold – all can have a significant impact on the strategy processes and strategies of companies.

Whilst assumptions about such events can be built into scenarios, companies have different levels of ability to predict and prepare for them. It is the ability to learn from events and to adjust both strategy and action that is of vital importance for companies. Managers need to understand that:

> *Strategy looks forwards, whereas learning looks backwards and should be used to inform strategy and action looking forwards.*

This learning applies not just to events but to changes in position of stakeholders in the Stakeholder Power and Willingness-to-use-power Matrix and what triggers them. Managers need to learn what events will trigger action by stakeholders and what that action is likely to be. This enables managers to prepare for that action or to avoid, where possible, the events that trigger action. It also means, of course, that it enables managers to trigger action where they believe it beneficial.

Learning also relates to what is happening in the market in terms of buyer needs and behaviours and the intentions and actions of competitors. As we have seen from the use of the basic strategic analytical tool the SWOT, a context for the company and its products and services has to be created. This can only be done through learning what is happening external to the company.

Too often learning is treated as the property of an individual or a specific team. This misses an opportunity for the company as well as for the individuals within it. The products of learning should be treated as a corporate resource. It is too often the case, however, that there is no systematic approach to learning or to sharing the products of learning in companies.

> *If the company's strategy is only as good as the strategy process supporting it and the strategy process does not include learning and the dissemination and use of that learning, how good will the strategy be?*

Strategies set the company's direction with intent. It is vital that they keep up with changes in the market. Without ongoing learning it is hard to see how strategies can remain relevant and useful. Where learning is not an effective part of the ongoing evolution of strategies companies are in danger of becoming disconnected from the market.

Strategic market disconnection occurs where the company's strategy does not evolve with changes in the market and the competitive environment within it. Managers within the company do not recognize the changes, learn from them and act upon that learning. Typically the strategic direction once set is maintained irrespective of the changes that are taking place. This leads to a growing gap between the external market reality and the company's internal reality and decision-making resulting in a strategic market disconnection.

The reasons for strategic market disconnection are many and include the strategy being the property of a single senior manager or small number of senior managers who believe that their power and status are linked to the strategy that has been set. They will consequently not allow any challenges to it and deviation from it.

Strategic market disconnection can result from past capital and revenue investment in premises, technology and branding making the cost of change prohibitive and being perceived by managers as a loss of or challenge to their reputations or status. In these cases the company has effectively built exit barriers to its own strategy and it consequently sticks with the existing strategy even though it is delivering less and less.

Companies sometimes have neither the organizational cultures enabling them to change nor the technology nor the competencies nor the leadership for change. They also may not have the strategy processes to enable them to recognize the need for change or to support and enable them to change.

An example of strategic market disconnection is seen clearly in relation to the impact of the internet on retail companies. Those who recognized that buyers wanted to increasingly shop online developed, as part of their strategy, an internet-based offer. Those that didn't develop this strategic option have suffered strategic market disconnection and are now desperately trying to catch up. In the UK Tesco was early in identifying buyer channel shift and built an online retail offer. Morrisons, by contrast, stuck to its traditional value bricks-and-mortar retail offer and has had to play catch-up.

## CASE STUDY

### Marks & Spencer plc

Marks & Spencer suffered strategic market disconnection because it was successful. Its success blinded it to changes in the market and in the competitive environment. It believed that it could carry on as it had always carried on. It believed that it would always be the retailer of choice because of its quality, service, value and choice. It believed its own rhetoric and didn't recognize either the changes in the buyer's requirements or the emergence of new retailers with different offers that were more attractive to buyers. It did not learn from the changes taking place in the market and the competitive environment but merely extrapolated the past to the future in its own terms. Crisis followed where the whole company was at risk. It narrowly avoided takeover and it is still trying to get back to where it once was in the market.

Strategic market disconnection often continues until a trigger event is reached. Stakeholders, generally based upon results, decide that their definitions of success and acceptable are not being met and that there is increasingly little chance of them being met. Those with high power choose to use it to change the leadership of the company and/or to force a change of strategy.

Companies suffering from strategic market disconnection can change strategy but often do not recognize the position that they have got into until they are at risk of failing. They become exposed to takeover as a turnaround opportunity or for break-up. Shareholders often lose a significant amount of value as a result of strategic market disconnection. Entrepreneurs and venture capitalists with the strategy and resources to address the strategic market disconnection and to pursue a new strategy often make a lot of money from such turnarounds or break-ups.

Learning has to both recognize and evaluate major events and changes and also the smaller cumulative changes that impact the company, its competitors and its markets. Learning needs to identify patterns of events and behaviours emerging over time as well as the large significant acute events. Whilst the large significant acute events can be game-changers and create new rules of the competitive game so too can the cumulative effect of smaller events and changes.

Learning in itself is useful but is not the prize. The prize is what results from the learning. Will learning enable competitive advantage to be gained or protect the company from losing its competitive position? As with strategy formation, corporate learning is a means to an end and not an end in itself. It must enable the company to understand the past, to change, to respond to change that affects it and to prepare for change. Managers should understand that:

> *Learning enables managers to rationalize and evaluate the past to inform preparations for the future.*

So many times we have heard people state: 'All becomes clear. I now understand what has happened and why it has happened.' As we say in the UK: 'The penny drops.' We suddenly understand. We learn and that learning changes our understanding of the context. We post-rationalize and evaluate.

Post-rationalization is an interesting concept as it involves looking back at events to put them into context. But which context? This is where the evaluation comes in. Managers tend to use their own contexts for evaluation which generally leads to a more positive outcome, eg it was not as bad as it could have been. It is, however, the company's context that needs to be used. As a manager my context, from a vested interest perspective, might be different from the corporate context. Think only of the existence of, and differences between, the official planned strategy and the unofficial planned strategy! Think of the post-rationalization for takeovers that promised synergy that is so frequently not achieved.

This contextualization will provide an important backcloth for how managers will evaluate, communicate, adopt, adapt and act upon the learning in the strategy process. Companies often need to address the issue of corporate learning to ensure that the learning is in the context of the company, rather than just that of individuals. This requires not only an agreed strategic market context to be used but learning, through post-rationalization and evaluation as a corporate, rather than individual, activity as part of the strategy process.

The ability of companies to learn from the past, whether it is from their own direct experience or the experience of others, is a factor of their organizational cultures and leadership. It is an important competitive and corporate competence of strategic significance.

Learning can only be effective if it is adapted and/or adopted for the company's context and influences strategy and action. Learning without positive decision-making is more likely to have a negative impact than a decision (appropriately communicated) to not act upon the learning. Learning in a corporate context takes effort and sometimes raises sensitive issues for individuals. It consequently requires individuals to understand that the effort of learning corporately is worthwhile. If it is believed that learning is just another process to be gone through without any tangible outcome it will soon lose credibility and become a token activity.

As we have seen contexts change and it is important to ensure that learning continues to relate to that changing context. It could be that the learning identifies different strategic changes and events that need to be recognized in the evolving context.

The learning dynamic can be illustrated as follows in Figure 14.4:

**FIGURE 14.4** The learning dynamic

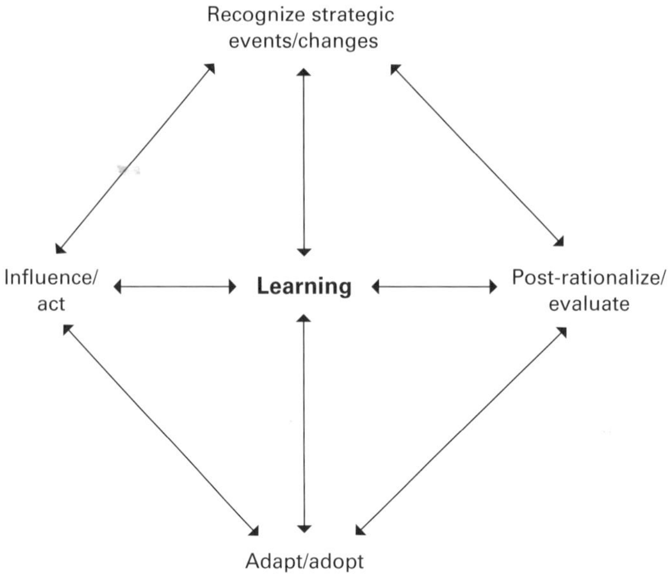


Single major events or changes in stakeholder power and the willingness to use it or a change to the definitions of success and acceptable can cause crisis and have a profound effect on strategy. It is often the cumulative effect of individual events, however, over time that changes strategy. This change occurs incrementally and implicitly rather than explicitly.

Behaviour often changes over time unrecognized but creating a new norm. Strategic leadership is about the ability to recognize this 'new norm' and to decide what to do about it; for example, the new norm may now be that we now buy in, assemble and apply our branding to more products than we make ourselves under our brand. Is this what we want the strategy to be? Are the competencies of the company now as a designer, brander and assembler of products rather than as a manufacturer of products?

## *4. The strategy in action can be very different from that originally intended and is the realized strategy at that time*

The above illustrates that there can be a significant difference between what is produced by a formal strategy process and what is being implemented in practice. Some of these differences can be planned whilst others evolve over time through acts and omissions. Not doing something can have as big an impact on a strategy as doing something.

People at different levels and in different roles within companies react to events. These reactions are often incremental and individually may not amount to a change in strategy. Cumulatively, however, these changes can result in a change of the company's strategy in action.

People, buyers in the market, react to events. These reactions again may be incremental and individually may not require a change of the company's strategy. Cumulatively, however, these changes if sustained may result in the company changing its response to the buyers and lead to a change in the strategy of the company by such actions. These buyer changes may also cause a change in the strategy of competitors, which consequently requires a change in the strategy of the company.

These changes are often not the result of a formal planned change in strategy but through an evolution of action over time. It is not strategic market disconnection but *strategic drifting*. Strategic drifting is where a company increasingly does not act consistent with its agreed strategy but allows its strategy to evolve with events, learning and the requirements of stakeholders with power and the willingness to use it. The strategy in action resulting from strategic drifting once recognized is often post-rationalized in terms of: 'It's what we knew we needed to do anyway'.

Whilst some might argue that strategic drifting is keeping in contact with the market it often happens as a series of unconnected, uncoordinated actions rather than as a coherent, coordinated, corporate approach. Again it is often the cumulative effect of the strategic drifting that creates problems. These problems are recognized only where they cause a crisis, such as when a company realizes that it has confused buyers about the brand, that it has made investments in products and services consistent with its official strategy but not with its strategy in action and it has not invested in the necessary competencies, capacity and capabilities to enable it to compete successfully and meet the definitions of success and acceptable of stakeholders with high power and the willingness to use that power.

Whilst sticking rigidly to a planned strategy can be dangerous for the company and lead to strategic market disconnection as market contexts change, so too are not recognizing and responding to strategic drifting. It is vital to ensure that the company recognizes both the changes to the strategic market context and how its strategy in action relates to it. It needs to be in a position to make positive choices about its strategy in action within the corporate strategic intent.

> *Strategic drifting is akin to casting a bottle with a message in it into the sea and hoping that the tides will take it to a shore where it will be found, selected from the others washed up there, the message read and a rescue initiated! Strategic market disconnection results from putting the message into a bottle and keeping hold of it whilst you wait for the right sort of tide and believing that when the right tide arrives it will take the bottle to where you want it to go.*

## Flexing in the strategy process

Positive choices about strategy in action are not just decisions about how to react to events and the like, but how to influence the market before they occur and after they have occurred (hence the importance of scenario planning). Flexing a strategy in action does not have to be a passive reactive process. Competitors that change the rules of the competitive game can be the big winners. Risk and reward have to be balanced as does the recognition of what it takes to achieve the change desired with the ability of the company to achieve it.

Strategies need to evolve over time and there needs to be, at the very least, a recognizable relationship between the official/hybrid strategy and the strategy in action. This evolution needs to be part of a positive strategy process that is ongoing within a framework of strategic intent.

As the values of a company should not change every five minutes so too the strategic intent of the company should not. Strategic intent is an important part of the company context and an anchor for the company, for its employees, for its stakeholders and for the market. It should not be like quicksand with no one certain where it is and whether they can rely on it.

The ability of a company to flex its strategy in action within its strategic intent based upon a corporate approach to learning and recognition of the events and changes in the market context is an increasingly important corporate competence. A competence that requires highly developed leadership skills to provide an organizational culture which creates a commitment to the corporate whole (rather than just parts of it), to communication, to learning, to a market focus rather than an internal focus and to positive decision-making within an evolving strategic market context. Leadership that creates a climate for constructive challenge and change and which ensures that the skills exist within the company to support an effective strategy process that leads to market-focused action.

This is a significant leadership challenge and reinforces the relationship between strategy and leadership. Leaders should not be the sole arbiters and custodians of strategy but should create the conditions necessary to ensure that the changing reality of markets can be recognized and owned within the strategy process to ensure that the strategy in action does not lead to either strategic market disconnection or strategic drifting.

This is a significant challenge between providing in-front leadership (I have a vision and we go this way to achieve it) and empowering followers to lead (How are we doing and what can we do better or differently to meet our company's objectives for the market?).

This *flexing approach to the strategy process* can be illustrated as follows in Figure 14.5 below:

**FIGURE 14.5** Flexing and the strategy process

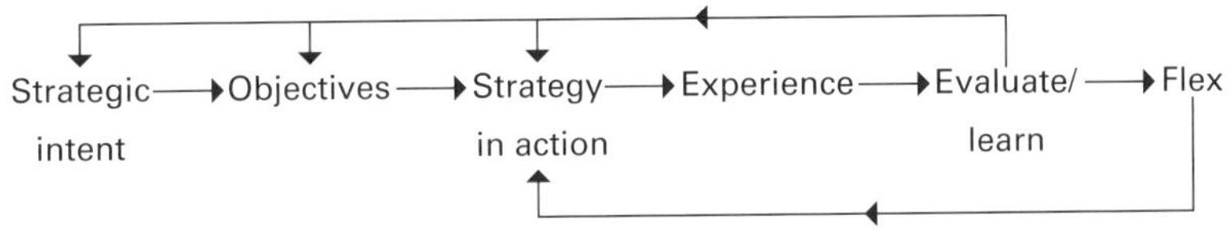


The strategic intent creates the strategic context for the company for the market and guides the development of its objectives and strategy for it. Experience gained in the market is evaluated in the context of the company's strategic intent, objectives and strategy so that the company can learn and then, if appropriate, flex its strategy in action.

This flexing needs to be understood as an individual action and cumulatively. Flexing is not a wholesale change in strategy but an incremental change. Flexing leads to further experience being gained and managers are encouraged within the boundaries of the strategic intent, objectives and strategy to innovate and to respond to the evolving market conditions. This additional experience is then subject to further evaluation and learning. As this cycle between experience, evaluation, learning and flexing continues it is important that there is an identification of whether or not the company should continue to flex its strategy in action or to review its strategy, objectives and strategic intent. This point is called the *strategy in action review point.*

Strategies in action, like materials have limits to their elasticity. There comes a point where the limit of flexing the strategy in action is reached and where a different approach is required. It is also the case that flexing of the strategy in action that is informal or outside the 'official' strategy process where evaluation and learning are limited to an individual or small number of people within the company and the action taken is maverick and beyond the limits of flexing, can lead to crisis. Continuing to flex when a fundamental change in the strategy in action is required is like putting a lid on a pan of boiling water. It might contain the water for a short time but the pressure will build and the lid will be forced off with unpredictable results.

If the leadership is empowering and the strategy process is effective those at the interface with the market flexing the strategy in action should be able to identify when this more fundamental evaluation needs to take place and be able to communicate this need. Too often, however, those at the interface with the market implementing the strategy in action do not have the knowledge, skills, confidence or systems to enable them to identify this need and to communicate it.

The identification of the strategy in action review point should become a part of the ongoing strategy process within the company. Clearly life cannot stop whilst a strategic review is undertaken but it is important for companies not to commit to major investment or new initiatives until the strategic intent and the objectives and strategy that flow from it are settled. If those within the company do not recognize the necessity for a strategic review, however, and such investments do occur there is a risk that they will constrain the ability of the strategic review to achieve change and/or that they will undermine the ability of the company to compete and flex its strategy in future.

There cannot be a prescriptive approach to the strategy process. This is why the strategy in action is often so different from the official strategy. Key to all of the above is to get to a position of a strategy process that works for the company and the people within it. Whatever the strategy process, if it is delivering the definitions of success and acceptable of the stakeholders with high power and the willingness to use it now and preparing the company to meet those definitions for the future, should the precise nature of the strategy process matter? Whilst it is always the case that potential will remain unfulfilled if you aren't aware of that potential, it is for the stakeholders to determine what is acceptable to them and how they view success. It is then for the strategy process to deliver those definitions in practice.

Leaders and managers have to decide how they are to operate the strategy process to meet the requirements of their stakeholders and the strategic market issues with which their companies have to deal both now and in the future. There cannot be a prescriptive approach or a one right approach.

Different market contexts and different company contexts require different approaches at different times. This is what makes strategic management and the strategy process so exciting!

The strategy process is a key component of the strategic management of companies and should play a key role in its ongoing evolution and success. A strategy process that is inadequate or dysfunctional is likely to lead to strategic market disconnection, strategic drifting, an internal company focus, internal turmoil and external confusion. No strategy process is perfect but an effective strategy process can reduce risks and provide a framework for the ongoing development of strategies that ensures that the focus of companies is on the market and puts managers in the best position possible to make decisions as the future unfolds.

## Practitioner's tips

1. Make sure that there's a shared understanding of what strategy is amongst those involved in its development.
2. Be clear about the importance of the *intent* necessary to convert the strategy into action.
3. Be clear about the context for the strategy both in terms of the key stakeholders' definitions of success and acceptable and the key strategic market and competition issues now and for the future.
4. Be clear about who should be involved in the strategy process and manage that involvement.
5. Recognize that the strategy process has to start with an external focus and that without an understanding of the key strategic market and competition issues now and for the future the strategy process will merely produce a promotional document of little practical use and credibility.
6. Recognize that there can be a difference between the official planned strategy and an unofficial planned strategy.
7. Recognize that different strategies can collide to create strategic turmoil that can create collateral damage if not addressed.
8. A strategy in action can be different from the official strategy and needs to be identified, managed and evolved within the strategic intent and objectives of the company.

9. A strategy that doesn't evolve merely becomes a position statement at a point in time and is likely to lead to strategic market disconnection or strategic drifting.
10. Strategy processes cannot be prescriptive, are a symbol of the leadership and organizational cultures of companies, of the strategic competence of companies and of their connection with the markets in which they seek to compete.

## Practitioner's questions

1. Do all of those involved in the strategy process have a shared understanding of what a strategy is and of the need to support it with the intent to act?
2. Does the company have the competence and organizational culture to operate an effective strategy process?
3. Is there a clear understanding of the key stakeholder's definitions of success and acceptable and what role those definitions will play in providing a context for the strategy process and the strategy?
4. Is there a clear understanding of the key strategic market and competition issues now and for the future to inform the strategy process?
5. How will differences between the official planned strategy, any unofficial planned strategy and the strategy in action be identified and dealt with by the company?
6. How will the strategy in action evolve to avoid both strategic market disconnection and strategic drifting?
7. What authority will be given to flex the strategy in action and how will that flexing be identified and evaluated within the strategic intent of the company?
8. How will the strategy in action review point be identified?
9. By whom and how will the strategy be evaluated to determine whether it has been successful and when?
10. How will the strategy process be evaluated to determine whether it is fit for purpose and evolving to meet the needs of the company?

# Competing in markets

15

## Introduction

The strategy in action represents the implementation of choices made. As we have seen from the previous chapters, for those who make those choices, it is important to understand that there is often a difference between the choices made by those formulating the official planned strategy and those implementing the strategy in action.

In both cases, however, the choice is based upon the formulation and evaluation of the options available for the context in which the choice is being made at the time. This reinforces the need for a shared understanding within the company of the market context, the competitive context and of the strategic intent of the company.

This chapter looks at the options available and their implications, the context in which the choice of options is made and why strategies based upon choices not focused on buyers and the market are doomed to failure.

## What are the options available?

In his book, *Competitive Advantage*, Porter (1985) identified the three generic strategies of cost leadership, differentiation and focus. Subsequent authors have developed other generic options including a hybrid option where competitors seek to both achieve low-cost production and differentiation. Regrettably, many of these generic options concentrate on the 'industry' rather than the market. An exception to this is Bowman's (1997) 'Strategy Clock', which refers to perceived added value being traded off against price.

Whilst companies compete against each other, it is what they are competing for that is important. Companies compete for buyers. The strategy (how they compete) therefore has to relate to the buyers – the market. Buyers are not interested if the company is the cost leader compared to the unit cost of production of all of the competitors. They are merely interested in the benefits that products and services give them at a price they are prepared to pay for them.

When considering the choice of options the nature of the choice being considered needs to be clear. Is this a choice about how the company is going to seek to meet the requirements of buyers in the market or is it a choice about the company's strategy to deliver the offer required to compete for buyers?

This distinction is important as it guides the approach to the development of the options available. Whilst being the cost leader for the production of products and services could provide competitive advantages, these advantages are only truly effective where competing products and services do not have a high degree of relative differentiation. Differentiation confers a value for buyers that does not always relate to the cost of production.

Being the cost leader of production for a product and service will only confer a competitive advantage for a company if the cost advantage:

1. is passed on to the buyer in the form of a lower price and the buyer, when comparing the price and benefits packages on offer from different products and services, decides that the product and service benefit packages on offer are at least as good as each other and so will buy the lowest-priced one;
2. is used to create additional buyer benefits (differentiation) from the product and service benefit package for the same price compared to competitor offers and the buyer sees these as creating more value for the price.

Differentiation is achieved on the basis of the functionality of products and services and on the evaluation of the benefits on offer from them. This is why so many companies spend so much money on marketing and branding. They seek to convince buyers that the product and service confer benefits in addition to functionality, eg seeking to convince buyers that being associated with the Mercedes brand is better than being associated with the BMW brand.

In the case of Mercedes and BMW the cost of production is important but they seek to keep prices high in the market to support the brands' values. Whilst the functionality of cars in the ranges of both brands may be very similar and their corporate strategy may relate to reducing the unit cost of production whilst maintaining quality and design, their market strategy will be to continue to reinforce and expand their differentiation and keep prices high.

The choices for competing in markets therefore have to relate to markets and not to the internal machinations of companies and how they compete with each other to be the lowest-cost producer, ie their corporate strategy. It also has to be recognized that being the lowest-cost producer doesn't always lead to the lowest prices as companies can decide to retain the benefit of being the lowest cost producer themselves in terms of margin retention!

The *Buyer Market Competition Matrix* below seeks to identify the options for competing in market segments. It is specifically called the 'Buyer Market Competition Matrix' as it reflects the need to look at competition from a buyer's perspective rather than a seller's perspective. The competition after all is for buyers!

It is important to recognize that competition often does not take place consistently for the whole market but varies between market segments, however they are defined (see Chapter 7). Consequently it is important to understand the key current and future strategic market issues and the competitive dynamic within these segments. This can be represented by the Buyer Market Competition Matrix below in Figure 15.1, which relates to individual market segments:

**FIGURE 15.1** The buyer market competition matrix

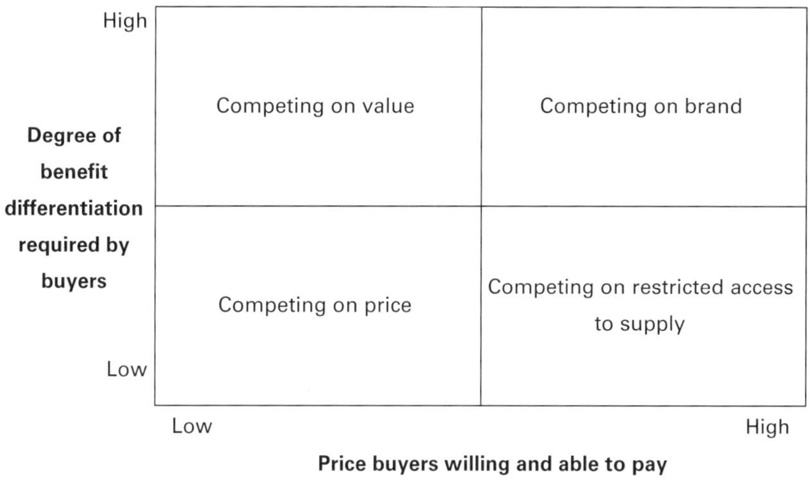


Taking each of the competitive strategies in turn:

## *Low benefit differentiation low price*

Where the degree of differentiation between the product and service benefit packages required by buyers is low, the lowest being commodities, competition for buyers will be on price. There is nothing else on which to compete.

When competing on price the sellers have to have low costs and/or access to significant resources to sustain the low prices. The market is volume driven with low margins. Barriers to the entry of new competitors are important as increased competition for a limited volume creates real pressure on margins. Pressure to exit the market increases with increased competition for reduced volumes.

Buyer-switching barriers by the very nature of the products and services being a commodity or having low differentiation are not high. Buyer churn could be a significant issue with a cost implication particularly where the costs of gaining new buyers is high.

This type of strategy might be pursued as a loss leader as part of a portfolio approach to meeting the wider needs of buyers where the retention of buyers leads to more sustainable margins in other parts of the seller's portfolio. Those, however, solely relying on a market with a strategy of low differentiation and low price will find this strategy very challenging unless they can achieve and sustain large sales volumes.

Many companies competing in this quadrant seek to develop some form of differentiation to create buyer loyalty and/or to achieve higher prices if possible, eg companies selling the commodity of petrol branding their petrol stations and including a shopping experience with it.

## *Low benefit differentiation high price*

On what basis is the buyer to make a decision to buy if they are able to get the same level of product and service benefit package for a much lower price? Where there is a ready supply of the product and service it is questionable whether such higher priced product and service benefit packages are actually competing.

The only way such product and service benefit packages could compete is where there is a shortage of supply in the market and the buyer is in a 'have to buy' situation and can only get access to a limited number of suppliers. It could also be a competitive situation where buyers with poor credit ratings may have to pay a significant premium price to be able to buy products and services benefit packages which are the same as those able to be bought by buyers with much better credit ratings.

For a market to exist there have to be willing and able buyers and sellers. This implies that the sellers have products and services to sell (as well as the willingness to do so). This ability to sell relates to the availability of those products and services to sellers and the accessibility by buyers to that supply. Supply can distort markets and can therefore have an impact on the competition within them. This in turn can affect the competitive strategy of sellers in terms of vertical integration to protect access to supplies and entering into supply agreements for the whole production of suppliers.

Regulatory issues may surface where a competitor seeks to acquire or merge with another competitor to gain a dominant position in the market and thus in theory be able to control a significant proportion of the supply to it. This provides the potential to increase and/or keep prices high.

The price elasticity relationship with supply is a well-trodden economic theory. High demand and short supply lead to higher prices. There comes a point, however, where the willingness and ability of buyers to pay that higher price are reached even in a 'have to buy' situation.

Restricted supply can also relate to geographical position. Take the price structures of food and petrol at motorway services. If travellers want to stop on their journeys for food, drink and petrol whilst on a motorway they have limited choice. The supply is limited and the prices of the food, drink and petrol are generally significantly higher than those to be found in towns where buyers have wider access to sellers of food, drink and petrol.

## *High benefit differentiation and low price*

Those product and service benefit packages that are differentiated for the same price as competing products and services compete on the value perception of the buyer. Sellers pursuing this strategy are seeking to give buyers the perception that their product and service benefit package provides more value for the same price as competing product and service benefit packages to encourage them to buy from them. Examples might include special edition cars where an upgraded engine is included for the same price and/or three years' interest-free credit are provided for the model. The product and service benefits package is improved for the same price to increase the buyer's evaluation of comparative value.

This strategy is often seen in market entry, to protect market share, to increase market share, as an alternative to a price war, to put pressure on a competitor to exit the market and to provide a barrier to entering the market. To pursue this type of strategy often requires a low cost base and/or access to resources to deal with squeezed margins. The sustainability of this strategy to create a new norm for the product and service benefit package needs careful consideration, particularly if it cannot achieve an increased price in time.

The degree by which a product and service benefits package has to be differentiated to achieve higher prices is a key judgement for marketers, sales professionals and managers. It is generally the case, however, that there have to be significant increases in the buyer's evaluation of product and service benefits packages to achieve significantly higher prices.

### *High benefit differentiation and high price*

Competition is on the basis of brand. Premium pricing requires premium differentiation. With this strategy the competitors often have similar premium product and service benefits packages and it is the brand values perceived by the buyer that are key to successful competition. In practice there is often little difference in the quality and performance of many premium-priced cars, fashion accessories, beauty products, etc. Whilst design and styling will always be subject to a personal preference, the core product and service benefits packages are very similar. The differentiator (and therefore the basis of competition) is the brand and the perception of it in the market and its impact on the buyer and the buyer's associates.

Brands are key competitive tools and create barriers to market entry, buyer loyalty to protect and build market share and provide the potential to diversify into other markets both geographically and in terms of the product and service portfolio, eg the Virgin brand has been leveraged to diversify from music to financial services and travel.

## Moving in the buyer market competition matrix

It is possible to move between quadrants in the *Buyer Market Competition Matrix* but often difficult and expensive to do so. It is often easier to move from competing on price to competing on value than to move from competing on value to competing on brand. The perception of buyers of the brand when a product and service benefits package is competing in the value quadrant of the Buyer Market Competition Matrix is often very difficult to change. Toyota recognized this by creating the Lexus brand.

It is also the case that products and services can be perceived by buyers to have moved quadrant and this can undermine their product and service benefit offer. Burberry suffered when its classic design became readily available and was adopted by buyers outside its target premium brand buyer demographic. Companies seeking to compete on brand and seeking to achieve premium prices consequently seek to control the channels through which their products and services are sold and the prices at which they are sold. Whilst the Ralph Lauren brand is a premium brand, is this branding supported by being able to buy the branded clothing through discount stores?

## CASE STUDY

### Toyota

Toyota recognized that its core brand values related to buyer value – a high specification and quality for a competitive price. To move the brand to one based upon differentiated benefits and premium prices would have taken huge investment and time and might have undermined its core product and service portfolio offer, which gave it profitability. A new brand was the strategy adopted with considerable success.

The Lexus brand represents its brand values as follows:

> Lexus has always focused on what matters to the luxury customer. This is why we build products that are not only admired on the outside but also highly refined on the inside. And why we don't simply produce fine cars but pursue perfection to create the finest luxury vehicles on the road. It's also why we don't merely offer an excellent dealership experience but one that is unequalled in the luxury automotive category. And why we promise to make the most of every moment our customer spends with us.
>
> This approach to building, selling and marketing automobiles is what has helped Lexus to remain just as relevant today as when we first introduced our pioneering vision of luxury in 1989. Today buyers place a premium on memorable experiences and time well spent. They value products and experiences that offer luxury, comfort and innovation, and demonstrate ultimate respect for their time. Not only do we share the values and priorities of contemporary luxury purchasers, we celebrate them.
>
> The Lexus brand vision and values are more than a set of shared beliefs. They also inspire and show how we express ourselves, and shape our customer's experience.

Lexus focused on not only the product but the services to support it. It sought to create a brand that was clearly set apart from the Toyota brand and which was sufficiently different from Toyota to enable it to compete with the luxury brands of Mercedes and BMW.

Toyota didn't move quadrants with its existing brands, products and services; it created a new brand for a new quadrant.

# Positioning in the buyer market competition matrix

The *Buyer Market Competition Matrix* relates to market segments. Companies often want to compete not only in different markets but also in different market segments. In seeking to do so they have to be very careful, if they are to pursue different competitive strategies in different markets and market segments, not to undermine their brands. Competing on value in one market segment whilst competing on brand in another might undermine the perception of the brand's differentiation and thus ability to achieve premium prices.

Positioning in the *Buyer Market Competition Matrix* is important and needs to be consistent. Companies can undermine their own competitive strategy by the actions that they take. Particular care has to be taken in the development of the marketing support for the product and service; for example, it would not be appropriate to see Hugo Boss suits being sold in a discount supermarket chain. A competitive strategy based upon a differentiated brand associated with a retail channel to market based upon price causes confusion for the buyers willing and able to pay a premium price and risks undermining the brand.

In deciding the strategy in the *Buyer Market Competition Matrix* the objectives of the company need to be clear. The company needs to be clear about what it wants to achieve, which markets or market segments it wants to compete in, which products and services it wants within its portfolio and its willingness and ability to collaborate or partner to pursue its strategy and its objectives.

To aid the company in deciding which markets or market segments it wants to compete in, the following *Market Segment Choice Matrix* helps:

**FIGURE 15.2** Market segment choice matrix

Current relative competitive strength in this context refers to the buyer's perceptions of the strengths and weaknesses of the competitors. It is important not to confuse relative strength with current market share. Market share is a means to an end and not an end in itself. Companies generally want (and need) to generate profit from their strategies. Whilst a certain current market share may support the achievement of that profitability, through crowding out competitors or deterring new entrants to the market, it is not guaranteed to deliver an acceptable level of profitability now or in the future and it is not the objective.

It is also the case that having a strength and realizing it in terms of profitable market share may be two different things. This is why the nomenclature is an opportunity. Having a relative strength compared to competitors provides the opportunity to convert that strength into profitable market share. How to do so is subject to the choices to be made as part of the strategy process and will depend upon the strategy in action leading to realized profit.

When putting relative competitive strengths in the context of market attractiveness it is the future market attractiveness that is important and not just current market attractiveness. Strategy looks forwards and not backwards. Options are identified and evaluated and choices made for the future recognizing that different timescales are used depending upon context.

## *High future market attractiveness and high relative competitive strength*

Where there is an assessment of high future market attractiveness (see Chapter 2 for the definition of market attractiveness) and the company has a high relative competitive strength the company should consider this an opportunity and look to invest in maintaining and improving its relative competitive strength, being clear that any such investment is targeted at getting an acceptable return from investing in such an opportunity. It is also likely that having such a clear strength in an attractive market is unlikely to be deemed unworthy of investment. Some companies, however, seek to merely cash in on the opportunity rather than invest in it. This often leads to a loss of relative competitive strength and of the opportunity in time.

## *High future market attractiveness and low relative competitive strength*

Where there is high future market attractiveness but low relative competitive strength compared to competitors there is an opportunity as long as there is a belief that investing to develop the strength is likely to lead to an improvement in that strength and a consequent profitable return from that investment. Realizing the value of the opportunity requires investment and clarity of objectives. It requires clarity of intent, an understanding of what is required to improve both relative competitive strength and the willingness of buyers to buy from the company rather than its competitors and the resources and time to make the investment necessary.

## *Low future market attractiveness and high relative competitive strength*

In the case of low future market attractiveness and high relative competitive strength this should be seen as a threat. A threat in that limited resources have been used (and unless action is taken will continue to be used) to develop a relative strength in a market segment that is not projected to be attractive in the future and that the return of that investment is unlikely to match that in more attractive market segments. A threat as being in such a position may be indicative of strategic drifting and as a tangible symbol of the company being out of touch with the market. In such situations investment should be limited, profits taken or skimmed where possible to increase the return on the assets employed and consideration given to disinvestment.

## *Low future market attractiveness and low relative competitive strength*

Where the future market attractiveness and the company's relative competitive strength are low, the question needs to be asked as to why the company would be in this market segment at all. Its presence in this market segment would represent a threat similar to that above and is compounded by the likelihood that it will consume management focus, time and resources. In these situations there is often a significant opportunity cost. The company should look to disinvest.

## *Corporate fit*

Sometimes the senior managers of companies decide, irrespective of the company's relative competitive strength or the future attractiveness of market segments, that the products and services are not part of the business going forward. They may decide that particular products and services are just not consistent with the type of business the company wants to be in the future. As we saw in Chapter 14, Marconi no longer wanted to be a defence contractor even though it had significant relative competitive strengths.

Diversified companies can decide for a range of reasons that they no longer wish to be so diversified and would prefer to concentrate on a more limited range of businesses. Promised synergies from mergers and acquisitions may not be realized and this can lead to whole businesses and product and service portfolios being sold.

The analysis and evaluation in the Market Segment Choice Matrix can inform the product and service portfolio decision or a corporate decision about the portfolio can rule the Market Segment Choice Matrix irrelevant. If the decision is taken corporately to disinvest because of corporate 'fit' then there is no need to undertake the market segment choice matrix analysis.

## Options for markets or market segments

In reviewing the product and service portfolio there are seven strategic options available:

1. Manage decline and/or exit from the existing market segments.
2. Seek to increase the profitable market share in the existing market segments.
3. Develop or acquire new or different related products and services for the existing market segments.
4. Develop or acquire new or different unrelated products and services for the existing market segments.
5. Penetrate new markets or market segments with existing products and services.
6. Penetrate new markets or market segments with new or different related products and services.
7. Penetrate new markets or market segments with new or different unrelated products and services.

One of the most difficult decisions for managers to take is to decide to leave a market. This decision is often difficult for psychological as well as economic reasons – psychological reasons because of personal vested interests, emotional attachment to products and services or markets and perceptions of failure. Management and leadership are about people and the decisions they make (or avoid making).

As with the assessment of relative competitive strength the challenge for leaders and managers in assessing whether or not to leave a market is to be able to balance their needs and ability to take an external view with internal needs and perspectives. Companies often need external help with this process.

Where a company has invested heavily in getting a position in a market or where a company has made a significant investment in product development, manufacturing plant, marketing and in a retail premises network, often using debt finance, there is a pressure not to write off that investment but to try to trade out of the difficulties being experienced. There may also be contractual relationships in place for the provision of services and materials that would be expensive to terminate. The financial pressures to remain in the market may be significant.

Staying in the market too long, however, can be like gambling where managers want to stay in the game for as long as possible to try to recoup their losses. This is evidenced by the exit from the market frequently being prompted by those providing finance and not by the managers of the business. If the company is in an all-or-nothing situation the exit has been delayed too long.

*Staying in a market too long trying to recoup losses can be like a gambler in an 'all in' position, effectively betting the whole business. If it's all or nothing, you've often left it too late.*

It is important for managers to be able to recognize when the costs and negative implications of staying in the market outweigh the costs and implications of exiting it. Managers of companies can be seduced by their personal commitment to products and services, believing them to be world beaters when the reality is that they are not.

A pressure to stay in a market and a barrier to exit are also affected by the portfolio requirements of buyers, the desire of sellers to protect or change perceptions in the market of their products and services and the cumulative risk profile of the company.

In business-to-business markets particularly, but also in some retail markets, the buyer wants a portfolio of products and services to provide a solution rather than merely parts of a solution. Access to this portfolio might be a qualifier in the decision to buy. Sellers need to be aware of this portfolio requirement and, where it is a qualifier for sales of their core products and services, arrange for access to the portfolio required whilst managing their risk.

This can mean that some companies are in some markets that they wouldn't choose to be in and which do not provide the level of returns that they find attractive. If, however, they have to be in them they must find ways of meeting the buyer's requirements. This can be via developing their own product and service portfolio or branding the product and services of others as their own or merely entering into collaborative agreements for access to them.

## CASE STUDY

### More than just products

This case study involves the buyers of a company providing a trading service to a wide range of buyers internationally. Buyers wanted to be able to buy products to be sourced from all over the world and to get them delivered to their premises for processing with minimal risk and cost. The buyer's procurement expertise was limited and their core businesses were largely manufacturing. They did not want to spend a lot of time and money on sourcing the raw materials but wanted to buy warranted materials for when they wanted them at a price that was competitive.

It soon became clear that the company's core trading business could not be successful if it didn't provide the buyers with access to insurance, finance and logistic services. In short the buyers wanted to have a seamless solution to their procurement needs.

The company could not provide logistics, finance and insurance services itself. It could, however, through strategic alliances provide access to the services required by buyers. These alliances were put in place and the company was able to meet buyer needs. The company's investment requirements to provide these services was small, its risk profile was managed and it was seen as a solutions provider by the market.

In negotiating these strategic alliances it was important for the company not only to recognize what the buyers wanted but what the potential partners in these alliances needed. The partners needed volume of business and margin to make it interesting to them. The services to be provided were the core business of the partners and they understood and could manage the risk and had the competence and capacity to deliver what was required.

The company developed its product and service portfolio offer to buyers through these strategic alliances but also redefined the business that it was in. It became a solutions provider in the eyes of the buyers and in doing so expanded its offer to its partners by becoming a channel to the market for them. It earned a margin from the buyers of product and from its partners providing complementary services to meet buyer needs.

The key point that the company had to recognize was that the buyers required a solution to their needs and not just access to products. The rules of the market were based upon providing a portfolio of products and services and not just a trading functionality. If you didn't have a portfolio of services to meet buyer needs then you couldn't compete effectively in the market.

In reviewing the product and service portfolios, companies have to decide both whether to diversify their products and services and how to do so. This can involve in-house development, development in collaboration or partnership working with others or through acquiring a company with the products and services required. Similarly, when seeking to enter new markets companies can either do it themselves, in collaboration or partnership working with others or through acquiring existing competitors in the market.

Each of these different approaches can have significant resource requirements and risks. The further a company moves from its core competencies, existing products and services and existing markets the higher the risk. Risk assessment is a key element of any option evaluation.

Sometimes it appears easier for managers to see reward rather than risk. It is also the case that seeking to pursue several of the options above at the same time within a company increases the risk as it distracts managerial focus and consumes large amounts of financial and other resources. It can also confuse the shareholders and investors whose time horizons for returns and appetites for risk may not be consistent with those capable of being delivered by some of the options above.

## CASE STUDY

### Tesco US expansion

Tesco announced in 2013 that it will incur costs of more than $1 billion if it can't find a buyer for its 'Fresh and Easy' foray into the US market. One of the most successful UK companies had identified the US grocery market as attractive and one in which it had or could develop high relative competitive strengths. As a result it decided corporately to pursue a new market entry option with related products and services.

Tesco focused its investment in the West Coast neighbourhood areas where other food retailers were not well represented. They did this to avoid battling with the likes of Walmart in its heartland and the highly populated but intensively competitive East Coast. It also went for a relatively small size format with limited choice to cater for shoppers that would pop into the stores several times a week as they do in the UK. The format did not play to how Americans shop – fewer trips to the shops but with larger volume purchasers. Even the mighty Tesco got it wrong.

In the end, to make a sale easier, Fresh and Easy was put into bankruptcy. In November 2013 the court signed off a deal whereby Yucaipa Cos, an investment firm, bought the approximately 150 Fresh and Easy stores for $120 million with a loan provided by Tesco! The total costs to Tesco of the sale were reported to be £150 million on top of the approximately £1.2 billion write-off already taken by the company.

The sale was welcomed by Tesco shareholders and analysts with the share price rising upon the announcement of the deal. It was generally reported that the sale would remove a distraction from the company's management so that it could focus on the ongoing businesses and draw a line under the losses incurred.

In the past the diversification of product and services and geographical markets was promoted on the basis of spreading risk so that if one product and service category hit a downturn it could be compensated for by another. The same rationale was used for being in different geographical markets around the world. Markets became attractive because of the potential ability they gave to spread risk.

It often takes a big investment to diversify the product and service portfolio and to enter new geographical markets. Not understanding the implications of cultural differences or the competitive and comparative advantages of existing players in markets abroad can make a market appear attractive when it isn't.

Some companies in seeking international expansion do so by only buying the number one and possibly the number two competitors in those markets. This is because the premium price required to buy them is countered by the reduced risk. Too many companies have seen the performance and potential market value in non-core markets as attractive based upon their misplaced belief that they can manage in different contexts or impose their business model abroad or compete successfully for profitable market share.

It is important that in looking at markets an external dispassionate view is taken to identify their challenges and opportunities. There is no substitute for knowing the market and being able to put your company's products and services within it from an external buyer perspective.

*Success in one geographic market does not guarantee success in another. Know the market as well as you know yourself.*

## Don't forget cumulative risk

Similarly it is important to recognize that risk is cumulative as well as individual. Companies, particularly those operating in different markets, tend to look at risks individually. If the cumulative risk profile is not recognized and managed the company may find itself overexposed and in danger of failure. It is important that cumulative risk is identified and evaluated.

It is also the case that competing in diverse markets often leads to a competition for resources. Those parts of the company that compete successfully for these resources may grow whilst the unsuccessful ones merely struggle on. In the worst case resources are just spread too thinly across the different markets or market segments and the company does not thrive in any of them. In a resource-restricted world a decision has to be taken on the basis that if resources aren't available to invest to the level required for success then the company should exit that market or look to share costs, risks and rewards through collaboration or partnership working with others.

The most successful diversified companies are able to do the above and to adapt to different market conditions. They understand how those markets work, how to market and adapt their products and services and how to overcome barriers to exploiting the opportunities available. They can also identify and evaluate threats in the market and know when to exit markets. Unsuccessful companies exit too late and do so surrounded by negative communications that can undermine their remaining businesses.

When corporately it has been decided which markets or market segments are to be invested in and which products and services are to be supported, the next stage is to decide, in terms of the options in the market competition matrix, which strategic option to pursue.

Before deciding the strategy in the Buyer Market Competition Matrix to pursue, the company needs to understand what is required to enable it to pursue each option and to compete successfully. The reality is that the present often constrains the future and as previously explored movement within the Buyer Market Competition Matrix is possible but not without challenge. Tesco, which researched the US market extensively and which is a successful and sophisticated company, did not get this right and this reinforces both the risks and the requirement to really understand what's required to pursue each option from an external market-focused perspective.

In reviewing the options the company needs to understand why each option would convince buyers to choose its products and services over those of its competitors, what the performance and intent of competitors are and how it is going to choose an option and then implement it. It has to be recognized, however, that there is never a perfect or complete knowledge of markets or competitors. As with the development of scenarios, assumptions have to be made which inform choices.

Options are evaluated on the basis of their suitability, feasibility and their acceptability. These are summarized as follows:

- **a** Suitability – does the option enable the company to achieve its objectives, to address the issues implicit in realizing the potential of the opportunity available, fit with its portfolio approach so as not to conflict with or undermine its brand or other strategies in action and fit with the company's strategic intent?
- **b** Feasible – is the company capable of pursuing and realizing the potential of the opportunity within the resources the company can access, its organizational culture and the timescales available?
- **c** Acceptability – will the option deliver the definition of acceptable by key stakeholders?

The evaluation of options generally follows the suitable, feasible and then acceptable cascade. An evaluation can conclude that an option is suitable and feasible but fails because it is not acceptable. Acceptable in terms of the amount of investment required, the risk that the option would incur for the company, the level of return from the investment or the timescales required to achieve the return on investment.

It is also the case that sometimes the issue of organizational culture is not given the consideration it deserves. Anything is possible in theory but organizational culture can be a major inhibitor of achievement. It takes considerable time and investment to change it and seeking to pursue an option requiring innovation and risk-taking in a culture dominated by technically oriented silos and risk aversion is not credible without recognizing the challenges of organizational cultural change.

Some managers want to be part of some markets or market segments as they believe that this can have a beneficial impact on the perception of them personally. A company's presence in a market or market segment should not be a 'vanity' strategic move but based upon an externally buyer-focused and driven strategic choice.

## Practitioner's tips

1. Recognize that if all of the strategic options are not identified they cannot be evaluated.
2. Recognize that vested interests may affect the identification of all of the strategic options, eg exit from the market or market segment.
3. Make sure that those identifying and evaluating the strategic options have a market focus rather than an internal company focus.
4. Ensure that corporate choices about the company's portfolio of products and services and market or market segments are clear before looking at the strategic options for competing.
5. Ensure that the company's assessment of competitive strength is in the context of the buyer's perception of strengths relative to all competitors.
6. Ensure that the implications of the different options available are understood in terms of the buyer's requirements, the resources required, the risks and the rewards.
7. Be realistic about the position of the company's products and services in the Buyer Market Competition Matrix and the ability to move within the matrix.
8. Recognize that the further a company moves from its core competencies, existing products and services and existing markets the higher the risk.
9. Recognize that risk is cumulative and not just individual product and service based.
10. Ensure that you understand what is involved in the evaluation of suitable, feasible and acceptable.

## Practitioner's questions

1. Who is to be involved in the identification and evaluation of the strategic options?
2. How is the 'fit' of products and services in the corporate objectives or portfolio to be determined to identify whether time and resources should be invested in developing options for the products and services being reviewed?

3 How is relative competitive strength to be ascertained and the future attractiveness of markets to be determined?
4 How are the risks, rewards and requirements of pursuing the different options in the Buyer Market Competition Matrix to be identified and evaluated?
5 How is the potential impact of different options to be identified on the cumulative corporate risk profile?
6 How is a credibility check to be undertaken to determine the ability to move, if necessary, within the Buyer Market Competition Matrix?
7 Where do the company's products and services currently sit within the Market Segment Choice Matrix and what does this illustrate?
8 Is the company able to manage the risks and requirements of moving from its core competencies, existing products and services and markets or market segments?
9 How are options to be evaluated for suitability, feasibility and acceptability?
10 How is the company to learn from the experience of others?

# Making strategic choices and corporate strategy

16

## Introduction

This chapter deals with making strategic choices and how rationale and logic are not always the determinants of the choices made. It goes on to deal with how the strategic choices are then used to inform the development of the corporate strategy. The relationships between competitive and corporate strategy are explored along with the competencies, capacity and organizational capability to enable companies to exploit markets for sustainable business growth.

### *If only choice were straightforward!*

In Chapter 15 strategic options were explored for the company's competitive strategy. Part of the evaluation of the strategic options was an assessment of suitability, feasibility and acceptability. Will the strategic option enable the company to achieve its objectives? Is the strategic option doable and is it acceptable to key stakeholders with high power and the willingness to use their power?

Logic dictates that the strategic option that is suitable, feasible and acceptable will be chosen but as with the difference between the planned official strategy and the planned unofficial strategy, the rationality of logic is not always the determinant of the strategic choice made. The reasons for this relate to the vested interests at play, the different interpretations of reality, the dominance of an internal focus over an external focus, confusion about what business the company is really in and the attachment that senior managers can have to products and services.

Why have companies failed when it was clear to outsiders that the strategies that they followed were obviously wrong and that parts of companies should have been closed or sold long before they went into crisis? Why, given all of the rational financial analysis illustrating that internet companies were loss-making and unlikely to make any returns on investment for years, if ever, did the value of these companies become stratospherically high before they crashed to earth? Why have some retailers continued to invest heavily in bricks-and-mortar shops and not invested in an online-based retail offer when the buyer channel shift has become so obvious?

Strategic choice is sometimes not rational. It is also sometimes driven by past choices that make it difficult for managers to change their choices – particularly where large amounts of capital have been invested. This is why the identification and evaluation of strategic options need to have an external focus and often be subject to external independent challenge or support.

## *Context, context, context*

Context is all and if the choice of strategic option is made within an internally focused context there is a danger that it will be too influenced by internal power structures, past decisions or choices and non-strategic issues. Strategic choices should be both strategic and positive (rather than choice by default) within a clear, competitive strategy context. The reality of managerial practice, however, is that the basis on which decisions or choices are made is too often based upon the dominant or imposed rationality of an individual or a small team of individuals chosen for the consistency of their view of the world and their 'fit' or compliance with the leader.

In making strategic choices we need to understand how managers make decisions. Managers make decisions through looking at issues through their paradigms to give data context, meaning and purpose, thus converting them to information. They then use their pragmatism filter to make decisions. This is illustrated in Figure 16.1.

We are all bombarded with data – facts and statistics. We receive all of these data and automatically either reject them or convert them into information using our paradigms. Paradigms act as a filter and use our assumptions, beliefs and experience to help us decide whether to accept or reject the data. For the data accepted the paradigm gives the data context, meaning and purpose to convert them into information.

**FIGURE 16.1** How managers make decisions

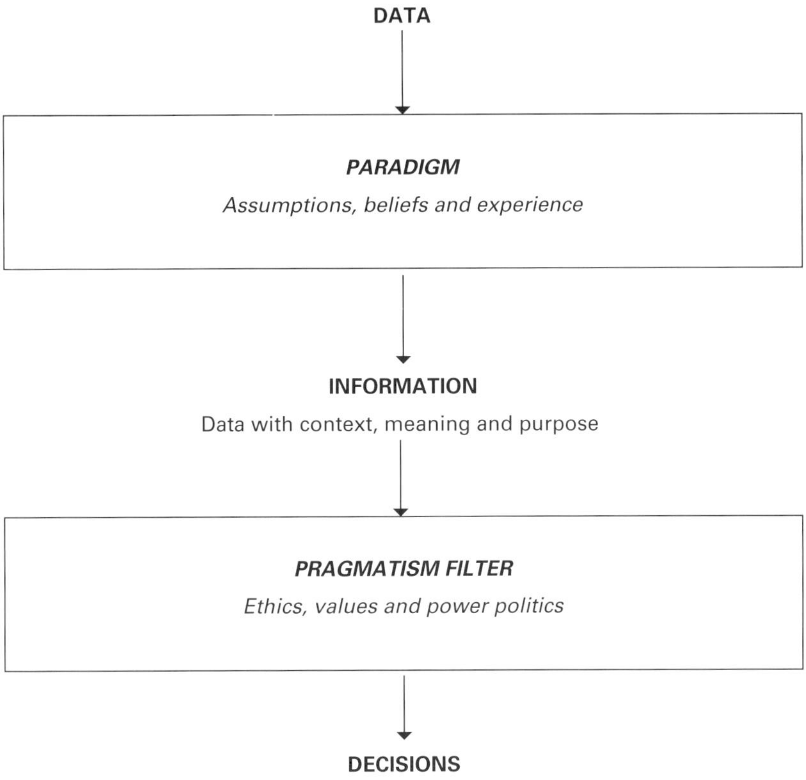


It is important to recognize that not all data are accepted. Kuhn (1962) identified that in the case of the history of scientific discovery, data that did not fit with the dominant scientific theoretical paradigm at certain times were rejected as anomalous. In rejecting the data, the dominance of the existing paradigm was protected and the scientific theory remained unchallenged.

Think of strategic drifting and how even successful companies ignore data that the market has changed and that the company's strategy is no longer appropriate. Managers may be looking at and listening to the market but if they are not seeing and hearing they will not be able to make decisions relevant to the market. It is the paradigm that acts as a filter for the acceptance and rejection of data. The paradigm is the interface between listening and hearing, looking and seeing, recognizing and understanding.

Managers apply their assumptions and beliefs about the company, the market and their roles to the data received. They also apply their assumptions and beliefs about the definition of 'acceptable' by key stakeholders and the willingness and ability of stakeholders to use their power to ensure that this definition is used.

Past experience is then used to further provide context, meaning and purpose to the data. Once the data have been passed through the paradigm and been imbued with context, meaning and purpose, they become information.

This information is then passed through the pragmatism filter. This filter is where personal ethics and values and power politics are applied to the information to determine what is the right choice and what is the best choice. Managers evaluate the options to determine what the right choice is for the company and/or the right choice for themselves. They also evaluate what is the best choice for the company and/or the best choice for themselves.

Managers need to understand the difference between what is right and what is best. Ethics and values play into what is right and power politics play more into what is best.

Where the option is the right and best choice for the company and the right and best choice for themselves, the decision is easy to make. Where, however, there is a conflict between what is right and best for the company and what is right and best for themselves, a value judgement has to be made.

There are circumstances where the option is the right and best one for the company but not in the interests of the manager making the decision. In these cases the manager has to draw upon their ethical framework and values. The strength of their ethical framework and values is then tested against the power politics context. Where should the balance between the interests of the company and those of the manager lie?

Seeking to balance what is right and best for the company with what is right and best for the manager often leads to compromise – decisions are made which are often not optimal, for either the company or the individual. Key factors in making these decisions relate to the strength of the individual's ethical framework and value set, the degree to which a compromise can be determined and the power of the individual to make the decision and to impose it.

How often have we seen managerial rewards, for example, fail to reflect the results of the company? How often have we seen it revealed post failure that managers have made perverse decisions about acquisitions or diversification when the fundamental data about the market and the company acquired have clearly been poor?

It is important to recognize that decisions are made at a point in time and that they may need to change as assumptions about the future become the reality of the present and the past. It is also the case that one decision compels another to be made and as the original decision and its impact become known, movements in the Power and Willingness-to-use-power Matrix might result, which can lead to a different balance being struck between the right and best decision for the company and the right and best decision for the manager.

The creation of information from data provides the ability to identify options. The pragmatism filter is then used to evaluate the options on the basis of suitability, feasibility and acceptability, to determine what is right and best for the company and what is right and best for the manager. This interface between the right and best decision goes to the very heart of the ethics of decision-making; the power in the company to determine the definition of acceptable; the transparency of decision-making and the interface between the manager and the company.

When managers agonize over decisions, the angst is not always created by deciding which of the options is right and best for the company. This angst is a result of the conflict between what is right and best for the company and what is right and best for the manager – a conflict between the ethical framework and values of the manager and the power politics within the company. It is also a result of evaluating, as part of the pragmatism filter, whether or not the manager can 'get away with' the decision made if it leans towards right and best for the manager rather than right and best for the company.

*It is vital that managers understand the conversion of data to information and how this then leads to decision-making. It is also vital that managers recognize the role of the pragmatism filter and how the filter works. The latter often involves managers asking themselves some searching questions.*

Information is not a once-defined absolute but changes with the context and as it is used. Data continue to be received and these data are constantly evaluated through the use of the paradigm. There is a never-ending process of data receipt, acceptance or rejection and evaluation to convert data to information. This information is then constantly evaluated through the pragmatism filter and converted into decisions.

This ongoing data conversion to information either adds to existing information, confirming, challenging or adapting it or provides new information, which might lead to the rejection of the previous information. All affect the decision-making process. The operation of the pragmatism filter also changes as managers and their contexts change over time. Whilst managerial traits often remain, the needs of managers change over time particularly as ambitions and achievements and contexts change. These changes can result in different balances being struck between what is right and best for the company and what is right and best for the manager making the choice and decision.

Communicating information to others might result in further context being provided. The paradigm uses this data to refine the information automatically. This evolution in use is important as decisions are taken at a point in time and within a context at that time whereas information continues to evolve and be affected by, as well as affect, the decisions made and the context. This is why, like the strategy process, the decision-making process particularly in respect of strategic choices needs to be understood and evolve as one decision may inform, constrain or significantly change the next.

## The relationships between competitive and corporate strategies

The above is relevant not only to the decisions and choices made as part of a company's competitive strategy but also to its corporate strategy. Corporate strategy relates to how the company is to organize itself to enable it to pursue its competitive strategy. The relationship between the two can be illustrated as follows in Figure 16.2:

**FIGURE 16.2** The relationships between competitive and corporate strategies

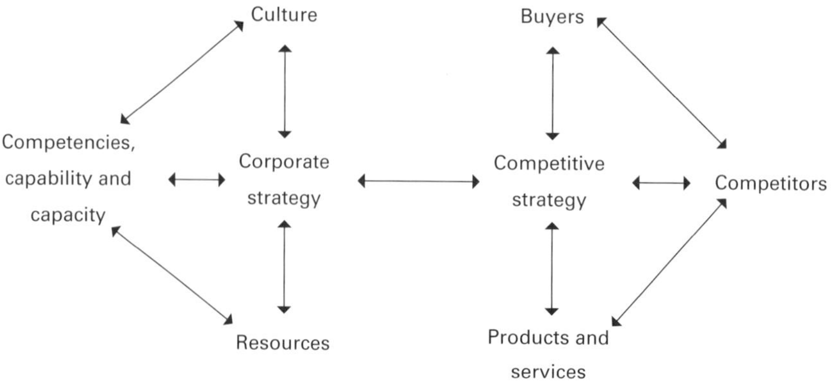

Competitive strategy can only be delivered if the company's corporate strategy is effective and consistent with it. The objective of the corporate strategy is to enable the company to achieve its objectives for the market. Whilst there will be specific operational objectives for the different elements of the corporate strategy, eg in respect of human resources, the context for the corporate strategy needs to be very clear. The corporate strategy is not an end in itself but part of the company's approach to achieving its objectives for the market.

There are three key elements to corporate strategy and these are: organizational culture; organizational competencies, capacity and capability and organizational resources. Together these support the delivery of the competitive strategy.

## Organizational culture

Organizational culture is often talked and written about in terms of esoteric 'feelings' within organizations, an abstract conceptual entity somehow binding the organization together. Organizational culture is tangible and is seen in what companies do and how they do it.

> *Organizational culture is represented by the values of the organization in action in the form of the decisions made and the behaviours of those within it.*

It is sometimes the case that organizations spend a large amount of time and money formulating the 'official' organizational values, only for the organizational values in action to be very different. This is similar to the difference between the official planned strategy and the strategy in action described in Chapter 14.

### *Leadership*

Many books have been written and many academic papers published on organizational culture. Many models of organizational culture are promoted. An organization's culture is a factor of the leadership of the organization. A despotic leadership style will support a despotic organizational culture. An empowering leadership style will support an empowering organizational culture.

The organization's culture has to be linked to the objectives of the organization and supports the delivery of the competitive strategy. Whether through leadership style, symbols, structures, focus or the use of power, an organization's culture needs to reflect and support the achievement of the organization's objectives and the values it seeks to guide the way it does business and promote itself both externally and internally.

## *Disconnect*

The more that there's a disconnect between the espoused values and organizational culture of an organization, the organizational culture required to support the pursuit of the competitive strategy and the organizational culture in action, the more likely it is for there to be internal discord and external confusion. Neither is good for the pursuit of competitive strategy!

If the values that guide the company's organizational culture are espoused as integrity, innovation and empowerment but the values and organizational culture in action represented by the leaders are untrustworthy, risk-averse and controlling, will it be surprising if problems arise? The perception of a company's organizational culture can have a big impact on buyer loyalty (particularly where it is based upon relationships) and the ability to recruit, retain and motivate employees.

Organizational cultures can be reinforced by the leaders recruiting people in their own image or people who are likely to conform unquestioningly to the wishes of the leader. The relationships between leadership, organizational culture and competitiveness are important to be understood and managed.

## *Complexity*

As the environment in which the company seeks to compete becomes more challenging and complex, the need for an organizational culture that supports the competitive strategy grows. It sounds like an oxymoron but the more that the competitive strategy requires innovation and flexibility, the more the company's organizational culture has to support that innovation and flexibility.

> *Leaders and managers increasingly need to support, live and symbolize through their actions and behaviours an organizational culture that gives employees the freedom to think, contribute, innovate and make decisions rather than creating an organizational culture based upon imposing a duty to conform with the power to make decisions concentrated in the hands of the few.*

Diversified organizations sometimes state that there's a single organizational culture. This is rarely the case, as different organizational cultures often exist within different parts of the company, whether in different functions or different geographies. The reality of this diversity needs to be acknowledged and managed as it can create internal tensions and external confusion. When companies make acquisitions or undergo mergers it is not just the physical assets that are being acquired or merged but their organizational cultures. Many acquisitions and mergers fail because of unreconciled differences in organizational cultures.

It is also the case that changing organizational culture takes significant time. These timescales may not fit with changes in competitive strategy and are a material consideration as part of the due diligence process for mergers and acquisitions and for the evaluation of strategic options. It is also the case that changing organizational culture takes the investment of resources and leadership.

Another point to consider is whether the leadership of the company is a symbol of the organizational culture desired and whether it reinforces the behaviours required through action. If not then it is doubly difficult to achieve organizational cultural change. Is organizational culture likely to change if leaders or managers are preaching the need for cost reduction but have not been affected by it?

## *Context*

Organizational culture, as with leadership style, relates to the context of the company, its objectives and its strategy. Different organizational cultures and leadership styles are required at different times in the evolution of companies and at different times in the context of the markets the company is seeking to be competitive within. There is, however, no 'right' organizational culture and no 'right' leadership style. The ability of organizational culture to cope with changes in the market/competitive dynamic is increasingly important.

It is also the case that as partnership and collaboration increase and where different parts of the value-creating process are subject to such extra-organizational inputs, managers have to be organizationally and culturally sensitive to make such collaborations/partnerships work and also be able to ensure that the brand values and competitive strategy the company is pursuing are supported by a portfolio of other organizations and their organizational cultures.

Take, for example, a call centre handling a company's interface with its buyers. The call centre company A is a separate company to its client B. If A in its dealings with the buyers of B does not represent the values and organizational culture of B and creates negative buyer perceptions, the buyers will believe that the values and organizational culture in action are different from those espoused by B. This can lead to a loss of reputation and business for B. Conversely if A in its interface with the buyers represents a more positive and acceptable set of values and organizational culture than B delivers in practice, this can also lead to buyer dissatisfaction and confusion.

Managing a portfolio of organizational inputs from different organizations into the corporate strategy to support its delivery is of growing importance. Unless there are consistency and compatibility of organizational values and culture at the organizational interfaces and at the interfaces with the buyers, conflict can arise that can cause disruption and negative perceptions amongst buyers. Having organizational cultural sensitivity and the ability to manage a portfolio of organizational values and cultures is an important managerial and organizational competency. This is particularly the case for:

1. managing diversified companies;
2. collaboration and partnership working to meet the needs of buyers;
3. the increasing trend for specialization for corporate services where specific services are outsourced;
4. serving different markets and market segments.

## Organizational competency

Examples of organizational competencies include a company knowing how to structure an acquisition to minimize the post-acquisition risk to the acquirer or a company being able to manufacture a component to within a micron. A company's competencies should relate to the achievement of the organization's objectives and its competitive strategy for the market – even for organizationally internally focused products and services, eg procurement. To have high levels of organizational competencies that are not relevant to the organization's objectives and competitive strategy begs the question: Why have high levels of organizational competency not relevant to organizational objectives and competitive strategy?

> *An organizational competency is knowledge or skill and should be relevant to meeting buyer needs, supporting the achievement of the company's objectives and creating and/or sustaining competitive advantage.*

It is sometimes the case that companies develop high-level competencies over a protracted period and that these become synonymous with the company and part of its organizational culture in terms of the regard in which it holds itself. This can constrain the delivery of the company's competitive strategy, as maintaining these competencies can inhibit the development of new competencies and the evolution of the competitive strategy.

## CASE STUDY

### Auto manufacture to auto assembly

In the auto industry of the past companies had high-level engineering and manufacturing competencies that were very important to those companies' competitive strategies. Indeed many of those companies even manufactured all of the nuts and bolts required for the manufacturing process for the company's product. Today the competitive strategy relies on competencies of design, procurement, logistics, marketing, product assembly, etc with manufacture of many components having been outsourced.

Mexico's emergence as a major auto manufacturer is an example of this change. Companies such as Volkswagen have located assembly plants in Mexico due to its comparative advantages. These plants largely assemble vehicles with 89 of the world's top 100 auto parts makers having production facilities in Mexico.

Today suppliers undertake 25–40 per cent of the research and development (R&D) within the auto industry sharing the costs of development but also, importantly, enabling the auto assemblers to focus on their core competencies. Increasingly auto manufacturers are becoming auto designers, brand developers and assemblers. Is it only a matter of time until the assembly process becomes totally outsourced? Are the joint ventures in China just one step away from this?

A review of the strategic options for auto companies in the context of their objectives has led them to identify the core competencies that they need to focus on and on the competencies where they can develop and sustain competitive advantage. Often a manufacturing competency (as opposed to assembly) is no longer regarded as core. Other companies are better placed to develop and exploit a manufacturing core competency. Perhaps the next stage is that they decide that as long as they control the brand, design and the quality of assembly, they no longer need to have an assembly competency.

Competencies need to be put into the context of the company's objectives, its competitive strategy, current and future strategic market issues and current and future market competitive dynamic. Having a high level of competency today does not guarantee its relevance or success tomorrow. The contexts created by the application of the models for the market and the competitors in the previous chapters are important and seeking to evaluate competencies on the basis that a manager thinks that they are good or useful is unlikely to be credible or useful.

> *Core competencies are those competencies of strategic importance to the company in achieving its objectives and competitive advantage.*

This means that the core competencies should be identified and evaluated in terms of whether they are:

1. fundamental to achieving the company's objectives and competitive advantage now and for the future;
2. at a level required to deliver the buyer's requirements (now and in the future);
3. better than those of competitors now and likely to remain so in future;
4. capable of being delivered consistently to the standard and cost required;
5. capable of ongoing development in the context of the future strategic market issues and future competitive dynamic to maintain their ability to meet the needs of buyers and their superiority over competitors;
6. hard to replicate by competitors in terms of the resources and timescales required;
7. capable of being sustained by the company within its resources;
8. concentrated in the hands of a few employees and thus vulnerable to the loss of those employees;
9. recognized within the company as an important source of competitive advantage and used as such throughout the company.

It is often the case that managers in different functions within companies identify and rank the importance of competencies differently based upon their own internal focus and roles. This is why the context for the identification and ranking of competencies needs to be external and not internal. It is also the case that as the competencies required to compete are fragmented through collaboration and partnership working, the importance of some external competencies is overlooked. It is vital that the focus for the identification and evaluation of competencies is external and based upon the key strategic current and future strategic market issues and the current and future competitive dynamic. Access to and control over a 'core' competence required for competitive success is a strategic issue. (See Hamel and Prahalad (1994).)

> *Managers must put the company in an external context or run the risk of being trapped by an internal context where there is a danger that the importance of past competencies constrains the recognition and development of the 'core' competencies required for the future to achieve competitive success.*

Competencies that exist in isolation may be useful but are unlikely to enable the company to achieve sustainable competitive advantage. If an employee with all of the knowledge leaves, so too does the organizational competence and competitive advantage. Whilst recognizing that knowledge and skills may be in the brains and hands of a few specialists, ways have to be found to retain and embed as much of that knowledge and skill as possible within the company.

It is also the case that those with the competencies need to have the willingness and ability to share and contribute their competence. This reinforces the importance of organizational culture and of the selection, development and motivation of employees committed to the company as a whole and willing and able to be part of the team rather than act as an island of excellence for which bridges are only built for the selected few.

Similarly, competitive advantage is often created not just by the existence of a competence but how it is linked in the process of creating value for buyers. It's not enough to be great at procuring or manufacturing products if the company can't get the right products supported by the right services in the shops for buyers to buy at the right time and at the right price!

Competitive advantage requires competencies to be linked together as part of a compelling and competitive offer to buyers in the market. These linkages are called organizational capabilities.

## Organizational capabilities

Organizational capabilities are the central nervous system of companies through which competencies are connected and by which those competencies contribute in appropriate ways to meeting buyer needs and creating and supporting the delivery of sustainable competitive advantage. A company can have great competencies but unless they are connected in ways that enable the company to meet buyer needs and create and support competitive advantage, the company will struggle.

> *Organizational capabilities are function- and organization-spanning systems and processes that support the development and use of organizational competencies to meet the needs of buyers and to create competitive advantage.*

No matter how good the company's organizational competencies are, unless they are connected by organizational capabilities in the context of the buyer's and market's needs companies will be at risk of strategic drifting and find it difficult to be competitive. Managers have to continually ask themselves how the company's competencies can be used together both within the company and with those outside it to meet buyers' needs.

Misunderstanding the balance that needs to be struck between organizational competencies and capabilities is like failing to recognize that products do not exist without services. The greatest products can be undermined totally by the inadequacy of the services needed to support them. Similarly the greatest organizational competencies can be undermined totally by the inadequacy of the organizational capabilities needed to support them.

Organizational capabilities need to be evaluated in an externally focused context. The starting point is to identify what buyers require and what the company needs to do to meet the buyer's needs in a way that provides competitive advantage. Information technology is increasingly important in providing a superhighway of organizational capability. It provides both external and internal communications, channels to and from the market, information about buyer needs and the linkages for value creation by both the company and its suppliers and/or others providing inputs for products and services.

Having the right products on the shelves at the right time to respond to changes in buyer requirements is vital and without the systems (capabilities) that technology provides companies would not have the flexibility and responsiveness required to compete successfully. Lean and just-in-time manufacture require effective information technology-based capabilities reaching far beyond the company.

## CASE STUDY

### Product development

A multinational company was experiencing difficulties and was consequently undertaking a strategic review. It had a range of organizational competencies that had received significant investment and which in their own right stood favourable comparison with any of its competitors. It frequently identified new product and service opportunities ahead of the competition, designed them to meet customer needs, manufactured them to a high quality and marketed them well. At every stage of the product development process the high-level competencies were evident.

The problem was that the product development process took two years. By the time that the company got its products and services to market the requirements of buyers had changed and competitors were ahead of it in the market. The key to this particular problem lay not in the level and extent of the competencies within the company, nor in the level of resource investment in them but in the inadequacy of organizational capabilities.

Different functions representing different competencies within the company didn't speak the same language, didn't give the projects the same prioritization, didn't work together to identify and address issues that arose through the process and didn't share access to information technology systems. It was as if the product and service were designed by a dysfunctional committee of sole traders with no shared commitment to or understanding of what was being developed.

One story of a frustrated manager summed up this approach. When finally a product had been designed and was ready to go to manufacturing, the manufacturing team announced that they couldn't make it for the cost allocated and consequently the price point at which it was to be marketed. At this point the marketing and sales teams had generated an anticipation of arrival of the product in the market with a high level of functionality. Reworking of the design

➔

was required along with a reduction of the functionality that had been promoted and this led to a delay in its launch and negative market perceptions. It was no surprise that the company was having difficulties.

Through working together, all of the teams involved in the product development process identified the relationships between competencies and capabilities from the buyer's perspective along with the implications for competitiveness in the market of failing to link competencies with capabilities. The product development timescale was drastically reduced with ideas for products flowing throughout the system. Islands of organizational competencies became linked through the development of organizational capability.

Information technology can provide the capabilities required by companies but they are only as effective as the use that people make of them and their fitness for purpose. Having been a senior manager in a technology-based company, I recognize that anything is possible technically given time and money but everything is not always required to provide competitive advantage. Think of the ICT projects that have gone over time and budget and those that have been abandoned after large investment in them has not delivered the returns and/or competitive advantage desired.

> *Information technology systems and organizational capabilities need to be focused and relevant to what the company wants to achieve in the market and the people using them need to have not only the competence and commitment to do so but a clear understanding of how they contribute to achieving the company's objectives.*

Core capabilities should be identified and evaluated in terms of whether they are:

1. fundamental to achieving the company's objectives and competitive advantage now and for the future;
2. at a level required to deliver the buyer's requirements (now and in the future);
3. better than those of competitors now and likely to remain so in future;

4 resilient and capable of being operated consistently to the standard and cost required;
5 capable of ongoing development in the context of the future strategic market issues and future competitive dynamic to maintain their ability to meet the needs of buyers and their superiority over competitors;
6 hard to replicate by competitors in terms of the resources and timescales required;
7 capable of being used easily and maintained by the company within its resources;
8 recognized within the company as an important source of competitive advantage and used as such throughout the company;
9 being subject to the performance of other companies and thus vulnerable to the performance of others.

In this latter case it is important that as the company develops collaboration and partnership working, the impact on the company's organizational capabilities in delivering competitive advantage is understood and controlled. UPS is the United States's most admired mail, package and freight delivery company and it holds the reputation of its thousands of customers worldwide in its hands. It is UPS that has an interface with the buyers and if they perform badly it undermines their customer's performance, their organizational competencies and their competitive advantage.

Buyers want a seamless delivery of products and services to meet their needs. Whilst they often have little interest in how the organizational competencies and capabilities are organized and managed to provide what they want, they soon recognize when they are not adequate and performing to the level required.

## Organizational capacity

It is also the case that a company can have great competencies linked together by great capabilities but if the organizational capacity is inappropriate the company will not be able to sustain competitive advantage. Whether inappropriate in terms of not enough or too much, both can have significant implications for the company's ability to create and sustain competitive advantage.

*Organizational capacity is the ability of a company to cope to the standard required with a volume of demand for products and services, competencies or capabilities in a timely and cost-effective way.*

Planning and developing access to an adequate organizational capacity requires an understanding of key current and future strategic market issues and the current and future competitive dynamic. Capacity building and reduction can take time and significant resources. Given the capital intensity and lead times for capital investment it is no surprise that oil and energy companies were some of the first and most advanced in developing scenarios so that they could understand key current and future strategic market issues and the like, to inform their investment in capacity.

Companies, having invested in developing capacity, are sometimes loath to write that investment off. They also seek to retain capacity in the hope that it will be required by a soon-to-be-experienced increase in demand for their products and services or see a certain level of capacity as a strategic critical mass issue. Retaining capacity when it is no longer needed, however, is a drain on resources and increases the unit cost of products and services requiring either a price increase, cuts in costs elsewhere or a margin reduction.

## CASE STUDY

### The shipping industry

Prior to the world economic crisis shipping was one of the most lucrative of businesses as a then-booming economy sent demand for the movement of commodities and consumer goods soaring. The economic recession and China's slowdown, however, have transformed the market leaving some of the world's largest ships empty. Yet huge container ships are still being built and delivered in the hope of better times to come.

In mid 2008 it cost $238,000 per day to charter a large cargo vessel. In 2013 it cost $7,764. New ships delivered increased from 600 in 2000 to

1,700 in 2008 and have remained at around 2,000 per year since. Every new ship exacerbates the capacity problem and huge amounts of debt are being written off by the banks and long-established companies such as Stephenson Clarke, with more than 280 years of trading, have gone bust. Yet still ships keep being built. Whilst new ships are more fuel-efficient – a major cost advantage – cost-cutting alone will not save companies. Capacity in the market will keep prices low. Should the strategic competencies and capabilities within shipping companies not have addressed the capacity issue and their analysis and evaluation of the markets that they are seeking to serve?

Increasing the capacity of competencies, eg accountancy, training accountants and enabling them to acquire experience takes years if done in-house or is very expensive to acquire through recruitment, merger and acquisition. A company seeking to develop, bring to market and support more products and services per year can require a significant increase in organizational capabilities.

Increasingly, companies want to be in a position to flex capacity to increase and reduce it at lower cost than if they were to increase or reduce the capacity themselves. This has led to new markets being created for a flexible workforce and for parts of the buyer value-creation process. External providers of organizational competencies, eg logistics, form part of the company's organizational capabilities to enable the company to meet fluctuating capacity requirements.

Only when companies are confident that the capacity required to meet the demand is likely to remain will they consider developing the capacity required themselves. A key consideration for this decision, however, is whether or not the competencies and capabilities required are core to the company and its relationship with the market. The more that strategically significant competencies, capabilities and capacity and the interface with the buyers are not controlled by the company, the higher the risk.

## *Focus and risk*

Competitive advantage can rest with the uniqueness of company competencies, capabilities, capacity and the relationship between it and the market. To put these in the hands of others the company must have full confidence that it is protecting that competitive advantage and not running the risk of undermining it through the performance of others or losing and/or diminishing them or the ability to continue to develop them.

It is often argued that the economic benefits of aggregating volume to drive down unit costs should be pursued or that outsourcing certain functions provides the ability of the providers of those functions to specialize and to reduce cost to the company. Whilst this can be true, it is also the case that the opportunity to aggregate volume is often qualified by standardization. This standardization needs to be seen in the context of the company achieving and sustaining competitive advantage.

Whilst certain aspects of the market offer can be standardized the key competencies and capabilities that provide the competitive advantage cannot unless competition is to be merely on price. Similarly, using specialist providers of competencies with a view to receiving reduced costs sounds attractive but is only so if it does not put the source of the competitive advantage into the control of the specialist provider and consequently undermine the company's ability to evolve and to protect the source of its competitive advantage.

Countries such as the United States have very clear rules that prevent what are regarded as strategic assets and activities from being controlled by foreign-owned companies. Those countries are acutely aware of the need to protect their ability to defend themselves from the commercial as well as military migration of technology and control. The same concerns need to be considered for the source of competitive advantage for companies.

> *Whilst the desirability to flex capacity is obvious, companies still need to ensure that in doing so as part of their corporate strategy they do not undermine their ability now and for the future to pursue their competitive strategies.*

## Linkages and clarity

The development of organizational competencies, capability and capacity has a direct relationship with organizational culture and the leadership of the company. Leadership and the company's organizational culture will determine the recognition of the importance of competencies, capabilities and capacity and how the company will respond to them. It will also determine how the resources in the company will be used as part of the corporate strategy.

In this context resources include finance, people, intellectual property, physical assets, technology and relationships. Corporate strategy seeks to provide access to the resources necessary for and align those resources to the company's competitive strategy. Competitive advantage and the ability of the company to compete in the market require access to resources and an understanding of key current and future strategic market issues and the current and future competitive dynamic.

As we have seen through the analysis and evaluation of the market and the development of scenarios, competitive strategy requires clear objectives and that strategic choices be made to create a competitive strategy. This strategy – how the company is to achieve its objectives for the market – needs to be resourced to meet current and future requirements.

The desired appropriate organizational culture, competencies, capabilities, capacity and products and services along with the ability to compete successfully in the market will only be in place if access to the resources necessary to develop and secure access to them is planned, secured and allocated consistently with the competitive strategy. Securing access to resources and the resource allocation process are absolutely crucial to supporting and maintaining competitive advantage.

## Resources

There are a limited number of sources of resources to invest in the creation of competitive advantage. These include reallocating existing resources from within the company, raising debt, raising shareholders' funds and selling assets. All have their own challenges.

Reallocating existing resources from within the company often means deciding not to do something totally or to reduce what is being done currently and to use the resources released to reinvest in other activities. Whilst efficiency gains should always be sought, freeing up existing resources to reinvest in the company often requires a larger-scale resource release. This often means that difficult choices about activities have to be made. It is often better in these circumstances to seek to identify what can be stopped totally than to reduce activities to a point where they are not able to function properly. The latter merely causes internal conflict and can cause external impacts due to falling performance.

Raising debt has become more difficult in recent years due to the worldwide financial turmoil. Financial institutions have become more risk-averse and companies have seen a greater emphasis on due diligence. Financial institutions want to see that companies (and their leaders or managers) have a full understanding of markets and have both competitive and corporate strategies in place that are credible and which illustrate clearly how the company can develop, sustain and deliver the economic benefits of their competitive advantage.

Many kinds of financial instruments can be used to raise debt requiring specialist advice. All debt is accompanied by conditions, which can be onerous, particularly if performance doesn't match expectations, and these conditions need to be understood. Whilst there is risk for financial institutions providing the money to companies, there is also risk for the companies in the event of things not going to plan. It is also the case that the gearing of companies, the ratio of debt to equity or assets, can have an impact on the assessment of risk and the cost of debt.

Raising money from shareholders can involve existing shareholders and new shareholders. Existing shareholders can be given the opportunity of increasing their investment in the company with the promise of returns later or shares can be issued for new shareholders to acquire from the company. Rights issues, share splits, initial public offerings, etc can be complex, costly and require specialist advice. They can also lead to changes in the Power and Willingness-to-use-power Matrix, with financial institutions and some shareholders moving position within the matrix to protect their interests and to influence both the competitive and corporate strategies. Using profit for investment rather than dividends is also a form of raising money from shareholders.

Selling assets can involve selling buildings, intellectual property and whole businesses. Understanding the relationship between those assets and the competitive and corporate strategy is important, as is understanding the differential return from the investment of resources in the current assets and those future assets in which the company is to invest. It sounds obvious but the contribution of assets to companies is sometimes not recognized until after they have been sold. It is also true that projections for the return to be created by the investment of resources from the sale of those assets in new activities sometimes prove to be optimistic! The sale of existing assets, however, can be symbolic of the intent to change, can provide focus for the company and change perceptions about the company both in the market and internally.

Resources can also be accessed through partnership working. Partners can agree to provide upfront investment with agreement to take returns on that investment later. They can also provide access to intellectual property, share the costs of its development and share channels to market, etc. Securing access to resources can take a number of forms.

## Flexible human resources

Access to the human resources with the competencies required and the behaviours and attitudes to contribute to the company is very important. Increasingly different forms of employment are being developed to provide flexibility for employers and to recognize the needs of people. As Handy (1995) predicted, employment patterns will change with more flexibility being required by both employers and employees.

There is a temptation in some companies to use consultants to fill competency gaps. Whilst consultants can contribute both competencies and capacity, companies need to be clear about whether such competencies and capacity are of ongoing strategic significance. If they are then they should be looking at ways to ensure that the competence and capacity of the company improves supported by those consultants rather than use them as a crutch, which when removed causes increased risk of the company falling. Do they contribute to the development of organizational capability?

## Achieving a balance

The important issues for companies to understand are the costs, risks and rewards, both now and in the future, of securing access to the resources required, what the implications are for their current and future competitive advantage and how their ability to achieve the returns on investment their key stakeholders require might be affected. They need to balance the returns the opportunity that the access to the resources could provide if they are secured against the risks and implications if they are not.

Without resources, whether they are financial, human, intellectual property, physical, technological, etc, companies cannot pursue their competitive strategies and maintain and develop the competencies, capabilities and capacity required. The question is not whether resources are required but how many, what type and how they are to be secured, allocated and used to support the competitive strategy and the achievement of the objectives for the market.

The resource allocation process is a powerful symbol of organizational culture and power within companies. Seeing a resource allocation process in action can bring human nature into very sharp focus and illustrate the values in action. As with the strategy process there is often a rational, espoused process but resource allocation decisions can often be emergent and relate to subjective as well as objective criteria.

Without corporate strategy to secure the resources, competencies, capabilities and capacity required and to ensure that they are operationalized within an appropriate organizational culture supportive of the strategic intent of the company, the competitive strategy will not be capable of being pursued and the objectives for the market achieved. Whatever the strategic choices made for the market now and in preparing for the future the corporate strategy needs to be aligned to the competitive strategy.

### *Corporate strategy supports the competitive strategy*

If the company does not have the right tools it cannot do the job it is seeking to do. Seeking to be a low-cost producer of products and services to compete on price often requires different competencies, capabilities, capacity, organizational culture and resources than seeking to compete on brand. The corporate strategy needs to deliver the competencies, capabilities, capacity, etc required to support the competitive strategy.

It is sometimes viewed as more interesting to develop competitive strategy than corporate strategy. Both, however, are important. Both flow from an understanding of the market now and how it is likely to develop in the future. Leaders and managers who ignore corporate strategy can create a strategic risk for the company that can undermine its ability to compete and to create and sustain competitive advantage.

## Practitioner's tips

1. Ensure that you understand the conversion process of data into information and how they relate to the decision-making process.
2. Recognize that some strategic options may not be considered because of the process in (1) above; try to identify what they may be and deal with the causes.
3. Ensure that there's a recognition that competitive and corporate strategies go hand-in-hand and are both seeking to deliver the company's objectives for the market.

4 Ensure that there's a clear understanding of organizational culture, competencies, capabilities, capacity and resources now and what they need to be in the context of the competitive strategy.
5 Evaluate organizational culture, competencies, capabilities, capacity and resources in terms of whether they contribute significantly to competitive advantage and need to be retained and/or developed or are capable of being outsourced to others.
6 Recognize that competencies may be valued in their own right but must be capable of being applied within the company's culture and be part of the company's capabilities.
7 Ensure that the company is clear that collaboration/partnership working does not undermine either the competitive or corporate strategies of the company.
8 Recognize the risks and rewards of securing and failing to secure access to the portfolio of resources required to support the competitive strategy.
9 Recognize that the implementation of the corporate strategy can affect external market perceptions as much as competitive strategy.
10 Remember that people both within and outside the company look for tangible signs of the corporate strategy in action and consistency between the espoused corporate and competitive strategies and the strategies in action. Consistency is likely to build credibility and confidence and vice versa.

## Practitioner's questions

1 Does the conversion of data to information provide the company with a full range of strategic options for decision-making and choice?
2 Are the linkages between the competitive and corporate strategies clear and fit for purpose?
3 Has the organizational culture required to deliver the competitive strategy been identified and evaluated in the context of the existing organizational culture to identify gaps and/or issues?
4 Have the competencies, capabilities and capacity required to deliver the competitive strategy been identified and evaluated in the context of the existing competencies, capabilities and capacity to identify gaps and/or issues?

5 Have the resources required to deliver the competitive strategy been identified and evaluated in the context of the existing resources to identify gaps and/or issues?

6 Does the company have a credible and effective corporate strategy to address the gaps and/or issues identified in (3)–(5), above?

7 How does the company need to change to enable it to implement its corporate strategy?

8 How are the risks to be managed in developing and implementing the corporate strategy?

9 What appetite is there to reallocate existing resources to be consistent with the priorities within the competitive and corporate strategies rather than seek new resources?

10 What tangible signs of the commitment to the corporate strategy are to be delivered and how is consistency of decision-making to be achieved within it to support the competitive strategy?

# EPILOGUE

Understanding markets and strategy needs to be more than just academic if that understanding is to lead to sustainable business growth and the evolution of the strategic competencies, capacity and capability of companies. This book has sought to create the ability for leaders and managers to embark upon a journey. A journey of discovery and development to create a practical understanding of markets and strategy. An understanding that enables a credible context to be created into which to place the company and its products and services. A context in which to identify and evaluate options for the future and in which to make strategic choices. It provides tools and techniques to support leaders and managers to develop their strategic understanding and to lead and contribute to the success of their companies.

It should be clear that developing strategic management competence as a leader and manager and as a company needs to embrace understanding markets and the organizational challenges to how people think, behave and act upon strategic thinking. This is often a considerable challenge for the leaders and managers of companies. Unless the leaders and managers are prepared to challenge themselves and are prepared to empower their colleagues to challenge taken-for-granted assumptions about the company, its products and services, its markets and its competitors, little progress will be made in creating a strategically competent organization with a credible strategy with the understanding and commitment necessary for it to be implemented effectively.

This strategic challenge is sometimes taken as a personal challenge to the power and status of the leaders and managers of the company itself. If this is the case it is highly unlikely that the company will be able to develop the strategic competence (never mind strategies) necessary for it to respond to its full potential to the future competitive dynamic within markets and the future key strategic market issues.

An effective strategy process needs an organizational culture that enables the company to put itself and its products and services into an external market context. A culture that allows past decisions, strategies, performance and investments to be seen in the context of the future and not just the past. A culture that supports challenge and learning and an ability to avoid decisions becoming frozen rather than part of an ongoing evolutionary context.

In the face of uncertainty and complexity there is a temptation for strategy processes to be either unrealistically rational and constrained or merely marketing fodder to be used either internally or externally to convince that a strategy exists. In both cases the strategy is unlikely to be implemented.

Strategy processes need to be fluid and recognize that events with strategic significance happen as the future unfolds. Where these events cannot be anticipated through the development of scenarios, the leaders and managers of companies need to be able to put them within a strategic market context and decide what needs to be done. Ignoring events and doing nothing or merely waiting to see what others do are rarely options that lead to success.

Understanding markets and strategy is not a science. It is more subjective than objective. It consequently needs an understanding of people, whether as buyers, suppliers, competitors, external stakeholders or colleagues within the company. Leaders and managers need to ensure that they resist the temptation to pursue a purely quantitative approach to markets and strategy.

Those who work at the interface with the market have the greatest knowledge of how the market is evolving and changing. They should be empowered to communicate these changes. They should also be given the training and support necessary for them to be able to understand and contextualize these changes in terms of what the company is seeking to achieve in the market.

As markets constantly change so too do the variables that affect a company's strategy. Strategy relates to the assumptions and choices made about the future. These assumptions and choices need to be regularly reviewed in the context of the market as the future unfolds. The focus has to be market first company second. What is happening in the market? How are the needs/desires of buyers changing? What is the company doing relative to competitors and the changing market now and how does it need to change to achieve its objectives? Should it change its objectives?

Strategic intent creates a framework for action. Action from resource allocations, prioritization, performance and behaviours through every part of the company needs to be consistent. Markets and people within companies believe what they see. Leaders and managers need to continuously create and reinforce their and their company's credibility by the consistency of their decisions, behaviours and action.

Power and the willingness to use it determines the definition of acceptability and success. As competition within markets increases, it is vital that leaders and managers understand who defines acceptable and success and their definitions. A disconnect between the definition of acceptable and success between those leaders and managers and stakeholders who have high power and willingness to use it can have a fundamental impact on strategy and the future direction of companies. It can also have a significant impact on the leaders and managers if they fail to deliver it!

Increasingly the value creation process for buyers under a company's brand requires inputs from different organizations. Buyers are not interested in how fragmented or not the value creation process is, only in what the brand promises being delivered. This means that the strategies and performance of all of those in the value creation process need to be aligned and deliver/exceed the expectations generated. Strategy implementation increasingly involves more than one company. The leaders and managers of the brand owners need to ensure that their company's strategy is capable of being delivered in a pluralistic fragmented organizational context.

Similarly companies increasingly operate in multinational markets and different channels to markets. Different markets, market segments and channels to market often require different strategies. Companies cannot credibly seek to have a generic strategy for all markets, market segments and channels to market. This means that their strategic competence, capability and capacity will increasingly be challenged.

The understanding-markets-and-strategy journey does not have a convenient end. It is a continuing journey that will constantly challenge and change. This book has sought to provide its readers with the tools and techniques to embrace and undertake that journey and to support them in building sustainable business growth.

Embrace the journey and ensure that you and your colleagues continuously learn and use that learning to challenge and change, to build an organization that delivers sustainable business growth.

# REFERENCES


Bez, U (2013) www.astonmartin.com/the-company

Bowman, C and Faulkner, D (1997) *Competitive and Corporate Strategy*, London, Irwin

Bryant, Chris [accessed 22 November 2013] Kaeser expected to restore calm at Siemens, *Financial Times* [Online] www.online.wsj.com/news/articles

Dudley, R (2013) www.bloomberg.com/news/2013-2-27/wal-mart

Goebel, B L and Brown, D R (1981) 'Age differences in motivation related to Maslow's need hierarchy', *Development Psychology*, 17, 809–15

Hamel, G and Prahalad, C K (1994) *Competing for the Future*, Boston, Harvard Business School Press

Handy, C (1995) *The Empty Raincoat: Making sense of the future,* London, Random House Business

Helstom, J and Shanley, M (2013) www.reuters.com/article/2013/11/28/us-cevian

ifpi Digital Music Report 2009

Kuhn, T S (1962) *The Structure of Scientific Revolutions*, Chicago, University of Chicago Press

Lexus Brand Guidelines

Maslow, A (1954) *Motivation and Personality*, New York, Harper & Row

Mintzberg, H (1994) *The Rise and Fall of Strategic Planning*, Harlow, Prentice Hall

*Official Journal of the European Union*, 5 June 2013, L152/ – L 15247

Porter, M E (1980) *Competitive Strategy*, New York, Free Press

Porter, M E (1985) *Competitive Advantage,* New York, Free Press

Reed, S (2013) *New York Times*, 26 November 2013 [Online] www.nytimes.com/2013/11/26/business

Rogers, E M (2003) *Diffusion of Innovations* (5th edn) New York, Free Press

Tang, T L, Ibrahim, A H and West, W B (2002) 'Effects of war-related stress on the satisfaction of human needs: The United States and the Middle East', *International Journal of Management Theory and Practices*, 3 (1), pp 35–53

# INDEX

NB: page numbers in *italics* indicate Figures